Larry Drost

The Eastern Panther

D1527628

The Eastern Panther

mystery cat of the Appalachians

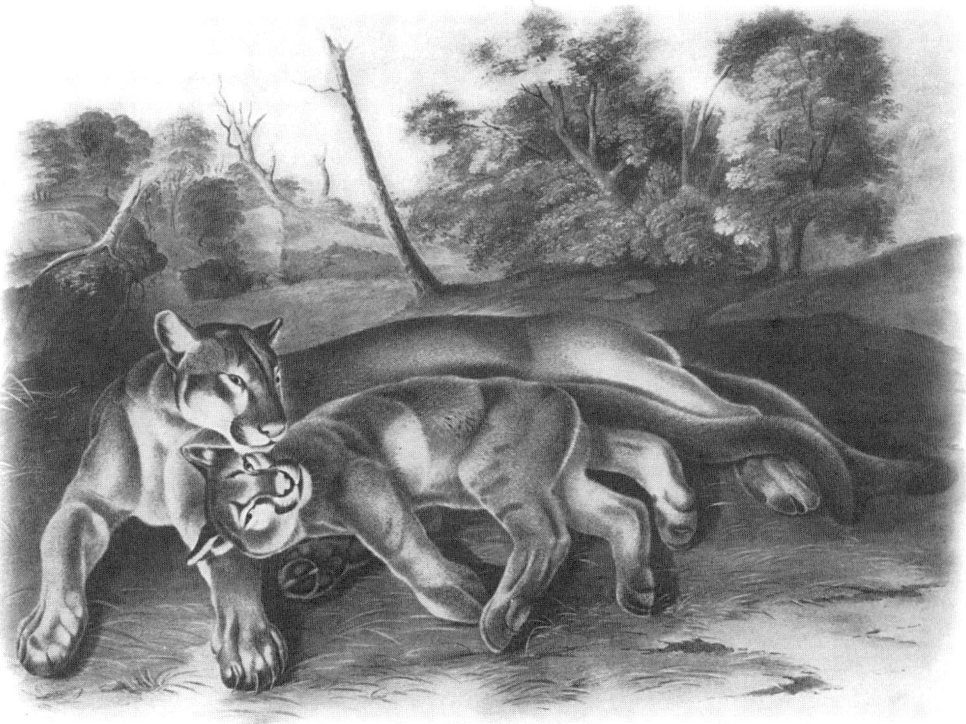

Gerry Parker

Copyright © Gerry Parker, 1998

All rights reserved. No part of this book may be reproduced, stored in a retrieval system or transmitted in any form or by any means without the prior written permission from the publisher, or, in the case of photocopying or other reprographic copying, permission from CANCOPY (Canadian Copyright Licensing Agency), 6 Adelaide Street East, Suite 900, Toronto, Ontario M5C 1H6.

Nimbus Publishing Limited
PO Box 9301, Station A
Halifax, NS B3K 5N5
(902)455-4286

Design: Joan Sinclair
Cover photo of panther (top): © Wayne Lynch
Printed and bound by Hignell Printing, Winnipeg, Manitoba

Canadian Cataloguing in Publication Data
Parker, G.R.
The eastern panther
Includes bibliographical references.
ISBN 1-55109-268-9
1. Panthers—East (U.S.) I. Title.
QL737.C23P37 1998 599.75'24 C98-950045-4

Nimbus Publishing acknowledges the financial support of the Canada Council and the Department of Canadian Heritage.

Contents

This book is dedicated to the memories of
Dr. Harold Hitchcock and Spencer Kraybill,
two dedicated and unselfish people whom I had the pleasure of meeting only briefly, but whom I admired and respected greatly. While Dr. Hitchcock spent many years pursuing the mystery of the panther in Vermont, Spencer devoted his energies to preserving and republishing the history and folklore of the state of Pennsylvania. They will be missed by many. I consider myself fortunate to have had the privilege of knowing them both.

Preface

When early European colonists first established their small settlements on the shores of America, they encountered an intimidating wilderness with mysterious and dangerous creatures. Faced with this threat, they chose the most obvious and, to them, most reasonable course of action: they cut and burnt the forests down. At first these small openings did little to the normal patterns of forest growth, and the responses of most wild creatures to these changes were insignificant. The small clearings provided pasture for livestock, room for planting crops, and an open and safe space between the settler and the dangers of this new world.

Things soon changed. A swell of immigration and an increasing demand for wood and minerals to feed industrial expansion produced a growing swath of deforestation west into the Appalachian Mountains and beyond; and they produced a variety of responses to these landscape changes among the wildlife that lived there. Some, like the passenger pigeon, were lost forever. Others, like the wolf, bear and panther, disappeared more slowly and less dramatically. A few, like the raccoon, fox and coyote, benefited from the open fields and miles of deforested hills and valleys. Lush young forests soon developed and mice, rabbits, berries and fruit were abundant.

A new environment was developing, a new world of changing opportunities for different animals. Two that come to mind are the coyote and the panther. No two medium–sized predators could be more different. The eastern coyote is an amazing mix of adaptability and craftiness. It is a prodigy of interbreeding, combining the cunning and flexibility of the plains coyote with the strength and social graces of the timber wolf. Deforestation and a fragmented landscape did little to challenge this shrewd predator and only encouraged its proliferation. However, like the wolf before it, the panther fell before the onslaught, a specialized predator unable to contend with human persecution, diminishing prey and a changing environment.

In an earlier book, I followed the amazing success story of the eastern coyote as it expanded its pre-European prairie range in North America and, within the past hundred years, colonized most temperate areas of the continent.[1] Although many hands were lifted against it, the coyote adjusted its behavior and needs to changing environments. On the prairies it fed on rodents and rabbits; as it crossed the Mississippi into the southeast it added poultry, young pigs, and melons to its diet; and in the northeast it preyed on hares and white-tailed deer. Its success is a fine example of ecological flexibility.

Meanwhile, in the eastern half of the continent, the panther was rapidly becoming a footnote to the chapter of environmental change. It too felt the wrath of human persecution and the consequences of a deforested landscape, but, unlike the coyote, it was unable to cope. As the forests fell to the ax, white-tailed deer, the panther's preferred food, also declined, and in several states these deer disappeared altogether. The fate of the inflexible panther was sealed. By the mid-1800s this great American lion was only a memory in most of the eastern states. Although a few stragglers managed to hold on in some of the more remote wilderness retreats of the Appalachian Mountains, they, too, soon slipped into the pages of history.

Or did they? Here lies one of the great wildlife mysteries of eastern North America. Did a few remnant eastern panthers manage to escape their tormentors and remain hidden away among the secret recesses and valleys of the Appalachian Mountains? Were those few survivors able to mate and maintain ancestral bloodlines down through the generations? Some people are convinced that with the reforestation of much of its former range, and surging white-tailed deer populations, this ghost cat of the east has made a remarkable comeback—hundreds, and even thousands, of sightings have been reported. Disbelievers say these are house cats, dogs, coyotes and assorted other animals misidentified as panthers, or escaped or released panthers from Florida, cougars from the western United States, or pumas from Central and South America.

Like many other people, the questions and mysteries surrounding the continued presence of the eastern panther have puzzled and intrigued me. A few, such as myself, have had a personal involvement in the issue by collecting, sorting and investigating panther sightings.

I arrived in New Brunswick shortly after the death of Bruce Wright. Bruce had for many years pursued evidence to confirm the continued survival of panthers in that province and had written two books on the subject. As a research biologist for Canadian Wildlife Service, a federal agency responsible for rare and endangered species, I continued to collect reports of panthers in Atlantic Canada from 1976 through 1984. Many of those reports were personally investigated, but no clear evidence of panthers was ever found.

Some people have seen what they believe to be a panther. Others embrace only a sincere and unabashed fascination with one of the few wildlife mysteries remaining in the diminishing wilderness of eastern North America. But what do we know of this mystery cat? How common and widely distributed was it? What do records tell us of its early presence? What evidence is there to suggest that panthers may still be found in remote regions of the east? Who are some of the people who devoted years of their professional and private lives to pursuing this feline mystery?

I have written this book for those who wish to learn more about this elusive cat of eastern North America and the debate that surrounds it. I have brought together stories of panthers from the past and the present which I hope will leave the reader with a greater appreciation of the history and mystery of this great American predator. This book is not about the life history and ecology of the eastern panther. That task would be rather difficult considering that the last of these mighty cats may have fallen more than one hundred years ago, and only a handful of musty specimens remain today, catalogued and stored away in vaults and glass displays of museums and universities scattered throughout the east. It is, rather, an attempt to bring together some of the early accounts of the eastern panther throughout its former range in order to provide the reader with an appreciation of its early occurrence and of when general consensus suggests panthers were last found in particular states, provinces or regions.

Most of the public remains largely unaware of the story behind this object of controversy, the importance the eastern panther held in the daily lives of early settlers, and the swiftness with which it fell before the onslaught of human persecution and deforestation. This book will not answer whether the panther still remains with us in isolated and remote wilderness retreats of eastern North America, nor was it intended to. However, I hope it will provide the reader with a greater appreciation of the issue. After years of involvement with this enigma, especially in Atlantic Canada, I remain optimistic. I accept the judicial wisdom that "absence of evidence is not evidence of absence," but at the same time I can understand the "I'm from Missouri, show me" school of thought. I have no illusions that critics from both camps may not find reason to claim this book incomplete, especially if their own arguments are not supported to their satisfaction. But I make no apologies. I believe, given the evidence at hand, that this book remains unbiased and presents a fair and impartial review of the "panther controversy."

Although the eastern panther has been the focus of countless articles in newspapers and magazines throughout the east, the two books by Bruce Wright remain the only authoritative references on the subject, and they were published more than twenty-five years ago. I thought it timely to review the story of the eastern panther mystery and update events since Bruce's efforts. I hope this book presents many of the facts, as best we know them, and allows the reader to decide if Klandagi, Lord of the Forest, might still be found somewhere amidst the wilderness solitudes of the Appalachians.

I rely heavily on early stories and accounts as they appeared in local papers, magazines and journals. I refer to the published efforts of early scientists, naturalists and historians. Many of these people have pursued the tangled web of circumstantial evidence in order to substantiate the continued survival of panthers in certain remote regions of the east. They have given us invaluable collections of reports and sightings which have been examined, studied and analysed in a manner which many of us can only respect and admire. Some may have shown their biases, but there can be no doubting their sincerity and propensity for hard work and the task at hand.

But before we begin our pursuit of panthers and panther legend and folklore, I must thank everyone who contributed to the preparation of this book. I am deeply grateful for the information contributed by many biologists and concerned citizens throughout the east. I have spoken and corresponded with a great many people over the past three years. During that time, it seems, I have received an equally diverse assortment of opinions, beliefs and sentiments. For all of that I am truly thankful.

I am also indebted to those who entertained me and endured my many questions during my search in June 1995 for those remaining few specimens of eastern panther now scattered far and wide behind glass cases and closed doors. Your generosity and hospitality, without exception, will not be forgotten. The following are a few of those who helped me: Joe Bopp of the New York State Museum in Albany; Bill Kilpatrick, University of

Vermont in Burlington; Kary McFadden at the Museum of Comparative Zoology, Harvard University; Carolyn Kirdahy of the Museum of Science in Boston; Bob Phillips at Oneonta State College; the staff of the Woodman Institute in Dover, New Hampshire; Edith and Armstrong Hunter of Weathersfield, Vermont; Roger Cowburn of Galeton, Pennsylvania; and the late Spencer Kraybill of Waterville, Pennsylvania and the late Dr. Harold Hitchcock of Middlebury, Vermont. Finally, I want to thank my wife, Sheila, for her patience, companionship and encouragement as I pursued the path of Klandagi over the past several years. Thanks to you all.

CHAPTER ONE

Introduction

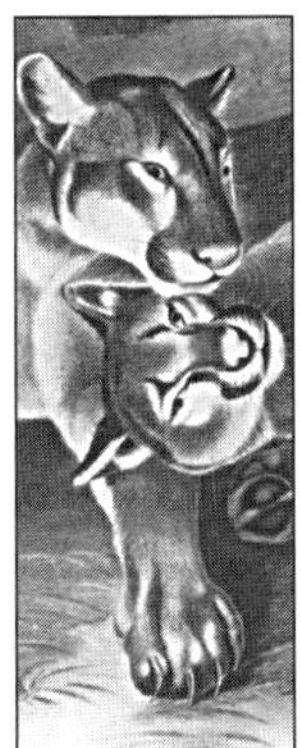

November 24, 1881

THANKSGIVING DAY a young man, living with Paul Crowell in Barnard, took his gun and went out to hunt partridges. A light snow had fallen the night previous and the tracks of any animals as well as that of a man could very plainly be seen. He had not gone far on the hillside when he discovered tracks of an unusual size. They were round and shaped like that of a cat, but enormously large. He followed them for about half a mile and came at once upon an immense great panther! Being startled and without any preparation for so formidable a creature, he hurried back and went to the house of Mr. Alexander Crowell's, a nephew of Paul Crowell's, and told his story. Mr Crowell, being an old hunter, immediately took his gun, loaded it heavily with shot, and with one of his boys started in pursuit.

They took the track near where the young man left it and followed it to the eastern part of the old Aiken place, a little north of Mr. Crowell's place. Here he was again found in the edge of some woods which are in sight of some houses. When discovered, he was crouched on his belly and forepaws lashing his tail and ready for a spring. There were low bushes in the way, some low spruces, and as Mr. Crowell had nothing but a shotgun and knew the charge would not amount to much except at close range he lay down on his belly and crawled under them and towards the animal. When within about twenty feet, he

> fired—the head being towards him—and broke his foreleg. He bounded a little, flew at the dog which was worrying him and then fell over on one side. Other parties coming up, he took a rifle and put a bullet through his head and finished [sic]. Mr. Crowell says he was tracked from the Pomfret poor farm, passed near the Lime pond in Barnard to the place he was first discovered. He thinks he has been prowling around the hills west of Barnard Village for some time as a good many sheep have been killed in that region. He does not think he had been seen until the day he was killed, but had been frequently heard in the night, giving a loud wailing cry not unlike that of a cat, only louder. Where he came from is a matter of a great deal of uncertainty. Probably from some section north and west of where he was killed.
>
> C. Dana[1]

And so was recorded the story of what may have been the last panther to have been killed in Vermont. Some suggest that it may well have been the last confirmed specimen of that magnificent race of "lion," which once roamed throughout much of eastern North America, from the cold spruce–fir forests of New Brunswick south through the Appalachians as far as the Great Smoky Mountains of North Carolina. The "Barnard Panther," as it was called, was so prized at the time of killing that it was mounted and exhibited around the state and drew rave billing such as "Monster Panther—Don't Fail To See Him—An Object Lesson In Natural History." A price of 10 cents was charged for its viewing! Today, the Barnard Panther is on display at the Vermont Historical Society Museum in Montpelier.

So, if the last confirmed specimen of the eastern panther fell to the gun more than one hundred years ago, should that not be the end of the story? Surely, if remnant populations of these large predators are still to be found in remote regions of eastern North America, something more convincing than personal sightings, occasional plaster casts of tracks, questionable photographs and a few scats would have been found by now. Surely, one or more of the millions of deer hunters who take to the woods throughout the Appalachian Mountains each autumn with high-powered rifles would have proudly returned bearing a carcass of this mysterious and elusive cat of the mountain. Alexander Crowell appeared to have little difficulty in tracking down and dispatching the Barnard Panther. And there are stories of early panther hunters in Maryland, Pennsylvania and New York who individually killed fifty or more panthers in their lifetimes. If the panther was indeed eliminated from the eastern landscape over a century ago, why are sightings, encounters and other circumstantial evidence for its presence continually reported to state and provincial wildlife agencies throughout the east? The eastern wood bison, elk and wolf were also once common in the Appalachian Mountains, but their demise following European colonization and land clearing was not followed by a legacy similar to that of the panther.

Is the panther today little more than an eastern Sasquatch, a mythical creature living more in the imagination than out among the darkened shadows of the forests? Many people think so; many others do not. The believers point to the thousands of people who have seen pantherlike animals over the past few decades—hunters, naturalists, doctors, farmers, housewives and biologists. How could so many people be mistaken? Some certainly, many perhaps; but all? Impossible! So say those in the "yes" camp. The nonbelievers, those in the "no" camp, point to the endless false leads which have ended up being a bear, coyote, bobcat, dog or housecat. What about positive identification of track imprints as those of a panther? Or the killing of panthers within the past thirty years in such states as Pennsylvania and New York, and in the province of Quebec? These are only released or escaped pets from occupied ranges to the west or from Florida says the no camp. So the yes and no camps remain highly polarized as the sightings of panthers pour in and accusations of indifference and coverup by government biologists and bureaucrats build.

The frustration expressed by people who in good faith report sightings of panthers to wildlife personnel, only to receive little attention or encouragement in return, is understandable. But that has nothing to do with concealed government plots or coverups. Rather, it has everything to do with other day-to-day priorities and real wildlife management problems related with very real animals and birds. Rare, endangered and threatened wildlife are high on the research and budget agendas of federal, state and provincial governments. I was there once. In the late 1970s and early 1980s, I was one of those "government biologists" who not only received reports of panthers in Atlantic Canada but actively solicited them and investigated many. I picked up where Bruce Wright left off. I corresponded with Robert Downing in North Carolina and shared his enthusiasm and optimism for confirming the presence of this mystery cat in the east. But hope fades after years of chasing down false leads and mistaken identities—bear carcasses, dog and coyote tracks, bobcat kills and scrapes, housecats. As much as I wanted to continue the search with the exuberance of youth, the years of false expectations took their toll. And my own professional work priorities changed, and the task was passed on to others. So it is with people who, during their daily duties as park wardens, state or provincial biologists, or game or conservation officers, receive reports of eastern panthers. Some, often the young and the keen, take up the challenge and, when other duties permit, knock on doors, search out leads and pursue this perplexing mystery. But mistrust, accusations and fingerpointing have no real place and make no positive contribution.

The greater question that begs answering is why, in the face of overwhelming scientific opinion to the contrary, have so many people reported seeing what they believed to be a panther? Why does this mystery continue to spawn and cultivate contention between the scientist on the one hand and, on the other hand, those who raise hope and aspiration above the pragmatism of analytical thought and reason? Some may suggest that people see what they want to see: a noisy squirrel can become a deer to an impatient hunter; and a half-wild farm cat at the edge of the field becomes a sleek and graceful 100-pound panther to those who want it to be there.

Others might suggest that human guilt has much to do with it as well. Most of us are aware of humankind's sad record of fellowship with other wild things on this earth. There has been a long struggle between an earlier attitude which saw the human as lord over all creatures, a being unique among all others for its powers of reasoned thought, emotions and communication, and a more recent perspective which sees ourselves as not especially different from, and certainly no better than, other life forms with which we share the planet. A growing number of people recognize the latter philosophy to be a maturing and certainly superior moral enlightenment. Others will disagree. But regardless of ideological persuasion, many of us do review our legacy of animal exploitation and mistreatment with varying degrees of shame and guilt. And perhaps, unknowingly, this guilt of perceived past misdeeds inflicted on our animal kin, especially many of the larger predators, may also play a role in the growing number of panther sightings. We not only want to see them, but their presence and survival may in some way lessen, or remove the mantle of insecurity and shame inherited from generations far less removed than ourselves from the struggle to survive in hostile environments.

Today, as we sit comfortably distanced from the personal and often bloody conflicts between humans and wild animals, we can afford to reflect on and debate such philosophical and spiritual musings. It is easy to see the beauty in all of nature's creatures until you're personally threatened. But shouldn't objective and rational reflection on the close interdependency of our ancestors and other creatures for human survival lessen or remove the underswell of guilt? Perhaps, but our perception of cruelty to animals, as seen from today's complacent detachment, may be seriously biased, some might say unreasonable, even smacking of ignorance, given that many of us, if we so choose, can now pass through life getting no closer to so-called animal cruelty and maltreatment than the local meat counter, or television's nature channels.

Early European colonists brought considerable cultural baggage to the New World. They believed that subjugation of wilderness frontiers was the only reasonable way to civilized edification. Living in tune with nature, taking only what was needed, practicing principles of conservation and recognizing the inherent rights of other wild beings were foreign doctrines to these early settlers. Perhaps this is why many of the customs of the aboriginal Americans—spirituality, conservatism and compassion towards other animals—were misunderstood and often ridiculed and rejected as primitive and inferior. Later, as European and American explorers plied the Arctic waters in search of the fabled Northwest Passage, similar rejection of Inuit ways of life and survival would lead to much unnecessary hardship and death. Only the few who chose to learn from the aboriginal cultures managed to live comfortably in one of the most hostile environments on earth.

So, to the early American settler, the eastern panther, or "painter" as it was frequently called, represented much of what was feared and hated about these wild and untamed new lands. It was the largest of native cats, sufficiently large, in fact, to carry off a fattened hog or sheep, and quite capable of taking a human life. It was a nighttime stalker of the darkened forests which would, on occasion, silently and stealthily intrude into the frontier sanctuary of the sleeping farmer. It was only in the morning that the bloody trail of a missing calf confirmed the worst of the farmer's fears, that "ol' painter" had indeed paid a visit and the winter's larder would be leaner because of it. The replacement of pristine forests with pasture and crops, and of deer and elk with sheep and cattle, hastened and intensified the inevitable conflict between settler and predator. The normal habitats and food sources for bear, wolf and panther were changing; to survive, the predator had to change its ways or perish. Yes, the predators did on occasion kill domestic livestock, especially those left defenseless and exposed in open pastures surrounded by forest. They still do. But where else could the predators turn? They could retreat no further into the vanishing wilderness; their normal sources of food were disappearing. Increasing conflict between predators and humans was inevitable. Little wonder that these great predators soon became the focus of hate and vengeance throughout much of frontier America. And the most hated, it appears, was the panther.

Years earlier, the European explorers who had plied the warm waters of the southern Atlantic and Gulf coasts first saw this long–tailed tawny cat and thought it to be a lion, a forgivable error considering that most of these adventurers were familiar only with the great cats of the Old World. On closer study it became clear that this large cat of the Americas was not a lion but was more like a dark leopard, or panther, as such black-phased or melanistic leopards and other great cats were then called. For lack of a better name at the time, this one stuck, and "panther" it became throughout much of its eastern range. Later, on closer study by European naturalists, it was given its own identity and was called cougar, but this name became common only in western North America. The settlers, farmers and frontierspeople throughout the Appalachians called it many things, but most often "panther," or "painter."

As settlement spread rapidly westward into the mountains and secluded valleys of the Appalachians, the panther, along with many other large predators which threatened human livelihood, became the focus of the settlers' wrath and persecution. It was not prized for the table like the deer, nor valued for its fur like the wolf and lynx. Rather, it was hunted and pursued because it was a feared competitor—it killed deer in the forests and, on occasion, sheep in the fields. To add more incentive to the chase, bounties were placed on its head, and a proud young hunter it was who rode into town with one or more painters lashed to his wagon. The legions of this great warrior soon became decimated, and by the early 1800s only the most isolated of wilderness retreats would provide safe haven. In a matter of a few short years these, too, would become violated and ravaged by the bite of the axe.

Through it all 'ol painter continued to play an important role in the daily lives of the early settler. Written records of that period were often considered to be incomplete without some mention of this feared beast. Panthers of legend and folklore flourished in the frontiers of early colonial America.

The following words by J. Herbert Walker, which appeared in the *Pennsylvania Game News* some forty years ago, may serve to set the scene as we begin our search for panthers and panther lore.

"The men who hunted the panther, who heard its eerie cry in the night, have long gone to their rest and few persons living today have any knowledge of this grand animal. Yet, in a small way, the memory of the panther remains. There are numerous Panther Rocks, Panther Hollows and Panther Ledges back in the mountains.... Mountain young bloods dared not pay court to the dark-haired, dark-skinned mountain girls unless they could boast they had killed a panther or two. Outside my study window tonight there is a heavy snowstorm and the winds are howling, blowing the snow into drifts. Before me burns a wood fireplace. It is a time for reflection of the days that are long gone—of the days of the panther and red-blooded frontiersmen and settlers who braved the rigors of snowy winter to seek out the great beasts and bring them down. The wind howls and it reminds one of the weird, piercing wail of the great cats as they traveled the ridges on cold, sometimes moonlight, nights. In imagination one can feel the fear that gripped mountain housewives in their lonely cabins in the hills when the voice of the panther carries far into the still night." [2]

CHAPTER 2

Klandagi, Lord of the Forest

THE YEAR 1865 brought to a close one of the bloodiest and cruellest human conflicts in American history. The young nation had been split, north against south, Union against Confederacy, father against son. In the spring of that year the trains wound their way north through the carnage, carrying the northern boys back home to their small settlements and loved ones left behind so many months before that had been a happier time, when they had confidently set off to teach those southern rebels some manners. It wouldn't take but a few months at the most, they boasted, be back before the crops need harvest. Oh, the self-delusion that so often inspires young sons and daughters! Battles are to be fought and won, and to be returned from in triumphant praise and glory; dying and suffering are someone else's fate. But in war, there are no winners, only losers. And some lose more than others.

It was the summer of '65, then, when we pick up the story of one of those young Union soldiers, Lewis Dorman, returning by rail to the small settlement of Lewistown in central Pennsylvania. It is of interest to us as we search early records for stories of panthers and panther hunters. It came to my attention as I searched the Pennsylvania State University archives, and came upon Henry Shoemaker's 1913 book, *In the Seven Mountains*, a collection of stories of early Pennsylvania as told to him by those who had cleared the forests, settled the land and suffered many hardships.

"The stage from Lewistown was three hours late; darkness had set in, all the windows in Bannerville were ablaze with light.... There was an oppressive stillness in the little town, the stillness of expectancy. The reason for this was that a dozen young men, natives of the village and surrounding country, who had been soldiers in the bloody war with the Southern States, which had lately come to a close, were due to arrive after their years of active service at the front. Their valorous deeds as reported by the county newspapers and letters home had already made them local heroes, superseding the grey-haired, middle-aged veterans of the conflict with Mexico. These old soldiers were in uniform tonight, anxious to do homage to the younger boys in blue. Fully a thousand persons had gathered in the little community, crowding around the porch of the general store and post office as there the stage would come to a halt.... Many of the young girls were dressed for the great occasion. They wore blue and white muslin gowns, red sashes, and some even had on red stockings. They wore tiny flags in their hats, and those who had donned coats, for the May night was a trifle chilly, had rosettes of colors in the lapels, or carried small flags....

"It was nine-thirty when the shout went up that the stage had been sighted. Fully fifty small boys ran up the hill, and along the ridge that the highway followed, to obtain an advance view of the important caravan. The few persons who lived along the road, who had not made up their minds to come to the celebration, could not resist the sight of the stage crowded with soldier boys, and dropped in behind it, forming an irregular guard of honor. The big driver, who himself had been a soldier for six months, had put on his uniform for the occasion, and kept cracking his long whip, which was draped with patriotic streamers....

"The crowd surged toward the oncoming conveyance, and the horses could scarcely travel. So slow was their gait that a hundred stalwart youths fairly pushed the animals from the traces, brushed them aside, and seizing the pole, drew the big stage to the post office. When it stopped, the young soldiers were dragged out bodily. They were embraced by parents, brothers, sisters, sweethearts, cries of joy mingled with hurrahs and songs. In the midst of this the tall leader of the band climbed to the post office porch and, adjusting his pine-torch, started his aggregation to playing, 'Ring the Bells of Heaven.' The soldier boys, after having been half kissed and hugged to death by their relatives and sweethearts, were now being congratulated by the Mexican war veterans and admiring friends. An old blind man, bent almost double, a survivor of the war of 1812 was helped through the throng by two of his grandsons, and shook hands with every young soldier. When the band ceased playing there was another cheer, and then a big dark-complexioned Lutheran preacher rapped on the post office porch floor with a broom handle and asked a prayer of thanks for the safe restoration of the local soldiers. After this the district attorney, who was also a congressional aspirant, who had come over from Swinefordstown for the occasion, delivered an oration. It was full of patriotic fervor and was frequently interrupted by applause. After the speechmaking the young and old veterans were escorted into the storehouse where an elaborate supper awaited them.

"One of the first of the young soldiers to alight from the coach was Lewis Dorman, the son of Widow Dorman of Dormantown, a village about three miles west of Bannerville. He was a handsome youth, of medium height and athletic build. He had clear-cut aquiline features. His straight black hair, which was worn parted on both sides, was brought down over his ears. He had piercing black eyes and wore a small black mustache of the style which has become so popular with young men in the big cities nowadays. His mother was the first to greet him when he emerged from the vehicle, and the scene between the two was affecting. On three occasions he had been reported missing after important battles, but wounded though he was, he had been able to creep back through the enemies' lines to his own regiment. Happy as he was to see his beloved parent, the young calvaryman kept casting his dark eyes about the crowd, as if looking for someone else. The fitful light of lamps and pine torches was dim enough, but the congratulatory throng crowding about him made it difficult to see very far. When he was able to climb on the post office porch, he obtained a good view of the assemblage; he presented a picturesque figure with his wide military trousers and blouse, his chevroned sleeves, cap in hand. After he had stood the suspense as long as he could, he turned to an aunt, to whom he had always confided his troubles, asking the whereabouts of Letty Lenoble. The good lady gazed at him in silence for a minute.

" 'Haven't you heard,' she whispered apologetically, 'she ran off with that Yankee who worked on Berkheiser's mill.'

" 'When?' said Lewis, turning deadly pale and letting his cap drop from his hands. 'Why, I only got a letter from her two weeks ago.'

" 'It's been about two weeks since she went away,' replied the aunt.

"His rosy color gone, the young soldier moved among the merrymakers like a ghost. Clammy-handed, he accepted their congratulations; he was the only person at the long table who did not eat; he was the only one in the throng of one thousand who was glad when the homeward pilgrimage began. He who had served his country well, had been promoted to be a first sergeant for general efficiency, [and] was a good and dutiful son, had been marked by fate for this sore trial."

The young lad's spirit was crushed at the news, and he spent the following days and weeks languishing with great anguish at his mother's home in Dormantown. At twenty-one, Lewis Dorman lost his ambition, willpower and self-esteem. He turned to the forests for solace and, with his bull terriers at his side, would wander off for days on end, no one certain just when he might return.

"The November of the year of his disappointment ... he killed an enormous brown bear in the 'sink,' a rocky desert in the White Mountains. This determined him to adopt the career of a hunter, to secure specimens of the fierce animals which were then making their last stand in the Seven Mountains. During the winter he trapped a dozen wildcats, a Canada lynx or catamount, thirty grey foxes, a pine marten and several opossums. His record was the envy of the boys of the neighborhood. His relatives encouraged him, saying among themselves that he would forget his unfortunate love affair in the forests. During 1866 he spent most of his time in the mountains. He went away in the spring, fishing and shooting waterfowl, exploring the least known streams and climbing the rugged peaks of each of the Seven Mountains. When he returned home in August he looked, so the neighbors said, 'like a wildman.' He had let his hair and beard grow; at twenty-two he could have passed for a man of forty. That fall he killed a brown bear, three black bears, one of the latter weighing, 'hog dressed,' 542 pounds. It was the 'record' black bear in the Seven Mountains for many years to come. He also killed a magnificent stag, with a wide spread and nine points on each horn, which was also a record head for a time. He engaged in several unsuccessful panther hunts; others ranging over the same territory had ... killed magnificent specimens the same year.... That winter he resumed his trapping operations, capturing in one month five Canada lynxes, the largest number ever caught by one hunter in so short a period in the Seven Mountains."

He returned home at Christmas, built a comfortable log cabin nearby and, having shaved and tidied up his appearance, became quite respectable. Folks were sure that Lewis would soon return to his former self. In the autumn of 1867 the troubled youth again left for the hills, determined to return bearing the hide of a panther, one of the few wild creatures that had thus far eluded him. Although details are sketchy, word was that the young Dorman had by chance crossed the path of his former sweetheart while trailing the path of a panther at the headwaters of Rapid Run in Centre County. She had married well and shone in the glow of happiness and success. This was too much for young Lewis, and he wandered aimlessly for the rest of the winter, arriving back home during the latter part of April 1868, unkempt and dejected. In an effort to arouse him from his misery, his family encouraged Lewis to take up again the hunt for panthers, a prize that would bring the family a $12 bounty for every animal slain.

"In September he consented to go on another hunt but affirmed with a laugh that he would not return until he killed his panther. He amused himself shooting wild pigeons, turkeys and grouse until there came a tracking snow, which occurred the first week in November. At the headwaters of Pine Hollow Creek, near the extreme eastern end of Centre County, Lewis's bulldogs located four panthers, by their tracks two were enormous males, two females. Their keen senses appraised them of the danger, and they separated, two traveling east in the direction of the divide above the head of Rapid Run, two moving west, along the ridge above Pine Hollow. The pair which moved west, on account of the tracks of the male being the largest, the young hunter elected to follow. He kept within half a day of them for three days when a warm spell set in, followed by a week of rain, and the tracking was spoiled. He could not believe that they would cross his 'line' and travel east, so he kept beating about in the vast pineries, gradually moving his position west. A week of good weather, Indian Summer, followed the rain, but despite the dreamy allurement of the atmosphere, the hunter never relaxed his purpose. The weather again turned cold, and another tracking snow fell about December first. He found the trail again on Round Top Mountain, following it along the ridges to Mount Stromburg, near Coburn. There a blizzard set in, and the crafty brutes, during its fiercest moments, doubled on their tracks, and started east. A thaw delayed his progress, but conditions soon righted themselves so that he again took up the trail which led over Paddy Mountain and along the ridges to Round Top. There the female left her mate, who moved northeast, across the Union County line towards Big Laurel Run. The hunt had now lasted nearly two months, the dogs were tired and restless, but Lewis Dorman was indefatigable. The male panther evidently tired of his solitary life, for on the night of the 23d of December he roared loudly and long from the topmost pinnacle of Shreiner Knob.

"Dorman, who with his dogs had bivouacked on a nearby ridge, never heard anything like this before, and sat awake all night by his fire, awed by the savage love-song.... He had often heard about panthers wailing and screaming, but there was a majestic melody to the awful sound which seemed to be the very voice of the wilderness. At the same time the panther is naturally a silent animal, rarely making an outcry except at its mating season. Just as the morning star grew dim, far in the distance came what at first seemed to be an echo, in a minor key; it was the answering notes of the female. Something in Dorman's blood told him that he would soon bring his quarry to bay. Muzzling his dogs, and placing them on leash, he crept on hands and knees through the snow. He descended the ridge, crossed the draft, and assumed a good location on the north slope of the Shreiner. At dusk he found the trail of the female, and followed it to where she had hidden herself in an inaccessible position in the rocks, evidently waiting for her fulvous-coated master. The full moon, which had been entirely obscured the night before, now rose and shone at intervals. Across its face swept sooty-colored clouds, the tips of the giant white pines soughed and murmured in the night wind. Dorman was certain that the male panther was in hiding near the summit, but would visit his mate that night. About ten o'clock he heard several short howls and moans and then, perhaps fifteen minutes later the two panthers emerged from the rocks. For a minute the moon-rays disclosed them, the male with blazing eyes, was licking the female's tawny coat and stroking her with his tail, in passionate ecstasy. Then clouds hid the light, [but] the chase was not yet ended. In the darkness came several fierce roars of wild rapture. Suddenly the moon became clear, revealing the male panther alone, stalking along the trunk of a fallen pine with head erect. Dorman's chance had come; he fired.

There was a hideous shriek of pain, echoed in treble key high up among the rocks. Again he fired; the wounded panther leaped twenty feet into the air, and with a resounding thud, fell in a lifeless heap in the snow. The hunter and his dogs hurried to the spot, and a cozy fire was soon crackling by the steaming carcass. While he was skinning it, far up on the rock-crested summit, came a sound like a woman's sobbing. Was it the pantheress, conscious of her bereavement, or a banshee wailing of dead sorrows?"

The story ends with young Lewis meeting another affectionate lass at a feast to celebrate his killing of the panther. Following the night of festivities, and a pledge of mutual love, "the young couple were driven to New Berlin where they were married, the happy bridegroom presenting the panther hide to the officiating clergyman. In that manner it found its way into the Natural History Museum of the old academy. When the Swinsfordstown stage reached Bannerville on New Year's Eve, several of Lewis Dorman's one-time army comrades were standing on the post office porch. When they saw the erstwhile 'wild man of the woods' clean-shaven, save for his little dark mustache, and dapper and jaunty looking, climb out, assisting a very pretty young girl, one of them remarked: 'What sights one sees when he hasn't got a gun.' That night the young hunter presented his bride to his family circle; it was a happy occasion. Within a week soft yellow lights were gleaming in the windows of the side of the little house in Dormantown that had been dark for so long." [1]

Thus ends the story of the slaying of the Dorman Panther, one of the few remaining relics of a bygone era, and which now resides in the biology building of Albright College in Reading, Pennsylvania. Dr. Edwin Bell of Albright College suggests that there might be some doubt that the panther was indeed killed by Lewis Dorman, as portrayed in Shoemaker's tale. But whatever its true history, the specimen represents one of the last of these noble creatures to be killed in Pennsylvania. Shoemaker's version of romance and tragedy surrounding the young hunter Lewis Dorman and the killing of this panther somehow befits the air of nostalgia and adventure we associate with a simpler and perhaps more innocent era.

This story of the killing of the Dorman Panther is more than a tale of a love-struck Pennsylvanian youth and his adventures in the backwoods of the Seven Mountains. It conveys the matter-of-fact dependency of many frontier people on wildlife, which were never far removed from their everyday lives. Deer, elk and turkeys were hunted for the table, the furs of wolves, lynx and bobcats provided winter warmth, and panthers and bears were pursued for bounty and prestige and to protect domestic animals. When the forests were cut during the late 1700s and early 1800s, the land lost more than just trees. It lost much of the wildlife native to the region. Deer were virtually decimated, and the settlers suffered because of it. Elk, wolves and panthers fell before the onslaught, and they would never recover.

To point fingers at what we now see as a complete disregard by our early ancestors for the rights of other creatures exposes a blind indifference on our part to the living conditions and mind-set of that era. Survival was indeed a struggle; certainty of anything other than the coming seasons was a fool's wish. To survive, one had to improvise, to make do with what was near at hand, including whatever wild creatures had to offer. Thoughts about the rights of other animals, cruelty and rules of fair chase had no place in the daily lives of early settlers. Such thoughts would have only proved counterproductive and shifted the odds in favor of the prey instead of the predator. A fleeting thought of sympathy for the quarry, a moment's hesitation, and the opportunity could be lost. No, the will to survive is as strong in the hunter as in the hunted. And we must never forget that most early settlers were hunters. There were no supermarkets, no truck deliveries, no social security nets. They lived by their wits and by what they had learned and did what had to be done. We can do them only a great injustice to now cast a shadow of guilt over their perceived disregard for holistic values, which have been conceived and nurtured by generations now benefiting from the fruits of their early labors. Our present role on this planet is two-edged. On the one hand, we enjoy the benefits that come from an exploitative culture, while on the other hand, as we have become so removed from intimate dependency on other creatures of the planet we are able to reflect on nature with a personal detachment which hints of hypocrisy.

But what of aboriginal Americans? What role did predators, and wild animals in general, play in the lives of the first settlers of the New World? Obviously, wildlife played an integral role in the religious and cultural lives of most aboriginal groups, and it was a relationship both intimate and personal. Many books have been written about early Native Americans and their relationships with the animals who shared their world. One of these is

George Laycock's *The Hunters and the Hunted*, a fine chronicle of the pursuit of game in America from precolonial times to the present. "We sometimes hear that Indians were the first conservationists, that they took no game they could not use and were never wasteful. But this may grace the image of the native American with a nobility foreign to him. Primitive people were opportunists. They had to be. Hunger was always near, and tomorrow might bring only a broth made from bones picked clean by vultures, or maybe nothing at all. Given the opportunity to kill a deer, duck, raccoon, swan, songbird, or buffalo, the animal was generally taken." [2]

But Early North American Natives were limited in what they could kill by the means at their disposal. Before the introduction of horses and gunpowder by Europeans, their means had been severely restricted, and survival was never certain. At the same time, of course, their influence on populations of North American wildlife was minimal, perhaps even negligible.

"In spite of the Indians' constant hunting, whether for bison on the plains, deer in the eastern woods, moose in the North, or salmon in the Northwest, fish and wildlife remained abundant. The land was wilderness. There were no massive alterations made in the landscape. Probably no more than a million people were spread across this vast land, drawing their sustenance from the forests, marshes, and grasslands, and from the lakes and streams.

"The human population had simply not reached levels that threatened many wild species. That threat would wait for a new breed of hunters, farmers, and developers driven by a relentless urgency to conquer the wilderness and people the land.

"The white man would bring a revolutionary new concept: the conviction that, instead of simply using the land or its products, people could divide land up among themselves and claim absolute ownership of it. The Indian believed that the land did not belong to people, but that people, like the bison and deer, the eagle and the wild geese, were part of the land. Now foreigners would arrive claiming personal ownership of land they wanted, building fences around it, and destroying the trees, grasses, soil, and water that had given life to the wild animals and the Indian people over seasons beyond counting. The face of North America was about to change for all time." [3]

Restricted as they were in what kinds and numbers of animals they could kill, early aboriginal peoples of North America developed close kinships with many of the wild creatures. Animals played important roles in their spiritual and cultural lives. Creatures were revered for their characteristics, or virtues: the eagle for its vision, the bear for its strength, and the panther for its cunning and stealth.[4] In lower California, Natives watched for circling vultures to locate the remains of animals killed by cougars, and in some respects depended on the hunting success of the great cat for sustenance. In contrast, Inca rulers considered pumas to be creatures which deprived them of game, and killed them at every opportunity. The Apaches and Hualpais of Arizona held this great predator in special awe and associated its wailing with death. Others used the dried paws to drive evilness from the sick. The gall of pumas was thought to increase the strength of the ailing, who, when recovered, would assume the fierceness of the cat.[5]

In *Mountain Lion: An Unnatural History of Pumas and People*, Chris Bolgiano carefully reviews the many and varied relationships between the North American lion and Native cultures. As diverse as these relationships were, however, there was one underlying theme. "Enemy, guardian, friend—facets of mountain lion glint and flash through myriad Native beliefs, but underlying them all is a single vein. Natives see the world as a whole in which every entity, animate and inanimate, plays a part. Every part is intimately involved in an unending, mysterious circle of life and death, and any feature of nature—plants, animals, mountains, waterfalls—might be addressed in terms of kinship. The lives of nonhumans have importance and power. Nonhuman life sustains human life.... Much of the sacredness in Native American thought about animals in general and lions in particular may have been wrenched away by half a millennium of disruption, but there's still an embarrassingly simple lesson at the core: live and let live."[6]

To the Creeks of the southeastern United States, he was known as Katalgar, "Greatest of Wild Hunters," and to the Chickasaws, as Koe-Ishto, "the Cat of God." The Zunis of the southwestern deserts called the long-tailed American cat "Father of Game." To the Cherokees of the southeastern states, he was Klandagi, "Lord of the Forest," and in the northeast, the Malecites of the St. John River called it Pi-Twal, or "The Long-tailed One."[7] To early European colonists the American lion represented all that was feared and respected about the new American wilderness. This rather colorful description of an eastern panther captured near the town of Roxbury, Massachusetts, in 1783 appears to be directed more towards the pockets of unsuspecting "Bostonians" than to the annals of scientific inquiry and fact: "To be seen at the Greay Hound Tavern in Roxbury, a wild creature, which was caught in the woods about 80 miles to the westward of this Town, called a Cattamount, it has a Tail like a Lyon, its Leggs are like a Bears, its Claws like an Eagle, its eyes like a Tyger, its countenance is a mixture of every Thing that is Fierce and Savage, he is exceedingly ravenous and devours all sorts of Creatures that he can come near; its Agility is surprising, it will Leap 30 Foot at one jump notwithstanding it is but Three months old. Whoever inclines to see this Creature may come to the Place aforesaid, paying a Shilling each, shall be welcome for their Money."[8]

It was only natural that the lion that roamed the length and breadth of the Americas fostered many human emotions—fear, admiration, hate—throughout its great range. It shunned the mighty jaguar to the south, and lorded over the smaller lynx and bobcat to the north. It was known and respected by all who shared with it the darkened recesses of the steamy jungles and the frigid slopes of the northern Rockies. Because of its large geographic range and its influence on so many early peoples, no other animal has been referred to by so many different names.

To me, the name Klandagi, Lord of the Forest, best describes the role and status of this great hunter of the American wilderness. But Klandagi was not always the "lord of the predators." In a much earlier America there were other now-extinct predators of larger stature and greater strength. The dire wolf, the short-faced bear, the New World sabretooth tiger and the American cheetah: not to forget the timber wolf and grizzly bear. It has been suggested that the timid demeanor and fear shown by American lions today towards the much smaller dog may well be a survival tactic inherited from those early ancestors that successfully lived among an assemblage of larger beasts of prey through tactical subordinance rather than bravado and challenge.[9]

Amerigo Vespucci—after whom the two American continents are named—while probing the coastline of Nicaragua in 1500 saw what he believed to be lions, probably because of their similarity to the African lion with which he was familiar. Two years later, on his fourth voyage to the New World, Christopher Columbus, while exploring the coastline of Central America, wrote: "I saw some very large fowls (the feathers of which resemble wool), lions (leones), stags, fallow deer, and birds."[10] His reference to "stags" probably meant elk, and "fallow deer" probably meant white-tailed deer—another example of how early Europeans inappropriately applied Old World names to the similar-looking but often quite different wildlife they encountered in the New World. The honor of being the first European to sight a "lion" in North America fell to Alvar Nunez Cabeza de Vaca, who in 1513, saw one near the Florida Everglades. "Tyger" was another name used for the American lion throughout the Carolinas, Georgia and Florida during the fifteenth and sixteenth centuries.[11] Captain John Smith left us one of the earliest references to the panther in the United States as he described the wildlife in Virginia about 1609-1610: "there be in this country Lions, Beares, woulues, foxes, muske catts, Hares fleinge squirells and other squirrels."[12]

But it was the early English naturalist John Ray who first attached a label on this new and mysterious American cat. In 1693 he used the native Brazilian name of "cuguacuarana" to describe the eastern panther, a move not universally endorsed by his English countrymen, who still believed that this creature was more closely related to the African lion. Later, in 1749, the French naturalist Count de Buffon called the panther "le couguar" and remarked that this large American cat was "smaller, weaker, and less courageous than the true lion."[13] This did not sit well with the great American statesman Thomas Jefferson. The soon-to-be president was quite offended by such frivolous remarks about an animal as courageous as the American lion, especially coming from a Frenchman, and he rebuked this not-so-concealed insult on more than one occasion.[14] Then, in 1771, Carolus Linnaeus, the early Swedish botanist who developed the binomial system for classifying living things, gave the panther its first and quite personalized scientific name, *Felis concolor*—quite simply, "cat of one color."

Further revisions of the species followed, but it was Stanley Young and Arthur Goldman's classic study of the species in 1946 that has been used as the accepted reference for the past fifty years. They examined hundreds of specimens stored away in assorted American museums and other institutions, many of which had been collected during early predator control programs in the western United States. They recognized one genus, *Felis;* one species, *concolor,* and thirty subspecies, of which fourteen are found in North America. They recognized two subspecies east of the Mississippi River: *Felis concolor coryi*, the Florida panther; and *Felis concolor couguar*, the eastern panther, the one we are most concerned with here.[15] Young and Goldman used the term "puma" to describe the species throughout its range in the New World, but recognized the abundance of local names, such as "cougar" in the northwest, "mountain lion" in the west, "panther" in Florida and "puma" in Central and South America. Because of the rarity of the animal north of Florida, they failed to recognize the name "panther" but used the term "eastern puma." Puma means "a powerful animal" in Quichua, an Inca language, and although it may have served to describe the great strength of this impressive predator, it is of little other use to us here. The early settlers of the Appalachians never used the term "puma" to describe this feared hunter, and we won't either. In all, the American lion has been known under eighteen native South American, twenty-five Native North American, and forty English names.[16]

As a rule of thumb, this large cat is called puma or "leon" throughout the Spanish-speaking countries of Central and South America, to distinguish it from *el tigre*, the jaguar. In North America it is called "mountain lion" in the western United States, "cougar" in the Pacific northwest and "panther" east of the Mississippi River. In the northeastern United States and eastern Canada it was often called "catamount," or "cat of the mountain," and "painter," a corruption of the word panther. It is believed that the name "catamount" originated from the Spanish *gat-monte*, meaning "mountain cat."[17] It seems just as likely that catamount is merely short for the descriptive term, "cat of the mountain," which the panther certainly was throughout much of the northeast.

Henry Shoemaker, an early twentieth-century Pennsylvanian historian, reviewed some of the early names given to the panther in that state: "The Pennsylvania lion was known by a great variety of names. William Penn called it the panther—why, cannot be imagined; it is colored very differently from the *panthere* of Northern Africa, which he probably had in mind. The backwoodsmen called it the *painter*; there is a Painter Run in Tioga County, a Painterville in Westmoreland county, and painter hollows and painter rocks innumerable all over the State . . . There have been a few Pennsylvanians who called the Pennsylvanian lion the cougar, and a still smaller number who alluded to it as the puma.. . . Others have referred to it as the

American Lion, Brown Tiger and Catamount. The last title refers more properly to the Canada Lynx, or big grey wild cat. The Pennsylvania Germans used to call the panther the Bender."[18]

It has also been called "Indian devil" and "Adirondack cougar" in the northeast, "Alleghenian cougar," "brown tiger," "tiger tail" and "long-tailed cat."[19] The list goes on.

An adult eastern panther would appear very similar to this fine specimen of western mountain lion. (HANSEN, 1992).

The term "eastern panther" distinguishes this northern race from the southern Florida panther. The Florida panther, the only breeding population presently confirmed east of the Mississippi River, is now restricted to several small pockets of wilderness in the southern part of that state, although the race is believed to have once been distributed through Georgia, South Carolina, Mississippi and Louisiana. It is likely that considerable interbreeding between the two races once occurred, resulting in only subtle differences between them in much of the south-central United States.

Before Europeans arrived in the Americas and pursued the large predators with trap and gun, these great cats ranged from Canada to Tierra del Fuego, from the coasts of both oceans to the peaks of the Appalachians, Rockies and Andes. The explorers were soon followed by the first European colonists, and these early settlers were also at a loss about what to call this great new cat. The few cats brought to the fortified settlements by early Native Americans looked like African lions, especially the female lion which did not have a mane. Like the explorers before them, they called them lions and at first wondered why those that were killed were all females. They soon realized, after closer inspection, that the male of this strange animal, like the female, was also maneless and was certainly different than any African lion they were familiar with. This new creature was indeed quite different. But what could they call it?

For reasons that have perplexed many who followed, they chose to call this feared creature "panther." Many people have wondered why. The word "panther" comes from the Latin *panthera*, which in turn comes from a Greek word used to describe the tiger's black stripes. So the words "black" and "panther" have a long and shared history. Although the word was used at various times and places to describe several of the large spotted cats, especially leopards and jaguars, and occasionally the striped tiger, it increasingly became the universal word to describe the black phase of the leopard. The black phase of any animal is caused by the production of a dark pigment in the fur called melanin, an uncommon although not rare condition known as melanism. Melanism is particularly common among several of the spotted cats, especially in the tropical regions of Africa, India and Central and South America. Panthers and large black cats became synonymous.

Why did the early settlers choose to call this tawny-colored New World lion a panther, an animal which has never been known to have a black phase? And why have I chosen to follow the same obviously mistaken path? For two reasons. The first is because this is a book on a great predator which played an important role in the lives of the early American settlers. It was their animal that I describe; it is their stories that I tell; and it is their name that I use. But I choose to call this great predator of the east a panther for more than just reasons of tradition. I think I understand why it was called panther.

Although melanistic leopards are black, or darkly pigmented, their spots are often still visible. In fact, for many years scientists were confused about the exact identity of these black-phased leopards with spots and often referred to them as separate from the more common and lighter-colored spotted leopard. Early American colonists would have soon become familiar with the short-tailed and much smaller bobcat and lynx. So when they saw their first eastern panther pelts, and they would not have seen many, they referred to them as lions. But the physical differences between the two soon became obvious. Young North American mountain lions (I will use "mountain lion" as a generic term for the species in North America, and "puma" for Central and South America), however, have distinct spots at birth which gradually disappear as they mature, although the spots may remain visible through the first six to eight months of life. Some suggest that the early ancestors of the North American mountain lion may have been striped or spotted, this characteristic now only remaining in the young and immature. Many of the early panthers brought into the settlements would have been immature, still showing visible but fading spots. The only other long-tailed cat of similar stature which also showed faint spots was the melanistic leopard, or, as it was then known, panther. Melanistic leopards are not always black but are frequently charcoal and sooty-colored. The eastern North American panther also varied in color from grey through tawny to rufous. Some early hunters spoke of the panther changing from a tawny rufous in the summer to a bluish grey in winter, much like the seasonal change in the color of white-tailed deer. To me, then, it was quite natural that the early colonists changed the name for this cat from "lion" to "panther." Both would have been the only two cats of similar size and color which showed, at times, various intensities of spotting. We can only speculate now. But "panther" it became known as, and "panther" is what I have chosen to call it here.

The name "panther" was originally used to describe the black, or melanistic, phase of the leopard.

(LOXTON, 1973)

Why is it now so often referred to as a "cougar" in eastern North America? The answer is quite simple: technology! The last of the true eastern panthers may have gone to life's reward a century or more ago, and certainly regular contact between panthers and early Americans was lost well before then. Reference to panthers in daily conversation fell from common use. It was not until the mid-1900s that this great American cat again made its presence in the eastern United States, and this time it was through radio, movies and television. The cowboys and frontiersmen of western America were often shown in battle with this mighty predator, which there, of course, was called a "cougar." The species was brought east and appeared in early carnivals, road shows and zoos. These captive animals retained their western identity as cougars, and reference to the eastern panther was relegated to long-forgotten prose and verse. But the significance of the eastern panther in early American life remains immortalized through the hundreds of places which still bear its name: Panther Mountain, Panther Rock, Panther Run, to name but a few. What are the stories behind these names? Did some brave soul slay one of these feared creatures on a faraway mountain peak and proudly bear his prize into town? Maybe some secluded meadow was renowned for the panthers which prowled there, where only the most courageous or foolhardy dared venture. Or perhaps some unfortunate mortal stumbled upon an unsuspecting panther and paid the ultimate price.

Most of us are familiar with the general physical features and coloration of North America's largest native cat. This animal of strength and stealth has been the symbol and logo for numerous commercial products and athletic teams: the University of Vermont Catamounts; the Pennsylvania State University Nittany Lions; the Carolina Panthers. Few western movies are complete without at least one encounter with this ferocious beast, most often at the expense of the lion. Maybe a little larger here, a little darker there, but given the vastness of its range throughout North and South America, this animal of many names is remarkably similar in appearance. Its name implies an animal of one color, and except for the black tips of the tail and ears and a white belly and rump, adults vary from a grey to shades of brown to red. Young kittens have rows of small irregular black spots that disappear as they mature.

As for size, the reported weights and lengths, like most so-called trophy animals, are often the product of considerable exaggeration. The largest documented western mountain lion was shot in Arizona in 1917 by a government predatory animal hunter. This male weighed 276 pounds and measured 8 feet, 7 3/4 inches, from the tip of its nose to the end of its tail. Theodore Roosevelt shot a male in Colorado in 1901 which weighed 227 pounds and measured 8 feet in length. Most lions, however, especially the panthers remaining in Florida, and the eastern panthers which were formerly common throughout the Appalachians, were considerably smaller. There are surprisingly few specimens of eastern panthers left for us to examine. Many of those available are in such a state of disrepair that colors have faded and features are distorted. We can, however, refer to firsthand descriptions left by America's early settlers, frontierspeople and natural-

Young North American mountain lions (Felis concolor) have spots at birth which gradually fade as the lion matures. A young spotted eastern panther would have appeared much like a leopard to early European colonists.

(HANSEN, 1992).

ists. It must be remembered, however, that we have no way to substantiate such records, and many may contain ample amounts of personal flair and embellishment.

We have already heard what one enterprising colonial promoter in the Roxbury area thought of this "fierce and savage" creature. Another early but certainly less opulent description of eastern panthers was left to us by Philip Tome, a hunter and outdoorsman of great repute who roamed the wilderness forests and valleys of the West Branch of the Susquehanna River in Pennsylvania during the early 1800s. Tome referred to the eastern panther as the "jaguar," "the American panther," or as it was often corrupted by early American hunters, "the painter." He described it as "one of the most formidable animals encountered in the forests of this continent." Tome noted the similarity in color between the panther and its main prey, the white-tailed deer. Both were reddish in summer but changed to a bluish colour in the autumn. Tome wrote: "They subsist entirely upon animal food, their usual prey being deer and rabbits. About the first of January is called the running season, being the time when they mate. When the first snows of winter come, they seek the rocky hills and sheltered places, where they remain until driven forth by hunger, when they frequently visit the farmyards of the settlers, and help themselves to any sheep or fowl that is within their reach."

Although Tome spent a lifetime in the wilderness of Pennsylvania, where panthers were common, he never found a den or "nest" with young panthers.

"I once saw a panther thrust her head out of a hole in an old hollow tree, but as I had no gun or axe, I went home, and in a few days returned and cut down the tree. I found in it a snug, warm nest, which she had occupied with her young but she had seen me, and removed them to other quarters. The bear is the only animal that can cope with the panther. I once witnessed an encounter between a bear and a panther. For its superior agility the panther had the advantage at first, but when the bear became enraged by his wounds, he grasped his antagonist in his powerful jaws, crushing and biting him to death almost instantly. When a panther is about to attack its prey, it creeps noiselessly along until within a few yards of it, when crouching flat, it pauses for a moment, with its eyes dilated, its tail quivering, and every muscle strained to its utmost tension, and then, with a sudden spring, it fastens upon its victim, which it soon dispatches with its teeth and long powerful claws. From this peculiar manner of attack, it is sometimes enabled to conquer even an elk and I have twice found elk, which had been killed by panthers; one of them so recently that it was yet warm, and I killed the panther within a short distance. I have attacked a panther with eight dogs, for which it proved more than a match, driving them all from the field. Notwithstanding its ferocity and strength, it is little feared by hunters, and many of the marvelous tales of its attacks upon men are undoubtedly without foundation. It may be that in some instances they have been driven by hunger to attack the human species, but with that instinctive consciousness of man's superiority which every animal exhibits, they will generally avoid him if possible."[20]

Henry Shoemaker interviewed many old-time panther hunters in Pennsylvania and left us the following description of the "Lion of Pennsylvania": a long, slim body and a large head; short but strong legs; tail long and tufted at the end; color greyish about the eyes; exterior of ears blackish; reddish shading to a dull grey slate in general body color. Shoemaker quoted the early French naturalist Georges Buffon, who referred to the *cougar de pennsylvanie* as being "low on its legs, has a longer tail than the Western puma; it is described as five feet six inches in length, tail two feet six inches; height before, one foot nine inches; behind, one foot ten inches."[21]

Shoemaker was told by one old hunter that the panthers he killed had heads like "bulldogs." When he describes the sizes of some of the panthers killed in Pennsylvania, it would appear that

This 48-lb., 7-month-old female panther, shot by John Gallant while hunting squirrels in Crawford County, Pennsylvania in 1967, clearly shows juvenile spotting. Early settlers from Europe probably thought such animals were melanistic or dark-colored leopards and called them "panthers".

(COURTESY ROGER COWBURN)

this Pennsylvanian historian may have accepted the word of some of these early hunters without question, as their estimates of lengths seem exceptionally large. He referred to an "Adirondack" Murray, who, about 1869, wrote that "the panther of the 'North Woods' often measured twelve feet from tip to tip," and to another panther caught in a trap near the mouth of the Beaver Dam run which measured "eleven feet six inches from tip to tip."[22] Shoemaker did admit that eight feet was probably a "good average size."

Dr. Clinton Hart Merriam was a respected American naturalist who devoted much of his professional life to collecting and describing the wild animals and plants throughout much of eastern North America during the late 1800s. Like others of his time, such as John James Audubon, Merriam was meticulous in his field observations and equally possessed by a burning passion to leave written record of the wild native creatures with which he shared a primitive but rapidly changing American landscape. Merriam traveled through the Adirondack Mountains of New York and there, from personal observation and word of mouth, he described in particular detail many characteristics of the "Adirondack" panther in one of the last retreats for this noble creature. He believed that a few still remained in the remote sections of the Adirondacks in the late 1800s, but their numbers had been severely depleted from the state bounty imposed in 1871. He remained optimistic, however, and concluded that "some years may yet elapse before the last Panther disappears from the dense evergreen swamps and high rocky ridges of this

Wilderness." Merriam travelled with E. L. Sheppard, an experienced northwoods guide and hunter "who has himself killed, or been instrumental in killing, twenty-eight Panthers in the Adirondacks." Much of what Merriam wrote about panthers was told to him during his travels with Sheppard.

"[Panthers] are either particularly fond of porcupines, or else are frequently forced by hunger to make a distasteful meal, for certain it is that large numbers of these spiny beasts are destroyed by them. Indeed, it often happens that a Panther is killed whose mouth and lips, and sometimes other parts also, fairly bristle with the quills of this formidable rodent. Porcupines are such logy, sluggish creatures that they fall prey to any animal that cares to meddle with them. But the Panther feeds chiefly upon venison, which he captures by 'still-hunting,' in a way not unlike, save in the manner of killing, that practised by its greatest enemy, man. Both creep stealthily upon the intended victim until within range; when the one springs, the other shoots."[23]

Stories of great feats of strength are part of the panther legend. Merriam tells us that Mr. Sheppard measured the length of one leap over snow of forty feet. The panther hit the deer on its fourth bound. The largest leap was sixty feet, although the panther had jumped from a ledge of rocks some twenty feet above its prey. Merriam noted that panthers in winter spread their toes, much like the Canada lynx, to keep from sinking in the deep snows. This gave the panther a great advantage over its main prey, the white-tailed deer, which flounders in snow over two feet deep.

A deer killed by a panther was often dragged into a nearby thicket or under windfalls for concealment, sometimes as far as one hundred feet. Upon killing a deer, the panther remained near its kill for a week or more, devouring it all. During this time the carcass was often covered by leaves and other forest debris between meals. Merriam described the hunting of a panther in winter: "Panthers are hunted during the deep snows of winter, when the hunter, on snowshoes, makes wide circuits in various directions till he finds a track. This he follows, leading the dogs, till he comes to the carcass of a deer which the Panther has recently killed and partially devoured. Knowing that the animal is not far off, he now "lets loose" the dogs, and as a rule the cowardly beast is soon "treed" and shot. Out of the twenty-eight panthers in the killing of which Mr. Sheppard was concerned, four refused to 'tree,' and were shot while on the ground. When attacked they never spring after the dogs, but merely act on the defensive. When a dog makes bold to come too near he receives such an energetic 'cuff' from the Panther's paw that he rarely solicits another."[24]

Although most of what Merriam wrote about panthers of the Adirondacks was learned by word of mouth, it has since proven to have considerable scientific merit, such as his description of its physical stature and reproduction: "In the Adirondacks, it is an uncommonly large Panther that measures eight feet from the end of its nose to the tip of its tail, and an unusually heavy one that weighs a hundred and fifty pounds. An adult Panther stands about two and a half feet high at the shoulders and is so slender that it generally appears to be very thin and gaunt when in reality it may be quite fat. The mother commonly has two kittens at a birth, sometimes one, three, or even four. The young are brought forth late in the winter or in early spring, and the lair is usually in a shallow cavern on the face of some inaccessible cliff or ledge of rocks. It is probable that they do not have young oftener than every other year. . . The young follow the mother till nearly two years old—that is until about two-thirds grown. She leaves them when hunting, and, after having killed a deer, returns and leads them to it. It is often stated that Panthers hunt in pairs, but on one occasion only has Mr. Sheppard found an adult male and female in company. This was early in December and the tracks on the snow indicated that they had been sporting considerably, and were probably rutting. He killed them both."[25]

In their classic 1946 book, Young and Goldman described the eastern panther as a medium-sized to rather large dark form. However, they also acknowledged that all skins examined had been exposed to light, so the exact pelage color was unknown for certain. It has also been referred to as "a small reddish race with a dark dorsal stripe."[26]

So the American lion that we call *Felis concolor* occupies a vast range with great differences in climate and vegetation. But, as we have seen, even with such extremes in environment, individual lions throughout the Americas showed a remarkable similarity in appearance and behavior. A little larger here, a little darker over there, perhaps the fur longer some place else, but a striking continuity in color and general physical appearance throughout. The eastern panther that struck fear in the hearts of the early colonists would have been nearly identical to the typical western cougars which most of us are familiar with today.

How much of a threat to human life was this American lion? Why did the early settlers refer to the panther as "one of the most formidable animals encountered in the forests of this continent"? Was this reputation earned, or unfairly awarded by pioneering folks whose lives were often threatened daily in their struggle for survival in a hostile wilderness? Surely a creature with such imposing claws and fangs, one which pierced the evening's stillness with its ghostly screams and, in the darkened shadows of night, stole away with the settler's sheep and cattle, must have been a threat to their safety. But let us look at the written record. What do we know of past and recent encounters between panthers and humans? What are the chances that early settlers, or you and I, might be attacked by a panther? Well, if you live on Vancouver Island in Canada's British Columbia, the chances would be very slim but possible, for it is there that attacks by western cougars on humans have been, and continue to be, most frequent. If you live in the mountains of California, the area with the second highest number of cougar attacks on people, again possible but hardly likely. But we're talking about the eastern panther, that elusive creature that many people believe lives more in folklore and the imagination than in the forests and mountains of eastern North America.

But let's put it into perspective. Paul Beier of the Department of Forestry and Resource Management at the University of California in Berkeley, summarized stories and accounts of attacks by cougars on humans throughout North America for the one hundred-year period from 1890 through 1990.[27] Beier searched both popular and scientific literature for accounts of attacks and corresponded and spoke with personnel of twelve western states and the two western Canadian provinces of Alberta and British Columbia. His extensive search uncovered accounts of nine fatal attacks and forty-four nonfatal attacks, resulting in ten human deaths and forty-eight nonfatal injuries (several attacks involved multiple victims). Ten human deaths in one hundred years! Bier compares the threat from cougars to several other wild animals: "Each year in the United States there are about 12 human deaths resulting from over 5,000 bites by rattlesnakes, 40 deaths due to bee stings, and three deaths due to bites of black widow spiders. Dogs annually kill 18-20 people and inflict suture-requiring injuries on 200,000 U.S. residents. In a single year (1979) there were 86 U.S. deaths due to lightening strikes."[28]

Each year, man's best friend, the domestic dog, kills twice as many people as cougars have in one hundred years! Bees kill four times as many! And the few documented attacks and deaths from cougars took place in the western states and provinces, areas where cougars are regularly seen, where cougars attack and kill domestic animals, and where they are frequently hunted and killed. What about the eastern panther? Did they ever pose a threat to the early settlers? Do records earlier than a century ago suggest that this feared predator may have earned its reputation? The answer, in short, is yes, but there are very few. There are lots of stories and tales, but few substantiated fatal encounters.

By the side of scenic Route 84, near English Center, Pennsylvania, is a monument whose inscription reminds travelers of the days when native panthers roamed much of that state. The bronze plaque on the face of a gigantic boulder reads:

In Memory of Dr. Frederick Reinwald
Dr. Reinwald was killed by a panther
at Black's Creek, four miles northeast
of this point, December 22, 1846, while
on his way to visit a patient. An unusual
example of the fortitude of pioneer physicians
and the hazards they faced in the performance
of their duties.

There is no information on the plaque about who placed it there. Nevertheless, it is a reminder that, despite what many may say to the contrary, panthers did—although infrequently—kill human beings. However, many of the tales of humans being killed by these great beasts may have evolved from circumstances where presumed victims died in the woods from other causes and their bodies were molested by animals some of which were panthers.

In an old cemetery at Lewisville, Chester County, Pennsylvania, is a tombstone with a crude image of a panther. Beneath this engraving is the following inscription:

Here lye the body
of Philip Tanner who
Departed this life
May 6, 1751 aged
58 years

It is believed that the unfortunate Mr. Tanner was killed by a panther at the edge of a patch of woods at a spot called Bettys Patch, near Lewisville, about one-half mile from the cemetery.[29] So the fear shown by early Americans towards the eastern panther may not have been completely misplaced. Legend has it that in 1903 a George Cunningham of Bedford County, Pennsylvania, was on his way home from Altoona by horse-drawn wagon. Suddenly, as the story goes, a large panther leaped from a tree and onto the back of one of the two horses. Mr. Cunningham, who was armed with a revolver at the time, drew his weapon and took aim at the panther, which was clawing and biting the horse. In the excitement of the moment, Mr. Cunningham's aim was less than he might have hoped, and he shot the horse in the head, whereupon it fell dead to the ground. The panther, meanwhile, escaped back into the forest. Mr. Cunningham managed to unhitch the dead steed and reach a nearby house with his now one-horse-drawn wagon.[30]

In a 1960 article in the *Pennsylvania Game News*, Herbert Walker treats us to a tantalizing taste of stories of pioneers and panthers: "In the north, its primary prey was deer, and, after several thousand successful years, coming into conflict with man, it became established in folklore as a bloodthirsty beast. There is a tale of a boy dragged from his horse by a panther along the Erie Canal. A Catskill story tells of a hunter who came upon the body of his companion's dog at the base of a tree where a panther lay stretched upon a limb devouring his missing partner. From Lewis County comes the story of an infant seized from its crib and carried into the night. The panther-kidnapper was unable to scale a rail fence with its burden and dropped the child unharmed. George Hinchley, while driving near Corinth in 1876, was attacked by a panther that leaped into his sled. As he grappled in hand-to-hand combat, as it were, the halter became wrapped around the panther's neck. The wildly careening cutter tumbled and Hinchley freed himself, but the panther was dragged away by the terrified horse and strangled. None of the tales, however, rivals an Ambrose Bierce story of a corpse carried from its bier by a panther. The following morning, the cadaver was found with a chunk of the panther's ear clenched firmly between its teeth!"[31]

Ah, yes. But perhaps we should return to the facts, as best we know them. Dr. Merriam, whom we have seen, roamed through the Adirondack Mountains of New York near the turn of the century, painted a less dangerous picture of the panther: "Though possessed of great strength and power, and naturally quick in his movements, the Panther is a positive coward. For all that, when seriously wounded, without being entirely crippled, all his latent ferocity is aroused, and he rushes fiercely at his assailants. But even at such times, when in an attitude of supreme anger and rage, and while lashing the snow impetuously with his long tail, anything thrust into his open mouth serves to divert his wrath from the enemy to his weapon. Thus on two occasions, once with an axe, and once with the muzzle of his gun, has Mr. Sheppard saved himself and his dogs from mutilation, if not from a horrible death."[32]

Merriam questioned some of the common fallacies of the day regarding the panther, especially its reputed fierceness and danger to humans: "Even as cautious and reliable a naturalist as Zadock Thompson quotes the following appalling and blood-curdling tale as an authentic narrative: 'Two hunters, accompanied by two dogs, went out in quest of game, near the Catskill Mountains. At the foot of a large hill, they agreed to go round it in opposite directions, and when either discharged his rifle, the other was to hasten toward him to aid him in securing the game. Soon after parting, the report of a rifle was heard by one of them, who, hastening toward the spot, after some search, found nothing but the dog, dreadfully lacerated and dead. He now became much alarmed for the fate of his companion, and, while anxiously looking round, was horror-struck by the harsh growl of a Catamount, which he perceived on a large limb of a tree, crouching upon the body of his friend, and apparently meditating an attack on himself. Instantly he levelled his rifle at the beast, and was so fortunate as to wound it mortally, when it fell to the ground along with the body of his slaughtered companion. His dog then rushed upon the wounded Catamount, which, with one blow of its paw, laid the poor creature dead by his side.' "[33]

But the stories and legends of this American lion grew as each new wave of early settlers pushed deeper into the darkened recesses of the Appalachians. It is a well-known fact that hunters, like fishermen, do on occasion embellish the facts of a chase or catch in order to better capture the attention of the audience at hand. A hunter who shot a panther hiding in a tree or cowering behind a boulder was much less respected than one who wrestled into submission a snarling beast that attacked him on the forest path. The following story of the killing of "'one of these insidious, pitiless denizens of the forest," which appeared in an 1876 edition of the *American Sportsman*, might serve as an example: " 'The wounded animal was emitting piercing cries, and its powerful tail was rapidly lashing its flanks. Again the hunter stepped out; it was but a moment's glance, but he saw the flaming eyes, the stretched and foam-dripping jaws, the ivory-white claws that riveted themselves into the great branch upon which the panther lay.' Such description is typical of dozens that stirred the hunter's imagination and created an image of the panther in the popular mind."[34]

This very large 217-lb. male mountain lion was shot on Jan. 15, 1927 in Colorado. Although there are stories of extremely large eastern panthers, they were a small race of mountain lion and seldom exceeded 7 to 8 feet in total length and 150 pounds in weight. Many would have weighed well under 100 pounds.

(YOUNG AND GOLDMAN, 1964).

The great American president and sportsman Theodore Roosevelt certainly did the reputation of the panther little favor when he described it as " 'a big horse-killing cat, the destroyer of deer, the lord of stealthy murder facing his doom with a heart both craven and cruel.' At the same time, however, some biologists who kept cougars in captivity were describing them as playful and shy. The truth may lie somewhere in between, as one naturalist suggested in 1912: 'After 31 years of more or less constant association with the beast, I have arrived at the conclusion that the cougar is the most incongrous mixture of courage and cowardice, boldness and stealth, wisdom and imbecility of any animal that runs wild.' "[35]

But attacks by mountain lions on humans do occur; most have been in the western United States and Canada. One such encounter took place in California in 1909. A physician, Dr. J.T. Higgins, treated a woman, Isola Kennedy, who had been scratched by a mountain lion. She had received her wounds when attempting to rescue a boy who was being attacked by the cat. Upon approach the lion turned its attention from the boy to his would-be rescuer. The courageous Miss Kennedy, held to the ground and being mauled by the lion, withdrew a hatpin of considerable length and proceeded to plunge this propitious weapon into the heart of her attacker. The two continued their struggle with the cat inflicting considerable damage to the lady from the claws of both front and hind feet. The battle was ended when a neighbor arrived on the scene and shot the lion in the head. By the time the doctor reached her, she had fifteen deep gashes reaching from her shoulder to her wrist. The doctor treated Miss Kennedy and assured all that she would survive unless her wounds became infected. On the road to recovery, the unfortunate lady took a turn for the worse some seven weeks after the incident. The lion had been infected with rabies, and Miss Kenedy and the boy both proceeded to die from the disease. This remains the only recorded instance of a human death caused by a rabid mountain lion.[36]

Today, mountain lion and human encounters are becoming more frequent in areas of increasing lion densities in western North America. As of February 1992, four Americans had been killed by mountain lions in the preceding twenty-one years, and fourteen had been injured. In British Columbia, ten people had been killed by mountain lions since 1900, most on Vancouver Island.

From 1992 to 1997, four more people died from attacks by mountain lions, two in California and two in British Columbia. In April 1994, a forty-year-old female long-distance runner was killed by a mountain lion in a recreation area forty-five miles northeast of Sacramento. The offending adult female mountain lion was subsequently hunted down and shot. Several months later, in December 1994, a fifty-eight-year-old woman was killed while hiking and birdwatching in Cuyamaca Rancho State Park near San Diego. That mountain lion was also tracked down and shot. The fatal attack followed several incidents in which mountain lions had chased or menaced visitors at the park. Several lions had been killed earlier in or near the park after officials declared them a threat to human safety. In July 1995, a mountain lion killed a thirty-two-year-old man riding a bicycle near Port Alberni on Vancouver Island, British Columbia. He was the fourth person to have been killed by lions on Vancouver Island in fifty years. And in August 1996 a mother sacrificed her life to save her six-year-old child when they were attacked by a mountain lion while horsebackriding in southern British Columbia.

Why does there seem to be a growing number of lion-human encounters? People have been attacked by cougars in Montana, Colorado, New Mexico, Texas and California. In 1990 alone, Montana officials recorded twenty-four separate non-fatal confrontations. A developing pattern in most incidences appears to be young lions with little fear of humans. Most immature lions do not have established territories and are more prone to wander into residential outskirts which are themselves expanding into the scrublands where lions live. Reduced hunting of lions in most states and outright moratoriums in others, such as California, have contributed to increased lion populations. Thus, more lions, reduced fear of humans due to lack of hunting, and residential sprawl into lion habitat have all contributed to the recent rash of lion attacks on humans. Deer, the preferred food of mountain lions, have also become established in many rural residential developments—another attraction for the hungry lion.

In a 1992 article in the *Smithsonian*, Susan Lumpkin offers some interesting insight into the growing conflict: "The sheer effrontery of some of these attacks is astonishing. . . The boldness displayed by mountain lions in attacking or killing people just doesn't square with the shy, retiring behavior familiar to those of us who have studied these animals. . . I think the hound or pack of hounds can play the part of a dominant predator in the mountain lion's life. . . Could it be, therefore, that cats are becoming emboldened in areas where they have had no recent experience with a dominant predator? . . . During the past 20 years, thanks to reduction in poisoning, increased protection and an abundance of prey, lions have moved back into their former range, including Yellowstone. With grizzlies and wolves essentially gone, the cats are now the biggest predator—the dominant predator."[37]

So mountain lions can indeed pose a threat to human safety.

But so do most wild animals, especially the large predators. We would be foolish to think otherwise. There is a certain degree of responsibility that comes with increasing wild populations of large predators, especially in areas where humans and the predators choose to cohabit. But how real is the potential threat to humans from panthers in eastern North America? Given the uncertainty that panthers even exist in most of the eastern half of the continent, it would be difficult, at the moment, to make this a credible public issue. If large wild cats of whatever origin are found in certain regions of the east, the potential for isolated incidents with humans is certainly real. But relative to the many other threats to human safety we face daily, it cannot be taken too seriously just now.

Justified or not, the American lion was feared by early Americans and was hunted down and destroyed whenever possible. In retrospect, much of that fear was probably misplaced, but while survival in the unforgiving American frontier was uncertain, there was little room for empathy. A fattened hog lost to a roaming panther or bear might well mean hunger or death during the long winter months ahead. But what do the records tell us of the passion and intensity of the war waged against the large predators of early America?

CHAPTER THREE

A Legacy of Persecution

THE MANY FRONTIERSMEN of early America lived much of their lives in the backwoods, among the lakes, swamps and mountains which lay between the settlements along the Atlantic coast and the vast reaches of the Mississippi River. They lived alone in isolation or left their wives and children in the shelter of remote cabins or small villages while they tramped the interior wilderness in search of wild game and adventure. Many lived harsh and short lives, and most passed through this life with no record of their accomplishments or failures. There were, however, a few hardy souls who chose, for some reason, to leave written testimony of their adventures and struggles in the forests and with the wild animals found there. One of these was Meshach Browning, who passed his travels and exploits on in his autobiography, *Forty-Four Years of the Life of a Hunter*.[1] This account of one frontiersman, hunter and slayer of panthers, although certainly impressive, may not be entirely unique, and the mountains and valleys of the Appalachians two hundred years ago most certainly contained many other men like him.

Browning was born in Maryland in 1781, lost his father when he was only two weeks old and was raised by his mother and, on occasion, by an aunt and uncle. He married at eighteen, and from then on, after the crops were in and other matters of summer tended to, he would strike off into the woods to fill the larder with wild game. His reputation as a master marksman and hunter stood unchallenged, and stories of his bravery and daring became legend. He could run down and wrestle to submission a wounded deer, and was known to battle wounded bear with knife and club. When he approached his eighties and his hunting days came to a close, he estimated that he had killed two thousand deer, four hundred bear and fifty panthers, along with many wolves and bobcats.[2] Browning, like most hunters of his day, relied upon the devotion, tenacity and companionship of one or more hunting dogs on most of his excursions. These dogs were of mixed pedigree, and were bred for their size, strength and bravery. Browning's dogs were a mix of English Bull and Greyhound. Few panthers, then or now, would ever be slain without first being treed or cornered by the pursuit of dogs.

Browning saw and shot his first panther in November 1798 at the age of eighteen years. The young lad had already slain many deer and bear and impressed those who traveled with him with his prowess with a rifle and his knowledge of the ways of wild game. Several years earlier at the tender age of sixteen he had clubbed a large wounded black bear into submission while his older but less daring, although perhaps more sane, hunting companions scampered up the nearest trees for their lives. The following matter-of-fact account attests to Browning's courage and humility:

"Not long after we had settled in our new home [he had just brought his mother and step-father to Maryland from West Virginia], there fell a light snow, when I took my rifle, and calling a dog which I had brought with me from Wheeling, which was of the stock of old Mr. Caldwell's hunting dogs, I went into the woods after deer. I had not traveled far before I found the tracks of four deer, which had run off; for they had got wind of me, and dashed into a great thicket to hide themselves. I took the trail, and into the thicket I went, where I soon saw the deer running in different directions. I got between them, in hopes that I should see them trying to come together again. I kept my stand perhaps five or six minutes, when I saw something slipping through the bushes, which I took to be one of the deer; but I soon found that it was coming toward me. I kept a close look out for it; and directly, within ten steps of me, up rose the head and shoulders of the largest panther that I ever saw, either before or since. He kept behind a large log that was near me, and looked over. But though I had never seen a wild one before, I knew the gentleman, and was rather afraid of him. I aimed my rifle at him as well as I could, he looking me full in the face; and when I fired he made a tremendous spring from me, and ran off through the brush and briers, with the dog after him.

"As soon as I recovered a little from my fright, I loaded again, and started after them. I followed them as fast as I could, and soon found them at the foot of a large and very high rock; the panther in his hurry, having sprung down the cleft of rock fifteen or twenty feet; but the dog, being afraid to venture so great a leap, ran round, and the two had met in a thick laurel swamp, where they were fighting the best way they could, each trying to get the advantage of the other. I stood on the top of the rock over them, and fired at the base of the panther's ear, when down he went; and I ran round the rock, with my tomahawk in hand, believing him to be dead. But when I got near him, I found he was up and fighting again, and consequently I had to hurry back for my gun, load it again, creep slyly up, take aim at his ear, as before, and give him another shot, which laid him dead on the ground. My first shot had broken his shoulder; the second pierced his ear, passing downward through his tongue; the last entered one ear, and came out at the other, scattering his brains all around. He measured eleven feet three inches from the end of his nose to the tip of his tail. This was the largest panther I ever killed, and I suppose I have killed at least fifty in my time."[3]

Several years later, in 1802, Browning tells another story of an encounter with a Maryland panther. He was then twenty-one years of age, lived in a remote cabin in Bear Creek Glades on the upper reaches of the Youghiogheny River in Garrett County, Maryland with his young wife Mary and their daughter, and in his words "lived in quiet and peace with the world, and ourselves, till fall came on."[4]

There they lived on the fruits from the land, "well provided with milk and butter, honey and venison.... I continued till fall, hunting bees and shooting turkeys and as many deer as I wanted. In September old Mrs. McMullen [Browning's mother-in-law] visited us, arriving in the afternoon; and Mary [Browning's young wife] said to me that she wanted some fresh venison, as she knew her mother was very fond of it; whereupon I took my dog and gun, and set out for an evening hunt.

"As the movements of my dog showed me, beyond a doubt, that there was game near, I ordered him to go on, when he bounded off to a large mass of rocks. I then knew it was not deer he was after, but that there must be a bear hid in those rocks. Gunner [his dog] presently came to a great crack in the rocks, and, after scenting around awhile, I told him to go in and fetch the animal out, believing that I should see a poor bear crawl out; for at that time all bears were poor. Down went Gunner, while I ran to the other side of the rock; but to my astonishment a panther bounded out, and, jumping from rock to rock, soon got out of sight. The dog followed among the rocks as best he could, and soon I could neither see nor hear anything more of them; but, after some minutes, the dog opened again, as if he was coming back on the other side of the rocks and laurel.

"Treeing and Shooting a Panther." *A sketch of hunter, dog and panther in Maryland sometime in the early 1800s.*

(BROWNING, 1859)

"I turned to follow the dog; but all again becoming quiet, I listened with anxiety, when I heard something moving behind me. I looked around, and beheld the panther coming toward me, but not near enough for me to shoot. He made a short turn, which brought him opposite me, and within ten steps; but he went on the off side of a rock, that covered him from my shot. As I saw he would have to come from behind the rock, and be exposed to my view, I held my fire till he came out; and as soon as he made his appearance, I let him have a shot, which I directed as near as I could for his heart. As the gun cracked he sprang into the air, snapping at the place where the ball had struck him; and then turning towards me, he came on till within about five steps of me, put his paws on a small fallen tree, and looked me full in the face. While he stood looking at me, I saw the blood streaming from both sides of his body. He stood but a short time, and then sprang up a leaning tree, where he sat only a minute or two, when he again came down to the ground, and disappeared.

I was really glad of it, for I found myself so nervous that I could scarcely load my rifle; and when he was looking at me, I was determined that, if he made an attempt to come nearer to me, I would seek safety in flight; for he would have been obliged to ascend a steep hill, and as I had at least five steps start of him, I don't think he could have caught me. If any man would run at all, I think that would have been as good a cause as he could wish for; and I know I should not have been distanced in that race. In the meantime my dog returned, and I sent him to see what had become of our enemy. He left me in great glee, and descended under a large mass of rocks, where I heard him worrying the panther. I then ventured to the den, and found the beast dead. He was a very large animal, and I felt sure that he had ranged these woods a long time; for many dead deer had been found there, which had been evidently killed by a panther, and after that fellow had been disposed of, no more deer were found dead in those woods."[5]

Meschach Browning, early panther hunter of Maryland, with flintlock and faithful hunting dogs. (BROWNING, 1859)

Browning and his wife Mary had eleven children, and many of his hunts were with his five sons. His first wife died in January 1839, following a long crippling illness from a fall from a horse. Browning was devastated with the loss of his beloved Mary and his "spirit for sporting was entirely gone"[6] He remarried in 1841, however, at the age of sixty, and "obtained as kind and industrious a wife [also named Mary] as any man ever had, and, in a word, one who suited me to admiration ... and I began once more to feel myself contented and happy."[7] He lived happily for another sixteen years until his second wife passed from him in September 1857. Mesching Browning died of pneumonia on November 19, 1859, at the home of his daughter in Johnstown, Maryland, at the age of seventy-eight years, eight months.

Before the advent of spear, arrow and a devious mind, our early primeval ancestors meant little more than an occasional meal to the wild cats, dogs and bears. These defenseless humans depended upon berries, plants, insects, small animals and whatever they could scavenge from the kills left by the true predators—a life of hiding in caves and trees, and being on constant vigil. But the wild beasts took the upper hand when the forests became shrouded beneath the mantle of night. We can only imagine the fear which coursed through the human soul as night's stillness was broken by the howls and barks of wild dogs and the screams of prowling cats. Death could be swift and unexpected. But even through the millennia of human evolution, as we became masters of all other creatures around us, a thread of that primal fear of the great predators has remained with us.

Later, *Homo sapian*, the lowly scavenger, became *Homo sapien*, the mighty hunter. This was especially true during the last ice age, when many large animals, such as the Woolly Mammoth, moved about in herds, and the reasoning human was able to capture and kill with the use of primitive weapons and anticipation. But temperatures moderated, the glaciers receded and many large mammals declined or disappeared altogether. Humans began to rely less on the chase and the kill, and more on cultivated crops which grew well in the newly exposed valleys and meadows. With less dependency on other animals for survival, it seems reasonable to assume that the human perception of animals also changed. Reliance on animals for survival lessened. Animals became more symbolic, and recognized and admired for their unique qualities. Humans continued to kill animals for food, of course, but the killing also became associated with elements of social and cultural significance—ceremonies of initiation and rites of passage, religious festivities, spirituality. Native peoples used animals for specific purposes, and the intent of taking the life of another animal was not motivated by fear, hate or vengeance.

So when Europeans first landed on the Atlantic shores of the New World more than five hundred years ago, they gazed out through their protective stockades onto an unspoiled wilderness teeming with wildlife, many of which were considered dangerous. The pristine American wilderness which sprawled before these pioneering Europeans, themselves encumbered with Old World prejudices, fears and biases, would never be the same. Early colonists believed, as one noted in 1709, that they lived amid "endless Numbers of Panthers, Tygers, Wolves, and other Beasts of Prey" that filled the night with "the dismall'st and most hideous Noise."[8] Over the next 250 years, humans proceeded to wreak havoc on the landscape and its wildlife. It wasn't until the early years of the twentieth century that federal, state and provincial governments slowly began to heed the words of early conservationists and apply the brakes to unsustainable exploitation of natural resources and the wanton destruction of wild animals. What humans hailed as technological achievements often meant tragedy and disaster for wildlife.

The flood of settlers who followed the earlier frontiersmen into the Appalachians was quite remarkable. Many took to the rivers which led them from the coast to the forested interior. One such watery route was the Ohio River, which in 1787 alone was estimated to have carried more than nine hundred flatboats, and eighteen thousand men, women and children and their belongings, including twelve thousand head of livestock, west into the Appalachians.[9] The number of people of European descent in Massachusetts, Connecticut, Rhode Island and New Hampshire increased from just over 30,000 in 1660 to over 90,000 by 1700. Natural population growth remained vigorous from 1700 through 1780, averaging between 26 and 28 percent per decade. Total numbers surpassed 115,000 by 1710 and 215,000 by 1730, and reached 450,000 by 1760.[10] America was on the move, and so were its people. Available agricultural lands around early towns became scarce, and young people moved to new towns to the north, west and south. The impact upon the land and its wildlife from this rapid demographic expansion was immediate and significant.

The early abundance of wildlife was short-lived because of clearing of the land and relentless pursuit by hunters. The Passenger Pigeon was to the east what the bison was to the west. Millions fell to the guns of market hunters. By best estimates, between ten and twelve million were killed each year from 1866 to 1876.[11] Securing wildlife was made easier by rapid improvements in the killing efficiency of firearms. Flintlocks replaced matchlocks in the mid-1600s and remained in use for 150 years. The Civil War ushered in an era of rapid gun development. The early frontiersmen of Kentucky and Pennsylvania carried flintlock rifles, some of which approached five feet in length, and had considerable accuracy. The advent of smokeless powder ammunition in the late 1800s ushered in the era of modern firearms.[12]

The mountainous frontierlands of the Appalachians which sprawled across Kentucky, Tennessee and western Pennsylvania were opened up by the famous such as Daniel Boone and Davy Crockett and by those of lesser acclaim. These men would leave their families behind in the small settlements and wander westward, searching out adventure for months or years at a time. They were hunters and trappers, and most were exceptionally proficient at their business. Years later, Theodore Roosevelt, the great sportsman and American president, would write: "Each backwoodsman was not only a small farmer but also a hunter; for his wife and children depended for their meat upon the venison

Early calendars and hunting magazines often used the panther as the ultimate trophy of the sportshunter.

and bear's flesh procured with his rifle.... The hunter's standard game was the deer, and after that the bear; the elk was already growing uncommon.... He lived out in the woods for many months with no food but meat, and no shelter whatever, unless he made a lean-to of brush or crawled into a hollow sycamore."[13]

Early fear of predators brought swift action in the form of incentives designed for their eradication. In the west, early Jesuit priests in California offered anyone killing a mountain lion a reward of one bull. The Massachusetts Bay Company put a penny-a-pelt bounty on the wolf in 1630 and, in Pennsylvania, William Penn first bountied the wolf in 1683. The state of Massachusetts was paying bounty on panthers in 1764. South Carolina, in its 1695 "Act for destroying Beasts of Prey," ordered every Indian bowman to hand over each year either two bobcat skins or the pelt of a wolf, panther or bear. Laggards were to be "severely" whipped.[14] And of all the dangerous wild creatures which these early adventurers encountered, none was more feared or hated than the panther. Stories of bravado and daring encounters between the hunter and these mighty cats were common. One such tale involved a hunter, Phin Temple, from Wayne County, Pennsylvania, who claimed to have killed 3,500 deer and 400 bears in his day. He supposedly was walking near Preston when a large panther stopped him right in the middle of the road. Without his gun at the moment, his dog drove the cat off. Curious at the unusually bold behavior of the cat, Temple searched the surrounding brush and found two young kittens, which he took home with him, one in each pocket of his coat. He returned to the spot the following day with one of the kittens and his gun. He secured the kitten and hid in the brush nearby. As he expected, the mewing of the kitten soon brought the old female in sight and within range, whereupon Temple reported, "I shot her plumb dead."[15] Perhaps not a sporting end to the tale, but to Temple and his colleagues, an appropriate fate for such a treacherous beast.

The Pennsylvanian historian and storyteller Henry W. Shoemaker stated that "From the earliest times the Pennsylvania lion has been unjustly feared. The first Swedish settlers ... could not but believe that an animal which howled so hideously at night must be a destroyer of human life....The limited range and the limited amount of wild territory in Pennsylvania set an early doom on the native lions. Gradually civilization closed in, and the number of hunters increased yearly. Panther hides were as prevalent on the walls of old-time farm buildings as woodchuck skins are today. Almost every backwoods kitchen had a panther coverlet on the lounge by the stove.… In an early day in Center County, hunters who had killed fifty panthers were of no rare occurrence."[16]

But it was the animal drives, or circle hunts, as they were often referred to, that inflicted some of the greatest losses on American wildlife during the eighteenth century. Communities would unite to hunt wild creatures for meat, sport and, in the case of the larger predators, hate and fear. Most such hunts were never entered in the written annals of history; record of their carnage was passed on only through spoken tale and legend. Perhaps the most notorious took place about the year 1760 in the vicinity of Pomfret Castle, a fort in Pennsylvania built about the year 1756 for defense against the Natives. Early records show that the infamous leader of this momentous event was a gentleman by the name of "Black Jack" Schwartz. Panthers and wolves had been troubling the more timid of the settlers, and a grand drive towards the center of a circle thirty miles in diameter was planned. More than forty panthers were slain in this one drive alone. At the center of this human circle was a cleared plot of ground into which the animals were driven. As many as two hundred hunters marched towards the center, all the while firing their guns, ringing bells and pushing all manner of wild animals forward to their fate.

We can only imagine the chaos at the center. It would not have been a pretty sight, nor a safe one, with animals running hither and yon, birds flying, and bullets being fired in every direction. The slaughter ended when the last animal had fallen or escaped back through the ring of fire. When all the dust and feathers had settled, the final tally often included a number of wounded and injured hunters. At Pomfret Castle it was estimated that several hundred buffalo broke through the circle and gained their freedom. Most weren't so fortunate. The final tally of carnage at Pomfret Castle, as recorded by Black Jack himself, was as follows: 41 panthers, 109 wolves, 112 foxes, 114 mountain cats, 17 black bears, 1 white bear, 2 elk, 198 deer, 111 buffaloes, 3 fishers, 1 otter, 12 gluttons, 3 beavers and upwards of 500 smaller animals. The large number of panthers and wolves in an area only thirty miles in diameter suggests that these large predators were indeed quite abundant in parts of Pennsylvania in the mid-1700s.

"The choicest hides were taken, together with buffalo tongues, and then the heap of carcasses 'as tall as the tallest trees,' was heaped with rich pine and fired. This created such a stench that the settlers were compelled to vacate their cabins in the vicinity of the fort, three miles away. There is a small mound, which on being dug into is filled with bones, that marks the spot of the slaughter, near the headwaters of (West) Mahantango Creek. Black Jack's unpopularity with the Indians was added to when they learned of this animal drive. The red men, who only killed such animals as they actually needed for furs and food, and were real conservationists, resented such a wholesale butchery. The story goes that the wild hunter was ambushed by Indians on a hunting trip and killed. Animal drives did not cease with Black Jack's death, but in some localities they were held annually, until game became practically exterminated. They were held in Northern Pennsylvania, which was settled at a much later date, until about 1830. After the great slaughter of Pomfret Castle, many backwoodsmen appeared in full suits of panther skin. For several years they were known as the 'Panther Boys,' and in their old days they delighted to recount the 'big hunt' to their descendants.... The panther uniforms were abandoned because they became favorite targets for skulking Indians. The savages, infuriated by the arrogance of the white newcomers, spared persons falling into their power occasionally, but gave no quarter to a 'Panther Boy.' The great slaughter of animals kept alive ill feeling between the two races in the region of the Firestone Mountains, and probably a dozen settlers lost their lives because of it. However, they went on with their animal drives, as the hardy settlers loved to do what the Indians hated.... In 1849 the last animal hunt or 'Ring Hunt' was held by the Pioneers at Beech Creek, Clinton county. Several panthers, it is said, escaped through the human barrier."[17]

The use of the circle hunt in capturing large numbers of animals appears to have been a common practice in many regions of early America. The following are the results of two such hunts in Ohio in the early 1800s:

"The literature is replete with accounts of the abundance of some mammals and the various methods of hunting or capturing them. The Rev. Timothy Howe described a circular hunt taken in 1825 in 'Gibbon's Deadening,' an area of 1500 acres in Harrison Township, Licking County, in which a group of men encircled the area to be hunted. Some of the men were on horseback, the remainder on foot, all converging on a common center. The 'bag' consisted of one 'large black bear, three wolves, forty-nine deer, sixty or seventy turkeys, and one owl.' The 'Great Hinckley Hunt' occurred on 24 December 1818 in Medina County, Ohio, principally in Hinckley Township.... 'Nearly six hundred men and boys' participated in this circular-type hunt.

This picture, which appeared in an 1890 Mobile, Alabama newspaper, clearly shows the hate and fear which humans felt for the eastern panther.

(LAYCOCK, 1990)

Four lines of men and large boys, each line five miles long, formed a hollow square, which converged inward towards a common center. Many deer and other mammals succeeded in breaking through the lines and escaping. However, 'An accurate enumeration of the game collected at the center resulted as follows: seventeen wolves, twenty-one bears, 300 deer.' Most of the turkeys escaped by flying over the lines, although a few were taken.... This hunt appears to have been well planned and executed. Some other hunts had more accidents in which 'quite a number of persons were wounded by careless firing of guns, and one or more killed.' "[18]

Circle hunting lost favor only when the game declined to limits which made them unprofitable. However, the tallies of animals killed in specific areas do provide us with some of the earliest estimates of wild game densities in North America. But the vendetta continued. The panther killed deer and livestock and was perceived as a threat to human safety. It was not only trapped and shot on sight but pursued relentlessly, especially in winter with dogs.

"Packs of panther dogs would soon spring up in the mountainous settlements, and the breeding of these animals would give an impetus to the canine industry in these regions. Small bull dogs are said to be the best for this purpose, though many prefer the ordinary whiffet or 'fice.' Aaron Hall, the 'Lion Hunter of the Juniata,' slayer of fifty panthers in Pennsylvania between 1845 and 1869, bred a race of panther dogs. They were part bull dog, part bloodhound, part Newfoundland, and part mastiff. They were so large that C.K. Sober, of Lewisburg, former State Game Commissioner, when on a visit to Hall at his hunting cabin on Rock Run, Centre County, was able to ride on the back of one of them. They were trained to hunt in pairs, and when the quarry was overtaken, to seize it by the ears on either side, holding the monster until the hunter appeared."[19]

A price was on its head. Time was running out. The stories were becoming fewer. By the mid-1800s the sight of a panther coming to town on the back of a wagon was rare indeed. By this time such a sight would be the talk of the county, and beyond. Many of these trophies were mounted, most quite grotesquely, and proudly shown in taverns, barber shops and sundry other public places. By 1860 the panther had become a rarity in the state of Pennsylvania, an area where less than a hundred years earlier over forty had been slain in the single day's hunt at Pomfret Castle. Clement F. Herlacher may have earned the dubious distinction as having killed the last of the Pennsylvanian panthers. Treaster Valley had long been known as one of the last strongholds of the Pennsylvania panther, and the panthers, which did little damage, were in a sense protected by the older settlers, who resented "outsiders" hunting or cruising about the valley. Clem Herlacher, a renowned hunter and trapper, followed a pair of panthers into the valley and discovered their "ledge" in the early summer of 1892. There he found and removed four kittens, which were about three or four months old. Returning the following year, he found two more young panthers in the same nest, which he also carried away. These are often referred to as the last panthers known to have been killed in the Keystone State.[20]

Klandagi, which once struck fear in the hearts of early colonists from eastern Canada south through the length of the Appalachians and from the muddy banks of the Mississippi to the rocky shores of the Atlantic Ocean, was rapidly fading from the eastern landscape. Today we may be left with only a few frozen reminders of a forgotten era. These fur-covered artifacts stare through glass eyes at the changing world around them. Some may have gnawed the bones of white-tailed deer on that fateful day in early April 1861 as the first shots of the Civil War were fired upon Fort Sumter. Others may have been prowling through the Allegheny mountains of Pennsylvania as General Lee crossed the Potomac, heading north for his showdown with the Union Army at Gettysburg. But these stuffed trophies of fur, plaster and wire may now be our only visual link with the feared and revered wild cats which once ruled with unchallenged supremacy throughout the Appalachians. Thousands of their brethren were slain for sport, fear and greed. Many of their hides were shipped to the rich European garment industry; others were spread on the cold plank floors of the settlers' cabins. They served as trophies of youthful bravery tacked to the walls and over parlor sofas or as a pronouncement on the skills of the settler whose shed was adorned by the tattered skins which flapped and blew away before the cold winter gales. Bragging rights were reserved for the hunter who brought his "painter" to town across the back of his wagon; a hero was he who earned a reputation as a slayer of panthers. The stories were passed by word of mouth, from village to village, and gained in color and daring with each telling.

In early winter the deer followed the snows down the mountain slopes and into the protective river valleys below, and after them came the great cats. It was then that the true cat hunter became serious about his business and struck out with snowshoes, rations and dogs in search of his quarry. These brave and hardy souls crisscrossed the slopes and hinterlands, hoping to cut a track or, better still, find the carcass of a deer freshly killed. The hunter knew then that his chances were good that the cat was not far away. Far more often the hunter would strike a track and follow it for miles, sometimes for days on end. Many such hunts ended with a new fall of snow. The most hardy and persistent, however, were on occasion rewarded with a fresh deer kill. The hunter loosed his dogs and the cat, if still nearby, was soon treed. The cat's fate was now sealed. A single well-placed shot brought the victim down from its lofty perch among the bawling and frenzied dogs. Most panthers would be skinned there, or just the "scalp," snout or paws were returned for a bounty. Colonel Henry W. Shoemaker captured many early hunting tales from the hills of Pennsylvania, the likes of Aaron Hall (1828-92), "The Lion Hunter of the Juniata," who was said to have slayed fifty Pennsylvania panthers, and Lewis Dorman, the "Panther Slayer of Schreiner Mountain."

"Among the Jefferson county hunters who killed fifty panthers may be mentioned 'Bill' Long, 'The King Hunter,' who died in May, 1880, in his ninety-first year. Even preachers and missionaries joined in the chase and some of them held high scores in the awful game of slaughter. Panthers insisted in returning to spots where they had reared their young the season before. The hunters were soon aware of the panther 'ledges' or 'clefts' and robbed them annually. They lay in wait for the old animals, killing them without quarter. A dog which would not trail a panther was held to be of small value."[21]

And so it was as humans continued to carve a swath of death and destruction before them as they marched through the Appalachians towards the Mississippi and beyond. The wild beasts of the deep woods, whose nighttime screams and caterwauling sped many brave soul on a hasty retreat to the sanctuary of their wilderness cabin, fell before the onslaught. The cat's great cunning and stealth allowed it to outlast the bison, elk and wolverine, but its days were numbered. The forests fell before the axe, saw and fire, and the deer, upon which the panther depended, became just a memory throughout much of its former range.

But stories of panthers being seen and killed in Pennsylvania and most other eastern states and provinces have continued right up to this day. Shoemaker compiled a list of only eighty-eight panthers bountied in Pennsylvania during the latter half of the nineteenth century. This number pales when compared to the legions which fell to the trap and gun in earlier times. Bounty payment records show that as many as fifty panthers were killed each year in Luzerne County alone from 1808 to 1820. Although these reports might best be viewed with a certain degree of discretion, they do serve to show that panthers were killed throughout most of nineteenth century, and in substantial numbers during the first several decades.

"To rid the frontier [of Pennsylvania] of panthers a bounty of $8 was placed on panther heads in 1805 and the pelt was worth $4. In 1819 the General Assembly increased the bounty to $12. In 1840 the Assembly passed an act 'to encourage more effectively the Destruction of Wolves and Panthers.' The bounty then was advanced from $12 to $14 for a full-grown panther and $9 for a panther kit. These incentives were conducive to bringing an end to the great beast."[22]

The war against the predators raged throughout the east. In Vermont, where panthers were probably never very abundant, the line had been drawn early. Accounts of their danger to domestic stock and human life did little to quell the growing tide of hate and fear. In *A History of Wild Game in Vermont*, Davis and Foote describe the interaction between panthers and the settlers and their livestock: "At the commencement of settlement of Vermont, wolves, panthers, bears and wildcats abounded in the state. To some extent, these animals were feared by the early settlers and undoubtedly did considerable damage to their livestock. Only the wolf was trapped and hunted for fur but panthers and bears were much hunted for sport in the early days. The panther … has never been abundant, but they were formerly much more common in Vermont than at present day and have at times done much injury by destroying sheep and young cattle. When the country was new, much precaution was considered necessary, when traveling in the woods in this state. In order to be secure from the attacks of this ferocious beast, travelers usually went well armed, and at night built a large fire, which served to keep this cautious animal at a distance. Under such circumstances a Catamount will approach within a few rods of the fire, and they have thus been shot in this state by aiming between the glaring eyeballs, when nothing else was visible. There are authentic stories of the fierceness of this animal and proof that when hungry it has pursued and attacked men on horseback. One instance of this kind occurred in Mt. Holly, another in Wallingford.… I find no record of a person having been killed by a panther, although they attack and kill horses. By February, 1779, at the first session of Vermont's legislature, a bounty of eight pounds was placed on adult wolves and panthers and 'four pounds for the whelp of a wolf or panther.' Shortly after Vermont entered the Union in 1791, a bounty of $20.00 was placed on both species 'and for the suckling whelp of every wolf or panther, the sum of ten dollars.'

Although the amount of payment was changed several times, the bounty on wolves and panthers remained until 1904.

"With the increase of settlement, wolves and panthers were more and more harrassed and their numbers diminished rapidly in the state. 'The howl of the wolf, once so familiar on these hills is (1846) fast dying away.... Since 1868, I find record of only one bounty paid on a wolf to June 30, 1894, a bounty having been paid for that fiscal year.' The more recent history of the elimination of the panther is similar to that of the wolf, but the former survived the latter in the state.... Although the last bounty was paid in 1896, panthers were nearly exterminated by 1850."[23]

Ranier Brocke, who teaches at the State University of New York College of Environmental Science and Forestry in Syracuse, seriously questions the accuracy of many of these early bounty records.[24] His arguments are both interesting and convincing. Brocke shows that in New York one man, a George Muir, collected 67 of the total of 107 bounties paid for panthers from 1871 through 1890! Brocke suggests that Muir and other enterprising persons like him often bountied panthers several times, traveling from community to community, taking advantage of vague bounty regulations and sympathetic county public servants.

"George Muir collected most of his bounties in 1882 and 1883. Muir made 17 visits to 5 villages to collect 27 bounties between May 10, 1883, and April 25, 1884. His frequent movement from one village to another suggests that individual cougar parts were bountied several times. He frequently bountied 2 pelts (or parts) in succession.... Muir alone collected most of his bounties during the summer months, while all others collected bounties primarily during the winter months. In the Adirondacks, it was the practice to hunt cougars with dogs in winter. Hence the pattern of bounty collection by all others tends to fit the normal hunting pattern, unlike Muir's efforts. During the entire period of bounty collection from 1871 through 1890, Muir collected 67 bounties, while 26 others collected only 40 bounties. The analysis strongly suggests that George Muir bountied each of his 'cougars' two or more times. At $20 per bounty, it must have been a lucrative pastime, especially during 1883 and 1884 when he collected 27 bounties for a total of $540 in a 12 month span.... It is my opinion that George Muir bountied as few as 8 and as many as 30 cougar or cougar parts for a total of 67 times, each cougar potentially providing a skull and a skin for bountying. It is probable that some of the bounties collected in 1871 and later were for cougars killed prior to 1871."[25]

Such possible fraud in New York and elsewhere is quite important when estimating the early abundance of this predator. Many past estimates were based on the numbers bountied. George Muir, and other backwoodsmen like him, in their own way, may have contributed to the apparent persistence of panthers throughout parts of the Appalachians long after the last fell before the relentless pursuit of the bounty hunter.

"By 1885, panthers [in New York] were scarce, but *Forest and Stream* argued for their complete eradication and editorialized for an increase in the bounty: 'For the sake of the deer supply, the

Vancouver Island, British Columbia is recognized as supporting perhaps the highest densities of mountain lions in western North America. These bounty hunters in Victoria proudly display lions killed on the island around 1929.

(SEIDENSTICKER AND LUMPKIN, 1992)

panthers should be systematically pursued and destroyed, and the bounty should be such as to encourage this.' The bounty hunters were successful. They generally worked in winter, spending days and even weeks tracking a panther through the snow. Ultimately, it was treed and shot. It was apparently a ritual business with little danger. The champion hunter was E.L. Sheppard, who survived twenty-eight encounters with Adirondack panthers."[26]

Although not a predator, the plains buffalo remains the nation's most embarrassing example of the ignorance of early Americans towards their wildlife heritage and the devastation they wrought upon it. As many as 60 million of these fine beasts may have once roamed the American and Canadian ranges when the first frontiersmen crossed the Mississippi. As late as 1830, some 40 million were still believed to be scattered throughout the vast unbroken plains and prairies of the midwest. Over the next forty years those millions quickly became thousands until, in 1886, a nation-wide search by Dr. William Hornaday of the National Museum revealed a startling count of 541! By 1900 only thirty-nine wild bison survived in the United States. What a sad chapter the nineteenth century was in the history of human stewardship of America's wilderness. Europeans were obviously unable or unwilling (probably both) to assume the custodial responsibilities thrust upon them as they seized control of resources from the Native Americans.

It didn't stop there. Even the wisdom of scientific reasoning did not stop us from defining wildlife in terms of "good" and "bad." Good wildlife included those animals which we liked to hunt and eat, or were pretty to look at. Bad wildlife, unfortunately, also needed to eat to stay alive, and we branded them as competitors. Predator control was an important component of most early wildlife management strategies. The first federal program of predator control in the United States began in 1915. At that time western stockmen succeeded in convincing Congress to appropriate $125,000 on the pretext of conserving beef for our allies during World War I by decreasing or eliminating populations of predators, such as wolves, coyotes and cougars.

"The U.S. Biological Survey, the predecessor of the U.S. Fish and Wildlife Service, was charged with the responsibility of hiring hunters and trappers to do the job. But it was the passage of the Animal Damage Control Act of 1931 that gave birth to the Animal Damage Control, or ADC, and provided the money and authority to expand 'the destruction of mountain lions, wolves, coyotes, bobcats, prairie dogs, gophers, ground squirrels, jackrabbits, and other animals injurious to agriculture, horticulture, forestry, husbandry, game or domestic animals, or that carried disease.'

"Between 1937 and 1970, federal employees of the ADC, derisively branded 'All Dead Critters' by some of their critics, killed 7,255 cougars; 23,830 bears; 477,104 bobcats; 50,283 red wolves; 1,744 lobo wolves; 2,823,000 coyotes; and millions of other animals. After 1970, control was focused primarily on cougars, coyotes, and bobcats, because the grizzly bear and wolves were placed on the endangered species list.

"Federal predator control efforts were supplemented by state hunters and bounty programs. Arizona originally considered the cougar an undesirable predator, and 2,400 were killed between 1918 and 1947. Efforts to eliminate the cat were accelerated in 1947 when the state began to offer a bounty varying from $50 to $100 per lion; between 1947 and 1969, over 5,400 cougars were slaughtered in Arizona. Federal, state, and private hunters killed 1,775 pumas in Colorado between 1916 and 1965. California paid out bounties on 12,452 cougars killed between 1907 and 1963.... British Columbia lays claim to the greatest carnage, with 16,633 cats slaughtered between 1910 and 1955. The bounty on cougar in British Columbia continued from 1910 to 1957; during that time the total kill probably exceeded 20,000 animals. According to statistics compiled by Ronald Nowak of the U.S. Fish and Wildlife Service, a minimum of 66,665 cougars were killed within states and provinces between 1907 and 1978."[27]

In Alberta a bounty on cougars existed between 1937 and 1964, during which time approximately forty to fifty were killed annually. A compulsory registration system was established in 1972 and the annual kill declined to about thirty. The threat of overharvesting certain regions of the province was addressed in 1990 by establishing a harvest quota system.[28] The state of California began paying twenty-dollar bounties on mountain lions in 1907, and in 1919 began employing hunters with dogs to drive the cats into trees and shoot them. One of these hunters, the famed Jay Bruce, was credited with capturing nearly seven hundred cougars. Bounty hunting of California mountain lions continued until 1963. Six years later California joined other western states in granting the lion protection as a big game animal. A complete moratorium on the hunting of mountain lions was enacted in California in 1972.[29]

And so the alarming saga of animal retribution is paraded before us, as if we are not allowed to escape the story of unbridled carnage which an earlier America inflicted upon many of our great predators, much in the name of wildlife management. But the eastern panther was not a target of the Animal Damage Control program whose main arena of operations was the western United States. No, Ol' Painter had already faded from the mist shrouded valleys of the Great Smokies and the snow covered mountains of the Adirondacks. Only a few tales from the old timers remained.

CHAPTER FOUR

Ghosts from the Past

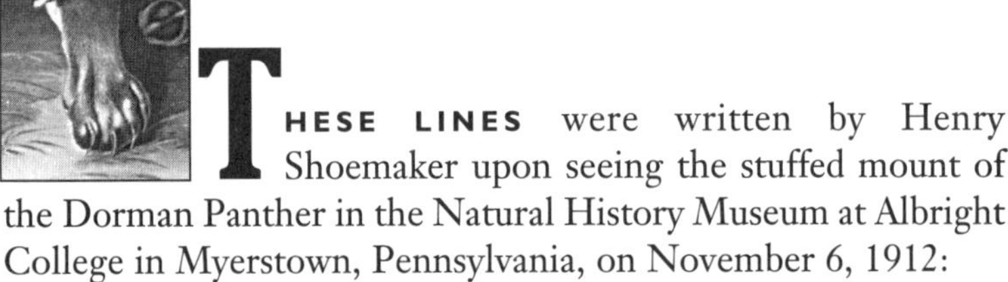

THESE LINES were written by Henry Shoemaker upon seeing the stuffed mount of the Dorman Panther in the Natural History Museum at Albright College in Myerstown, Pennsylvania, on November 6, 1912:

Ode to a Stuffed Panther

At twilight when the shadows flit,
Within the ancient museum I sit,
Gazing through the dust-encrusted glass
(While hosts of savage memories pass)

At your effigy, ludicrously stuffed.
The fulvous color faded, the paws all puffed,
And bullet-holes in jowl and side
Tell where your life blood ebbed like some red tide;

A streak of light—the last of day—
Gleams through a window on your muzzle gray,
And lights your glassy eyes with garnet fire.
You almost stir those orbs in fretful ire

Which gape into the sunset's dying flame
Towards the wild mountains whence you came;
Revives old images which dormant lie.
Outside the wind is raising to a sigh

Like oft you voiced in the primeval wood.
In your life's pilgrimage, I'd trace it if I could
In white pine forests, tops trembling in the breeze
Like restless sable-colored seas,

Beneath, in rhododendron thickets high,
You crouched until your prey came by.
Grouse, or sickly fawn, or, even fisher-fox
You rent, and then slunk back into the rocks,

And on cold wintry nights, lit by the cloud-swept moon
Your wailing to the music of the spheres attune,
Rose to a roar which echoed over all,
Beside which wolves' lamenting to a treble fall;

And through the snows your mate so slim draws nigh
Noiselessly, with strange love-light in her eye
You lick her coat, and stroke her with your tail,
Whispering a love-song weirdsome as the gale,

You leave her with a last long fond caress
Adown the glen you go in stealthiness,
… A loud report! another! how you leap;
With a resounding thud into the snow you fall asleep.

Your blood-stained hide the hunter bears away,
The virile emblem of an ampler day.
The golden eagle picks your carcass dry,
Wild morning glories trellice on your ribs awry.

Your meaning is a deep one—while your kind live
men shall rule.
There will be less of weakling, runt or fool,
No enervation will our rugged courage sap.
We will not dawdle on plump luxury's lap,

But as your race declines, so dwindles man.
The painted cheek replaces coat of tan,
And marble halls, and beds of cloth of gold
Succeed the log-cabins of the days of old;

When the last panther falls then woe betide,
Nature's retributive cataclysm is at our side,
Our boasted civilization then will be no more,
Fresh forms must come from out the Celestial Store.[1]

In the Vermont Historical Society Museum in Montpelier, the Barnard Panther is on proud display as the last of his brethren killed in the state. Curious patrons stop before the glass case and stare at this odd-looking relic from a long-forgotten era. The once smoldering eyes and fanged jowls form now a grotesque, almost smiling death mask hardly befitting the magnificent creature that fell to the bullet of Alexander Crowell on Boxing Day in 1881. How far removed this great creature is now, a curiosity behind glass on public view for all to see. The imperfections of early taxidermy and the harsh treatment of time are magnified by the spotlight's glare and the flash of the camera. This was a beast at home among the silence and shadows of the cool forest slopes and hidden valleys. It once paused to drink from the clear mountain streams, and sprang from its ledge-top perch with such speed and ferocity that the deer was dispatched with skilled precision. It had no equal in strength and speed, and feared no other beast. He was indeed, Lord of the Forest.

Monuments to this once proud race of North American lion are few. Skulls, bones and bits of skin are scattered around the east in various collections, but mounted specimens are rare indeed. This is perhaps surprising, given the numbers slain and the trophy status assigned to this feared predator. But many mounted specimens became tattered and in disrepair, a result from many years of neglect on open display in village stores, barber shops and assorted other public places. The glossy cinnamon reds and tawny browns of their sleek pelts soon became bleached and brittle from years of sun and dust and picking and patting. Teeth cracked and crumbled from the damp and the heat. The ears, which once flexed and scanned the sounds of the forests, became like stiff flaps of cartonboard, the fur became worn, wires protruded. Many mounts were prepared locally by amateurs with little training and few proper materials. And so many specimens of eastern panthers were discarded before their true worth was known. The few relics which survived the ravages of time did so more by chance than design. Several have passed the years in seclusion behind the closed doors of museums and university basements and storage rooms. A few others were fortunate to fall into professional hands and have been preserved through the efforts of trained curators.

I've always been somewhat of a dreamer—not the dead of night, sound sleep type, rather the let-the-mind-wander gaze-out-the-window wish-I-were-there type of dreamer. Thinking back to those wonderful and impressionable early school years in southwestern Nova Scotia, my thoughts then were just as likely on the woods and rivers outside with all their springtime distractions as anything the teacher may have had to say. But somehow I struggled through those academic years, and, to the surprise of most who knew me, even through university. Today I have no doubt that it was the nostalgic flair for things romantic and challenging that attracted me later to the Canadian Arctic and a life-long career as a wildlife research biologist. And it was that same passion that spurred me on in a personal quest for those few remaining panther relics from frontier America. A book on eastern panthers, I thought, should search out the resting places of those that remain with us—those that we can see, touch and count. And so I set out to compile a photographic and written testimony of those remaining denizens of a bygone era. There was a trail of sorts to begin on. Several well publicized specimens were on public display, like the famous Barnard Panther at the Vermont Museum in Montpelier. Others had received only vague recognition in obscure journals or local newspapers. It was, however, a start.

The only mounted specimen of eastern panther that I was aware of when I began my search was the Little St. Jean specimen. This rather peculiar creature was first uncovered by the late Bruce Wright, having been captured by a trapper from Quebec on the Maine side of the international border at Lac St. Jean around 1938. It stood on display at the University of New Brunswick for many years and has only recently been deposited at the New Brunswick provincial museum in Saint John. The only attempt to catalogue existing specimens of eastern panthers that I was aware of was an obscure 1950 paper on specimens of the "Adirondack Cougar." The author, the late Dr. Stoner of the New York State Museum, left us with an interesting account of seven intact specimens, and the scattered locations of several other unmounted skins, skulls and bones. So here is a roll call for what may well be all that remains of that once proud race of American lion. A rather unstately tribute, perhaps, and certainly incomplete, but it is a start.

THE CHAPMAN PANTHER

The Annie E. Woodman Institute sits comfortably in downtown Dover, New Hampshire. It was formally opened in 1916, named after the lady who bequeathed a sum of money for the creation of an institution for the study of local and natural history and art. The Woodman Institute, as it is now commonly called, boasts one of the finest exhibits of natural and local history on display in New Hampshire. Warmly greeted at the door by staff of this private historical museum, a sense of sincere interest and concern towards our preoccupation was immediately apparent. A huge mounted polar bear towered over us as we entered this stately but aging edifice in the middle of town. Shown into an adjacent first-floor display room which supported an assortment of wildlife specimens, the Chapman Panther stood at the far end in a glass case with several other smaller creatures. Rather large and domineering in appearance, this ancient warrior sported a fierce sneer beneath large, bulging, yellow glass eyes. The fur had long since lost its luster and had a faded and drab light-brown color. The long sharp claws added a sinister touch to this creature but certainly were not a natural feature of a walking cat, which this one was. It appears that early taxonomy was intended more for viewer impression than actual replication. The broken and tattered ears drooped awkwardly, casualties of years of abuse and neglect. But a panther it was, and a very large one at that. The caption on the glass case read: "This was the last cougar killed in New Hampshire. It was shot on the Cartland Farm in Lee by William Chapman of New Market in the Fall of 1853. The body was a gift to the Institute of Sewall D. Chapman, his son. It is an example of the crude taxidermy of that time."

However, a 1927 paper by Ned Dearborn in the *Journal of Mammalogy* describes the circumstances surrounding the killing of this panther in greater detail: "About the year 1900, I heard of a mountain lion that had been killed, years before, in southeastern New Hampshire by William F. Chapman, who was then living at New Market, New Hampshire. As it was the only instance of the actual killing of this animal within the limits of the state that had, or has, come to my attention, I visited Mr. Chapman to learn the particulars. I was shown the mounted skin of the beast, greatly over stuffed, which for years had been shown at neighboring fairs, but was then secluded in the attic of the Chapman home. At that time, Mr. Chapman, though aged, was in full possession of his faculties. He showed me the 14-gauge double, muzzle loading gun with which he turned the trick.

"Mr. Chapman was an enthusiastic fox hunter. On the morning of November 2, 1853, he started out with his hounds after foxes. In the township of Lee, Rockingham County, his dogs gave voice, and before long were evidently close to something either treed or holed in a growth of young pines among which were several large, wide spreading trees. Approaching noiselessly over the pine needles that covered the ground, he beheld the great cat standing with two feet on one branch and the other two on another branch of one of the big trees. Swaying its tail from side to side, it was giving its entire attention to the dogs. Bringing his gun to his shoulder, the hunter approached slowly and silently till within a few feet of the lion. Suddenly the lion looked down at the man, and at that instant a number four shot passed through the lion's eye and entered its brain. For a bit, it hung by one foot, then it dropped and proceeded to tear up the ground as head–wounded animals often do. It weighed 198 pounds and measured 8 feet and 4 inches from tip to tip."[2]

I started in fascination at this this effigy of an eastern panther. Somehow this relic from the past seemed comfortable and at home among the assortment of other creatures from another era. Mounted heads of caribou and moose and creatures from the sea, displays of moths and butterflies and even specimens of the now-extinct passenger pigeon and Eskimo curlew were but a few of the wide assortment of wildlife subjects which made up the displays.

The friendly and generous curators of this private institution provided the added touch of down-home charm and mystique to this final resting place of the last confirmed lion of the White Mountains of New Hampshire. Later, as we drove west through New Hampshire and into Vermont, my mind drifted back 150 years to an era when panthers and wolves roamed these forested slopes and valleys of the Green Mountains. How foreboding and inaccessible these wilderness sanctuaries must have been before they felt the bite of the lumberman's axe. But just how elusive was this wild beast. How long could the American lion continue to survive and breed successfully in the face of growing intrusion by humans? How much of his wilderness retreat could be lost before it, too, became only a footnote to the historical record of greed and exploitation which so quickly changed the face of much of the Appalachian uplands? Could it have retreated to those few enclaves of safety, hidden away, as many people believe, somewhere unbeknownst to its human tormentors and there continued to hunt the deer and to raise new generations of panthers, waiting for the scars on its wilderness haunts to heal so it could then go forth, multiply and reoccupy its former kingdom? Is it possible for any creature, panther or other, to live in such close proximity to humans, those intelligent evolutionary misfits, for so many generations without allowing "proof positive" of its presence? To believe so did seem to stretch the limits of reasoned thought.

THE WEATHERSFIELD PANTHER

Low clouds and a light rain clung to the fresh green slopes of the Vermont hills as we followed the winding trail of the Valley Road from Springfield up towards the Weathersfield Congregational Church. There, among stately red oaks and behind a winding, rustic stone fence, I met Edith and Armstrong Hunter during the Sunday morning post-sermon social hour at the far corner of the church. Armstrong had just finished delivering the morning service, and as I approached the chatting parishioners, Edith pointed at me and exclaimed, "You must be the panther fellow." After an initial exchange of pleasantries, we strolled across the road to the Dan Foster House, now the site of the Weathersfield Historical Society Museum. The Dan Foster House is typical of many such efforts by citizens across America concerned with retaining records and artifacts of local historical significance. Edith was president of the Weathersfield Historical Society. As we wound our way to the second floor, she enthusiastically showed us photographs, furniture and other items important to the early history of the Weathersfield area. The value of the Edith Hunters to the preservation of early American culture, lifestyles and folklore cannot be overstated.

There, under glass case and the dim glow of a lamp, stood the Weathersfield panther. Like the Dover Panther before, this old warrior looked tattered and worn. The pelage had long since faded to a bleached sandy color. Edith graciously searched the albums and records for pictures and stories of the panther. The history of this specimen has been recorded in detail, and because of the interesting but perhaps not entirely unique history of this eastern panther, I give you the following story prepared by Betty

Murray which appeared in the January 31, 1966, edition of the local paper:

"Just 99 years ago the famous Weathersfied Panther was roaming the hills of Vermont. How long he padded about the countryside will never be known, but on January 31, 1867, he was shot in a cave on Pine Hill near Downer's Four Corners. This stuffed panther is an accepted resident at the home of George E. Robinson at the intersection of Routes 131 and 106 in Weathersfield, but a startling sight to visitors. The large, fierce-looking beast with teeth bared, snarling down at the household from the top of an upright piano, has small, close-set ears, tawny colored fur, large paws and a long, thick rope-like tail.

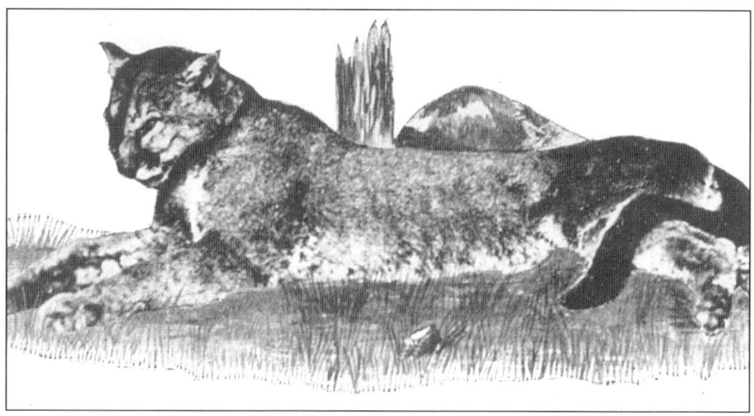

The Weathersfield Panther, shortly after it was killed on January 31, 1867 near Downer's, Vermont.

(COURTESY EDITH HUNTER)

"From his stand in the living room, the Weathersfield Panther can look down Route 106 toward Panther Rock on Pine Hill, where 99 years ago after climbing the steep bank from the Black River, he crossed the road and went into the woods where he hid in a cave. The slanting part of the rock, known as Panther Rock, was blasted away during some road widening, and now a hemlock tree towering above helps identify the rock by the road-side.

"Robinson said he was about nine years old when he first saw the stuffed panther, which was kept at Downer's Hotel. He and his father had delivered scythe sticks to Bellows Falls and were returning home at night. Young Robinson was asleep in his father's wagon when they stopped at Downer's Hotel, presumably for his father to get some refreshment. Robinson recalled the incident thus: 'Old Rosewell Downer owned the hotel. That panther was up over a doorway, I looked at the panther and was scared half to death. Ran out and got back in the wagon.' Later,

Robinson and his wife Elsie, used to attend dances at Downer's Hotel, which had a spring dance floor on the second floor of the building. At that time the panther was kept in the dance hall where it watched the dancers who often stayed until dawn. When Downer's Hotel burned, some fellow lugged the panther out, but some of its fur was singed. A new house was built on the site of Downer's Hotel and the panther was moved into the new house and came into Robinson's possession when he purchased the property.

The Weathersfield Panther on the veranda of the Downer's Hotel, sometime near the turn of the century.

(COURTESY EDITH HUNTER)

"The story of the capture of the Weathersfield Panther in 1867, as told to this writer by the late William E. Covell of Perkinsville, follows: 'My father, Lucius G. Covell, was going from his place up above the Upper Falls, down the back road to Perkinsville to do some shopping, when he saw these tracks sunk deep down in the snow. They went from Hawk's Mountain across the meadow towards Pine Hill, as straight as you can crack a whip! They were about half way between Edwin Roy's place and Frank Foster's. The snow was very deep that year and he couldn't see how the tracks looked. When he got to the store, where there were always a bunch of whittlers sitting around, he told about the tracks. Some of the men went up and followed the tracks across the ice on the Black River, up over the back, across the road and saw where the unknown animal had jumped up on a huge rock, now known as Panther Rock. In those days the rock extended down nearer the road; now it has been blasted away, so only the upper part remains. Well, from Panther Rock, he went back apiece and his tracks disappeared in some ledges. It was near night on January 30, so the men plugged up the entrance with whatever stuff they could get, so the animal couldn't get out.'

" 'The story got noised around that night. So the next morning, January 31, a whole bunch went up with guns, this heavy crow bar with a round top on it, and a black dog. They didn't dare open the entrance to the cave, because they didn't know what they were going to find. So they pried around in the snow

The Weathersfield Panther has been of great interest through the years. Here, several young boys pose with the trophy in 1939. It can be seen today at the Weathersfield Historical Society display at the Dan Foster House, Weathersfield, Vermont. (SPARGO, 1950)

and tried to find a place to dig. My uncle, George Walker, went punching around with that iron bar and that bar slipped and fell into the cave and the men heard the animal snarl and spit. So they dug a hole and put the dog in, but he came right back out. He was cut up pretty badly.

" 'After the dog came out, this fellow Gardner ... looked down into the hole and saw the animal's eyes gleam and sparkle. Gardner stuck a double barrel shot gun in the hole and shot the critter in the left eye. And that was about the end of him, besides pulling him out,' Bill Covell finished with a smile. Then he continued: 'That panther was skin poor. It was midwinter and he hadn't had too much to eat. He only weighed 122 1/2 pounds and measured 7 feet from the tip of his nose to the tip of his tail. Folks everywhere were excited about the panther and took him around and showed him in different towns and collected money for mounting him. Don't know why he was kept at Downer's Hotel.' Downer's Hotel changed ownership a number of times between 1838 and 1916, but in the later transactions was mention that the sale also included the 'Catamount' or 'North

American Lion' now in said hotel."[3]

On December 24, 1916, one month after it was last sold, Downer's Hotel burned to the ground. Although slightly singed, the panther was saved and remained in the house that was soon built on the site. When the property was auctioned off in 1973 by George Robinson, Jr., and his wife, Elsie, a group of Weathersfield citizens purchased the panther for $175 and donated it to the Weathersfield Historical Society, and it has resided at the Dan Foster House ever since.

We left the Dan Foster House and drove the short distance down the road to Edith and Armstrong's large rambling farmhouse. In Armstrong's studio he generously made copies of old newspaper clippings and articles. What a source of historical information Edith proved to be, and, as president of the Weathersfield Historical Society, I felt that the community will be hard pressed to find a replacement with equal enthusiasm. We said our good-byes and motored down the winding Weathersfield road to the interstate turnpike and on towards the capital city of Montpelier.

THE BARNARD PANTHER

As we crossed west through the Green Mountains from White River Junction, the overcast skies gave way to the sun and warmth of a mid-June New England day. The green slopes were bathed in the midafternoon blush of sun after a brief summer shower, and I marveled at the expanse of closed pine-maple forest. How different these same mountains must have looked 150 years ago, before most of the forests had fallen before the lumberman's saw and axe. There must have been small sanctuary for wolf, panther and deer. Did the killing of the Barnard Panther in 1881, which waited for us at the Vermont Historical Society Museum in Montpelier, represent the last panther to have roamed these rugged uplands?

The museum sits elegantly on Central Avenue of downtown Montpelier, the capital of Vermont. The massive building with its expansive two-tiered verandahs laced in a decor of potted plants and flags, retains the stateliness and elegance of a century ago. Entering the main door, and to the right of the vestibule, resides the famous Barnard Panther, killed at Barnard, Vermont, by Alexander Crowell (the details of which were given earlier). In contrast to the two previous specimens, the Barnard Panther actually looked like a large cat, probably much like it did to Alexander Crowell on that eventful November morning of 1881as he squinted at it down the barrel of his shotgun. The contrast between creamy neck and chest and the tawny rufous-colored back and flanks was prominent. The taxidermist had captured the animal in mid-stride. Inside, at the information desk, the personable attendant handed me a one-page description of the panther display with the added remark that panthers are believed by some to still roam the mountains of Vermont. In fact, he himself had seen large tracks in the snow which could only have been those of a Vermont panther.

Our stay at Montpelier was short, almost clinical in nature compared to our visit earlier in the day when we had chatted and exchanged stories with the Hunters at Weathersfield. We continued on to Burlington for an appointment with Dr. Bill Kilpatrick of the Biology Department at the University of Vermont.

Alexander Crowell poses with the famous Barnard Panther, which he shot on November 24, 1881, at Barnard, Vermont. Many believe this to have been the last eastern panther killed in the Green Mountain State.

(VERMONT HISTORICAL SOCIETY)

THE BURLINGTON PANTHER

The University of Vermont has a beautiful small campus cradled on the eastern slopes of Lake Champlain. We met Bill Kilpatrick in his third-floor office of the Marshlife Science Building, as planned, and our initial pleasantries soon led into tales of panthers, wolves and coyotes, with all of which he was well acquainted. Bill is very enthusiastic, and his research and teaching have taken him far afield, from Alaska to Pakistan. His understanding of natural history was immediately evident. We chatted around and into the question of panthers in Vermont and the northeast in general, and Bill's empirical approach became clear. He did not believe panthers could have ridden out the storm of persecution for the past 150 years without anything more tangible than questionable circumstantial evidence such as tracks and reports of sightings. We strode across campus to the university specimen of an eastern panther, encased within cramped storage quarters with such monoliths as polar bear and bison. Claws protruded unnaturally from this ragged specimen. The original teeth were cracked and broken behind a faint sneer. The only information on this old fellow was that it was collected somewhere in the Adirondack Mountains of New York. In the case, beside the panther, was a mount of the extinct passenger pigeon, perhaps appropriate, given the current status attributed to the eastern panther by Bill and his learned colleagues at the University of Vermont. The University of Vermont Catamounts carry the ferocity of their namesake into athletic battle, a symbolic gesture of respect for this legend of the Green Mountain State.

We headed south down Route 7, following the eastern shore of Lake Champlain toward the city of Albany and the New York State Museum. As we stopped for lunch at Middlebury, Vermont, I called Dr. Harold Hitchcock in hope that I could meet with this elder statesman. Dr. Hitchcock, a retired professor at Middlebury College, had spent years recording and compiling observations of panthers in Vermont, and a more impassioned and resolute panther believer would be difficult to find. I had written Dr. Hitchcock and received copious quantities of panther news from him, and I dearly wanted to meet him. As good fortune would have, my noon hour phone call was timely, and Harold and his wife Martine welcomed me to their lovely home and manicured grounds near center Middlebury. Although in his nineties, frail and confined to a wheelchair, there was no mistaking his quickness of mind and passion for panthers as we enthusiastically traded news and tales of panthers in the northeast. Dr. Hitchcock had a scientific and inquiring mind equal to that of the renowned academic, Dr. Kilpatrick, but the approach of these two scientists to the question of the survival of the eastern panther could not have been more different. So how, then, I asked, can there be a definitive yes or no to this panther debate, when minds of similar knowledge can track such divergent paths? Each highly respectful of the other, they continued their reasoned course and convictions. Little wonder those of lesser knowledge and experience are often heard the loudest in this debate; a little knowledge can be a dangerous thing. I was saddened to learn that Dr. Hitchcock passed away on September 13, 1995.

The Bernard Panther, killed by Alexander Crowell in 1881 and now on display at the Vermont Historical Society Museum in Montpelier, Vermont.

(G. PARKER)

We left Middlebury for Bennington, where I wished to see the site of the former Catamount Tavern and the bronze statue of a panther, or catamount, which was erected to mark the site of this historic structure. The actual history of the tavern, and of the statue on Monument Avenue in Bennington which has become synonymous with it, is a colorful story and one which I share with the reader as told by the late John Spargo, former director-curator of the Bennington Historical Museum and Art Gallery: "When the Bennington Historical Society was incorporated in 1875 it had an extensive program. One of the important items in that program was the marking of the site of the tavern that was kept by Stephen Fay [erected about 1769], in which the Council of Safety held its meetings; the place where Ethan Allen met with his Green Mountain Boys, from which he set forth on his memorable expedition to capture Fort Ticonderoga. The old house had been burned to the ground in 1871, after having been permitted to deteriorate so badly that its end was fitting enough, even though it was brought about by an incendiary."[4]

The following story helps explain the selection of a catamount by the town for the design of this marker: "In the course of the long and bitter controversy between the settlers on what were known as the New Hampshire Grants and the province, later state, of New York, a catamount was killed in the town, somewhere near the foot of Mount Anthony. It was the object of great curiosity and the skin was stuffed, no doubt crudely enough, since skill in taxidermy was not likely to have been an accomplishment of any of the settlers. For some time the stuffed beast was exhibited in the barroom of the simple little tavern kept by Landlord Stephen Fay. One day some of the habitués of the taproom of the tavern, in a boisterous mood, took the stuffed animal and fastened it to the top of the tavern signboard, where it remained for some months, until by the action of winds and rains it disintegrated. They set the stuffed animal so that it faced westward in the direction of New York. This was a symbolic act. They said the beast was grinning defiance to the 'Yorkers.' "[5]

Spargo believed that the panther fastened to the top of the Landlord Fay's sign may have been the same one killed in Bennington in 1785 as reported in Samuel William's 1794 History of Vermont, being one of the earliest reports of a panther killed in that state. This story, and the excitement over the killing of a panther in West Wardsboro, Vermont, in 1875 (specimen described later), were probably responsible for public opinion favoring the choice of a panther as the symbol for the Bennington monument in 1876. Ironically, the small inn and drinking establishment at Bennington was known only as Landlord Fay's House for many years, later becoming known as the Green Mountain Tavern. It was not until long after the structure was lost to fire in 1871 that it became affectionately known as the Catamount Tavern.

Another interesting twist to this catamount saga is the apparent resemblance of the feline figure to that of a lion, rather than of a panther—a not so insignificant point somehow overlooked by the artist who chose as a model for his work, not the mount of the recently killed Wardsboro panther, but rather a living African lion residing at the New York Zoo. After considerable public criticism and ridicule, a prominent tuft at the end of the statue's tail, characteristic of lions but not panthers, was removed in 1897.

I examined this interesting edifice, and the serene site on which it now stands. The simple inscription reads "Site of the Catamount Tavern, 1767," although the date of the building of the tavern by Landlord Stephen Fay appears to have been 1769, and the actual site of the tavern lies 45 feet to the east upon which now rests a private residence. The present-day monument

The author beside the bronze statue of a panther which marks the site of "Landlord Fay's House," a small inn and drinking establishment in Bennington, Vermont. The "tavern" was built about 1769 and burned to the ground in 1871. It became known as the Green Mountain Tavern and later, after it was destroyed by fire, as the Catamount Tavern.

(G. PARKER)

marks an important gathering place for the early farmers and laborers of eighteenth-century Bennington, a spot where news and gossip of the day were passed around freely over an ale or two and, of course, "everyone knew your name." It's comforting to know that some things never change.

THE NEW YORK STATE MUSEUM PANTHER

We left the Green Mountain State and motored west into upstate New York and the industrial sprawl of the Hudson River Valley. The Dan Fowler House and the Weathersfield panther tucked away in peaceful seclusion among the towering oaks and maples of Vermont now seemed far away as we maneuvered among the growing throng of automobiles rushing towards the outskirts of Albany.

The next morning, after the early rush of traffic had subsided, we ventured into the downtown sprawl and a visit with the New York State Museum. The museum sits elegantly at one end of a very modern city complex where government offices in high-rise glass and stone towers border acres of concrete encased water and fountains, all set within walkways of marble. Lovely indeed, but I still preferred the natural freshness of the Vermont mountains. However, this was the apparent resting place of an eastern panther killed in the province of Ontario, and we had a meeting with Joe Bopp, assistant curator of mammals in the Biological Science Section of the museum.

Personable and informed, Joe showed us a stack of "panther-related" papers and articles that he and curator Dave Steadman thought might be of interest to us. Joe led me to the back rooms where most non-display items were meticulously tagged and stored. The Ontario panther was locked rather awkwardly inside a metal storage cabinet. On removal, a fine specimen it turned out to be. Reclined, and in remarkably good condition, this mount was the most realistic specimen seen to date, with the dark reddish brown on the back and tail intact and conspicuous, as was the creamy white neck and black-tipped tail. The only information on this specimen was that it was a female collected in Ontario in 1908. It, and another from Washington State, had both been purchased from Ward's Natural Science Establishment in Rochester. It was photographed and returned to its metal tomb. We bade farewell and sped west on Interstate 88 towards the more rural and relaxing landscapes of upstate New York.

THE PANTHERS OF ONEONTA

By early afternoon, under a hot and hazy June sky, we approached the well-groomed campus of Oneonta State College, where we were to meet with Bob Phillips of the Biology Department. Snuggled among the lovely Catskill Mountains, this small college had somehow fallen into possession of five panther mounts, some or all of which were believed to be of the eastern race. Although a day earlier than expected, Bob had collected the specimens from their assorted places of storage and had them "gathered" in a laboratory near his first-floor office. And a rather bizarre sight it was. Mounted in various postures of defiance and pugnacity, it was apparent that these apparitions had been prepared by the same taxidermist. The following are all we have as a written record of their origin.

A letter from Professor Johnson of Oneonta State College dated April 22, 1937, reads in part as follows: "There are in the Normal School museum five mounted specimens of cougar. Two of these are without doubt, I think, of the Rocky Mountain form. The remaining three appear to be Eastern. One of these is an immature. Unfortunately we have no records of this museum material.... Our entire collection of about 1600 birds and mammals was purchased and brought to the school in 1895. They were from the estate of one James A. Hurst who seems to have lived in Utica but was a former State taxidermist.... One of these specimens which appears to me to be a very typical Adirondack specimen ... was mounted in the act of killing a partial albino white-tail deer. Since the representation was very crude, I recently separated the two specimens."[6]

Dr. Stoner of the New York State Museum summarized the inconclusive history of the Oneonta State Teachers College panther specimens: "Definite locality and other data concerning the taking of these animals as well as much of their subsequent history are lacking. Examples of cougars and other species collected at about the same time were, however, evidently mounted by Hurst. Remains of certain of these mounts are now in the New York State Museum. The available data on the latter indicate but do not prove that they were collected in that State. They, too, were mounted by Hurst and, while the mounts at the New York State Museum were destroyed as such (skulls only retained), certain of the Hurst mounts originally retained in the mounted condition by that taxidermist were subsequently purchased from his estate by the Oneonta State Teachers College and now repose in the museum of that institution."[7]

From the assortment of motley creatures which stood before me, I could not see how anyone, including Dr. Johnson, could have identified western from eastern specimens. They all looked alike to me, and they were certainly old. Three were faded and quite in need of repair. One was small with noticeable spots on its legs, obviously a young panther perhaps in the early winter of its first year. The fifth specimen was a much larger and darker animal, mounted in a reclining position, but with the defiant snarl characteristic of them all. I photographed them collectively and individually. A rather rumpled and disheveled assembly, but how often does one have the opportunity to walk among a "pride" of eastern panthers?

Four of the five eastern panthers which are stored at Oneonta State College in New York. The history of these panther relics is uncertain. They were probably collected in the mid- to late 1800s in the Adirondack Mountains of New York, mounted by a James A. Hurst of Utica and deposited at Oneonta College in 1895, along with some 1,600 others birds and mammals from the estate of Mr. Hurst. (G. PARKER)

We thanked Bob for his efforts and encouraged him to persuade the college to consider this unique collection of panthers for special attention and display. He was equally enthusiastic, and we left with the feeling that perhaps we may have contributed in a small way to ensuring that others will share the experience of viewing these peculiar but unique tributes to an earlier era.

THE LYCOMING PANTHER

The rugged mountains and valleys of Pennsylvania appear to have been the heartland of the eastern panther range. It was here, in the remote interior forests which cradled and nurtured the vast reaches of the Susquehanna River, that tales of panthers and panther hunters, many preserved and made popular by the prolific writings of Henry Shoemaker, abound. And it was here that our search for relics of this once-proud race of American lion had brought us.

Straddling the Susquehanna River lies the city of Williamsport, once a bustling center for the lumbering industry. Since the 1940s, however, Williamsport has gained recognition as the site of the World Series of Little League Baseball. But here also is the Lycoming County Historical Museum. We stopped here to view the interesting exhibits of early Lycoming County natural and cultural history. At the entrance to the museum is an attractive display of mounted specimens of wildlife and, much to our surprise, among the exhibits was a panther! This reclining and well-preserved specimen, I thought, must be of the western race. Certainly the fine taxidermy, when compared to many of the worn specimens seen recently, would suggest a rather recent origin. On inquiry I was surprised to learn that, although supporting documentation was absent, it was believed to be a local eastern panther. It was suggested that I should go next door to the tourist information bureau and speak with panther enthusiast Beverly Fronk for further details. Beverly understood that the panther had been killed near the Loyalsock River just north of Williamsport around the turn of the century. It was on display in

The Lycoming Panther, shot near Williamsport, Pennsylvania, near the turn of the century and on display at the Lycoming County Historical Museum at Williamsport.

(G. PARKER)

a public school during the early 1900s, but when the school was destroyed in the 1940s, the panther was moved to its present location in the Lycoming County Museum. Not a large specimen, it is considerably faded except for a rufous-colored tail tipped in black. I wondered how many other specimens of eastern panthers might be tucked away in county and small-town museums or collecting dust in someone's attic or barn.

We continued west to visit with Richard Yahner and the Brush Panther at Pennsylvania State University. Before roaring into the land of the Nittany Lions, however, we veered north on Route 44 towards the small village of Waterville. This quaint little village lies nestled beside the Pine River within the Tiadaghton State Forest. I had corresponded with Spencer Kraybill, proprietor of Pine Creek Historian, a business through which Spencer was republishing early accounts of Pennsylvania history, and I took the opportunity to pay a visit. Spencer and his wife Marie lived in a lovely chalet on immaculately flowered grounds. Our brief visit with Spencer was filled with stories and tales rich in the lore and heritage of the Keystone State. I could only marvel at his enthusiasm and ambitious publishing agenda. I left wishing him well in his efforts to help preserve and disseminate a literary chronicle of Pennsylvanian history and culture. I was shocked to learn later that Spencer passed away in November 1995.

THE BRUSH PANTHER

The forested mountains of central Pennsylvania embrace the beautiful campus of Pennsylvania State University. Home of the 1995 Rose Bowl champion Nittany Lions, the panther, like the catamount of Vermont University, carries the team colors into athletic battle. An enormous limestone sculpture of a panther watches over the manicured campus greenery beneath a canopy of oaks, maples and elms. Richard Yahner's office is on the first floor of the Forest Resources Building, and I entered to find him rushing off to a meeting. Apologizing profusely for the scheduling conflict, he assured me that his secretary would show me to the panther and provide what documentation she could find. On the second floor, the old Brush Panther was still wrapped in cardboard and packing as it had only recently been returned from the Carnegie Museum in Pittsburgh.

I was impressed with the high quality of the early taxidermy, and although the tattered ears and broken tail spoke of years of handling and travel, it was in remarkably good condition. Tawny in color, a darker rufous stripe ran from the neck down the back and tail. The end of the tail was tipped in black; the throat and chest were cream. It was a large animal, as the records suggest, an aggressive crouch made even more intimidating by open jowls

The Brush Panther was shot by Samuel Brush around 1859 in northeastern Susquehanna County, Pennsylvania. The specimen was shown at the 1893 Chicago World's Fair and was on display at the Carnegie Museum in Pittsburg from 1953 to 1993. It is now stored at the Forest Resources Building at Pennsylvania State University. When photographed, the panther was still in partial state of transit. (G. PARKER)

and fierce sneer. The Brush Panther has an interesting history (the story of which appears later). What we know for certain is that it was shot around the year 1859 by George Brush in Susquehanna County, Pennsylvania. The panther was supposedly a male and an old one. He was a large specimen, weighing approximately two hundred pounds. The story of the killing, as related to us by Don Stearns in a February 24, 1966, edition of the *Montrose Independent* newspaper continued:

"As the news of the killing of the lion spread, everyone was asking the same question. From where did the lion come, why was he here, and were there more around? There had been no mountain lions in Susquehanna County for more than a quarter of a century. Why did this one lion suddenly appear? There has been much conjecture on this subject, but, at this late date, we will never know the truth.

"Sam Brush took the dead lion home, and bringing the carcass into the little settlement of Brushville created a bit of excitement. He skinned the lion out and left the pelt intact for mounting. Doctor Latham Smith, a medical doctor in New Milford who evidently had acquired the skills of taxidermy, mounted the pelt for Sam.

"The mounted lion specimen was kept in Sam Brush's home in Brushville. It was exhibited at gatherings and was an excellent conversation piece.... All of the children in the neighborhood played with it, rode it and wrestled it. Occasionally they would use it to frighten some visiting youth who had never before seen it.

"Stanley Sutton [in his nineties when this article was written in 1966], as a boy, played with this mountain lion.... Mr. Sutton says that the lion specimen was still in Brushville in 1888 [at which time Mr. Sutton moved from the area]. The next word on the specimen is a brief note in an 1892 issue of the old 'New Milford Advertiser,' which states the lion has been taken to Chicago for exhibition at the World's Fair. We now know that the lion was part of a Natural History Museum Collection exhibition at the 1893 Chicago World's Fair by Pennsylvania State College. How, why and when did the lion specimen get from Brushville to Penn State? Extended research has revealed no clue to this question, nor any connection, at that time, between anyone in Brushville and Penn State.

"After the 1893 World's Fair, the lion specimen and the other specimens of the museum collection were housed on the first and second floors of the 'Old Main' Building at Penn State. When the Old Main Building was rebuilt in 1929, the collection was salvaged by the Zoology Department and stored in the basement of Watts Hall. About 1938 the specimens were retrieved from Watts Hall and used in the Zoology Department."[8]

In 1953 the lion was loaned to the Carnegie Museum in Pittsburg. In 1993, forty years later, the Brush Panther was returned to the Ferguson Building at Penn State University. The January 2, 1857, edition of the *Lewisburg Chronicle and West Branch Farmer* reported that Sam Brush shot a 147-pound 7-foot 4-inch panther in New Milford Township, Susquehanna County, near Oakland, two weeks earlier, on Sunday. This places the killing of the Brush Panther just prior to the Christmas of 1856. The celebrity status given to the killing of the Brush Panther certainly illustrates the rarity of such an event even then, nearly one and a half centuries ago.

Roger Cowburn is the proprietor of the Railroad Crossing Antiques roadside store several miles west of Galeton on Route 6, in north-central Pennsylvania. On Spencer Kraybill's advice that anyone interested in panthers in Pennsylvania should talk with Roger, we drove northwest from scenic Loch Haven, through Hyner State Park, and climbed into the Alleghany uplands. We passed through forested retreats with such charming names as Black Forest, Hyner Run, Oleona and Kettle Creek. Near noon we drove west from Galeton, not certain where Roger's store was. We confidently turned at the sign which read "Wanted—Cougar and Panther Sightings."

Roger's antique shop is a marvel to behold. His knowledge of collectibles was rivaled only by his broad interest and knowledge of panthers in Pennsylvania. Acquainted with most of the "believers" and "non-believers" in the panther issue, there is certainly no misunderstanding where Roger stands on the issue. A map on the wall positions the sightings of panthers in the state, along with pictures of deer and goat kills attributed to panthers and several pictures of catlike animals claimed to be panthers. In a glass display case rests an assortment of plaster casts of tracks of a variety of known and unknown animals. I soon learned that Roger is quick to test your ability at track identification.

I spent the better part of the afternoon swapping stories and theories with Roger and his friend John Olson about panthers, coyotes, wolves and other wild creatures found, or thought to be found, in the wilds of Pennsylvania. Both Roger and I knew that we disagreed on a number of issues, but that did not prevent us from engaging in an open and respectful dialogue on many aspects of panthers in eastern North America. Whereas I am an optimistic fence-sitter, Roger is an outspoken believer. We both are working towards the same goal.

Roger believes that panthers probably have returned to Pennsylvania from Ontario and Minnesota. I suggested that, if panthers are here, they probably never left. The vast wilderness reserve that many Americans relate with Canada is in many ways, misleading. Forestry operations have changed the face of much of eastern Canada, especially New Brunswick, at a heretofore unheard-of pace. Many parts of eastern Canada are forecasting timber supply shortfalls as public and large freehold lands are cut at a nonsustainable rate. Deer, the main food of panthers, have declined appreciably in recent years, probably due to severe winters and predation by the recently established coyote. Although hairs from a scat were recently identified as those from a panther, this region hardly represents a reservoir from whence migrants might replenish depleted lands to the south. If panthers have moved from southern Canada into the United States, I suggested that their status might be one of refugee rather than colonist! My observations suggest that the reforested wilderness areas of Pennsylvania, Vermont and New York, where deer abound, represent far more acceptable habitat for panthers than the ravaged landscapes of eastern Canada.

We left Roger and John that scorching June afternoon, happy to know that the issue of panthers in Pennsylvania will not be left as a footnote in natural history books. It was not the trained scientist that brought the issue of unsustainable and unacceptable loss of old–growth forests from logging to the forefront. It was the untrained but dedicated citizen's groups and the more radical environmentalists that were instrumental in saving thousands of acres of old-growth temperate rain forest from industrial greed and political ignorance. The scientific community followed closely but safely behind. So it is with the eastern panther. If panthers are still in the Appalachians, it will most likely be confirmed through the efforts of the nonscientific community. They will keep the issue on the front burner and promote legislation which will avert further losses and initiate scientific research to ensure its survival. We left Roger's shop knowing that we would be in touch again, hopefully to exchange more positive news of panthers in eastern North America.

THE DORMAN PANTHER

We arrived at Albright College in Reading, Pennsylvania, early Monday morning. We were unable to meet with Dr. Edwin Bell; in fact, the entire campus seemed deserted except for a maintenance crew at the Biology Building, and they knew nothing of any panther. I suspected that it must have been in storage, but our schedule did not allow us to wait longer. (An historical version of the killing of the Dorman Panther, as recorded by Henry Shoemaker in his 1913 book, *In the Seven Mountains*, was presented earlier.)

Dr. Edwin Bell of Albright College, where the panther now resides, suggests that there is some doubt that the panther was indeed killed by Lewis Dorman, as portrayed in Shoemaker's tale. Dr. Bell believes that the panther may have been killed in Penn's Valley, Center County, east of Aaronsburg by a Mr. Motx, probably around the date of December 24, 1868, given by Shoemaker. The mount was transferred to Albright College from its ancestral institution, Union Seminary. Whatever its true history, the specimen is known as the Dorman Panther and represents one of the last of these noble creatures to be killed in Pennsylvania. Shoemaker's version of romance and tragedy surrounding the young hunter Lewis Dorman and the killing of this panther somehow befits the air of nostalgia and adventure which we associate with a simpler era. The story seems especially fitting given the whimsical image we associate with the eastern panther.

THE AMHERST PANTHER

The rolling Pennsylvania landscape from Reading through Allantown and on to the Water Gap Recreational Area of the Delaware River is not your typical "panther country"—a patchwork of farmland and a maze of roads would put the run to any wilderness-seeking animal, especially the shy and timid panther. The Pocono Mountains provided welcome relief to the endless miles of billboards, roads, small towns and farmland. We finally reached Westfield, Massachusetts, our stop for the night before proceeding north in the morning to Easthampton.

Bright and early the next day, we drove through Easthampton towards the Arcadia Wildlife Refuge a few miles east of town. The narrow lane into the refuge reached a comfortable parking lot with a visitor's sign and building at the far end. Upon entering this attractive rustic quarters, an assembly of mounted mammals and birds were on display overhead, including that of the Amherst Panther.

Upon explaining my interest to the Sanctuary Director Mary Shanley Koeber, she and volunteers Dave McLean and Sally Kieszek helped me remove the panther from its lofty perch and into the sun and heat of out-of-doors. There we measured and photographed this medium-sized panther which had been killed in Massachusetts in the year 1858 or sometime earlier. Originally in the National History Museum of Amherst College, Massachusetts, it was transferred to the Arcadia Wildlife Refuge, along with many other preserved specimens, around 1970. A letter to Dr. Stoner of the New York State Museum from

The Amherst Panther was shot in 1858 near Amherst, Massachusetts by W.S. Clark. Dr. Clark was a professor, and later president, of Amherst College. For many years the panther was in the National History Museum of Amherst College. In 1970 it was donated to the Arcadia Wildlife Refuge near Easthampton, where it is now on display. (G. PARKER)

Professor Harold H. Plough, curator of zoology at Amherst College, and dated February 4, 1938, says in part: "We now find that the [panther] was received by gift from Professor W.S. Clark in the year 1858. Professor Clark was professor of chemistry and zoology in Amherst College and was later first president of the State College. The data along with the accession record show that the [panther] was shot by Professor Clark near Amherst. The indications are that the specimen was collected in the year it was received, but concerning the date and the actual place of collection we cannot be at the present time more precise."[9]

James Cardoza, Wildlife Biologist with the Massachusetts Division of Fisheries and Wildlife, wrote me the following on April 5, 1994: "There is one probable Massachusetts specimen of the eastern cougar. Several years ago I contacted Amherst College. I was informed that the specimen did exist, but was transferred to the Arcadia Wildlife Sanctuary of the Massachusetts Audubon Society in Easthampton. Upon contacting them, I was informed that they did have the specimen. I went there and examined it. It is unquestionably a mountain lion, and indubitably old. I have no doubt that it is the specimen from Amherst College; the paper trail is sound. However, there are no data with the specimen. According to Stoner's account, it was shot 'near Amherst' prior to 1858, and I tentatively accept that.... I am somewhat uneasy since the Amherst area was largely open and agricultural at that time, not the place I would expect a wandering cougar to show up. But then, the record states 'near Amherst', and that could be some distance away."[10]

The Amherst Panther, like many of the others that we had seen on this trip, had been through its share of wear and tear. Someone had substituted porcupine quills for its whiskers which had been plucked or worn away through the ages. The true value of these rare historical remnants, artifacts of a race of wild feline which may no longer be with us, is seldom understood. When told of its rarity and biological uniqueness, however, I was encouraged by the sincere enthusiasm of those to whom its custody had been entrusted. I left Arcadia Wildlife Sanctuary with the promise to Mary that I would return my concern for the Amherst specimen in writing. She assured me that such a gesture would help to establish the historical significance of this specimen in their collection, and its importance to the natural history of Massachusetts.

THE RHODE ISLAND PANTHER

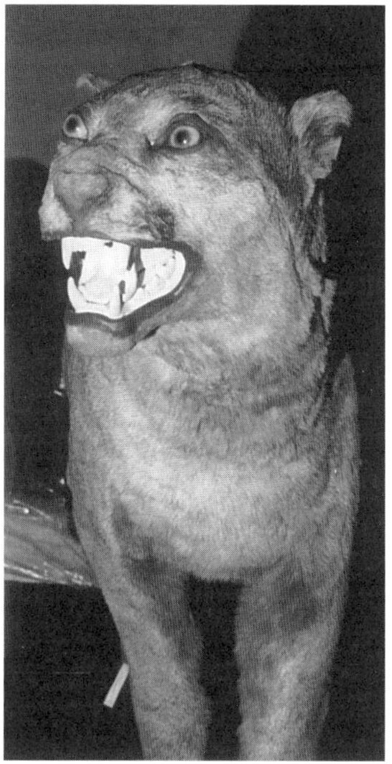

The Rhode Island Panther was shot by "one of the James Brothers" in Rhode Island in 1847 or 1848. It is part of the collection at the Museum of Comparative Zoology at Harvard University, Boston. (G. PARKER)

We arrived mid-morning of the next day at the grounds of the Museum of Comparative Zoology on Oxford Street at Harvard University, a city within a city—quite different from the pastoral setting of State College and Penn State University nestled among the Alleghany Mountains of central Pennsylvania. On the fourth and top floor, back among the walls of specimen cabinets, animal mounts and skeletons, we found Kary McFadden diligently cataloguing the growing inventory of specimens and data. To reach the Rhode Island Panther, we followed Kary up yet another flight of stairs through a hatch to an attic storage room. The temperature took another sharp turn upwards. At the far end of the cramped and stuffy room full of mounted heads, skins and other such collectibles stood the Rhode Island Panther under a clear plastic protective covering. It was a fine large specimen, and the dark rufous on the back, in contrast to many of the faded specimens seen earlier, remained strikingly prominent. This was one of the larger specimens seen, and the taxidermy was good. It stood 29 1/2 inches at the shoulder and 7 1/2 feet from tip of nose to tip of tail (the tail measured 31 1/2 inches).

The Rhode Island Panther was shot by "one of the James Brothers" in West Greenwich, Rhode Island, in 1847 or 1848. It was given by a Tillinghost Olmey to the Franklin Society of Providence, Rhode Island, and thence to the Boston Society of Natural History. It became part of the collection at the Museum of Comparative Zoology in July 1946. The skull was removed by a researcher from the Smithsonian Institute for taxonomic studies in 1982 and was apparently confirmed to be of the eastern subspecies.

Christopher Raithel, Senior Wildlife Biologist with the Rhode Island Division of Fish and Wildlife, believes that this is the only mounted specimen of eastern panther from Rhode Island. Mr. Raithel finds it remarkable that a panther would have been found in Rhode Island at that time, as much of the state was deforested well before 1847. Grey wolves had been eliminated from Rhode Island by the early 1700s. By the mid-1800s, deer, the stable food of panthers, had become scarce from loss of forested habitat and relentless and uncontrolled subsistence and market hunting.

However, we must accept the written records that were left us, and although possible errors in such early accounts should be acknowledged, they remain the only ties we have between many early specimens, such as the Rhode Island Panther, and their origin and history. The genealogical uncertainty which surrounds many of these early specimens forms part of their lore and mystique.

THE WARDSBORO PANTHER

"A PANTHER KILLED

"Be it remembered that on the 20th day of November A.D. 1875, Henry N. Fitt, Stephen S. Perry, Nathaniel B. Johnson, Homer B. Johnson, Louis G. Putnam, Erwin L. Putnam, Marshall S. Haskins, Alonzo K. Smith, Charles H. Rider, Daniel W. Streeter, George W. Putnam, Elwin Johnson, Irwin B. Putnam, Clarence Torry, Lucius Lyman, John Streeter, [and] LaFayette H. Haskins killed a panther within the limits of the Town of Wardsboro and near the dwelling house of the above named Daniel W. Streeter and between said house and Stratten Line in a piece of woodland, the shot fired by said Stephen S. Perry giving said panther his death wound.

"The length of said panther from nose to tip of tail measured six feet and eight and one half inches—height two and one half feet, weight one hundred and five pounds.

Attest. A.J. Dexter, Town Clerk

NOTE: The measurement of above panther was erroneously reported. The measurement according to the rule for measuring such animals was 7 feet in length from nose to tip of tail and 33 inches in height.

Attest. A.J. Dexter, Town Clerk"[11]

The Wardsboro Panther was hunted down and shot by a group of townsfolk from Wardsboro, Vermont, on November 20, 1875. It measures 6 feet and 8 1/2 inches and weighed 105 pounds. It is now in storage at the Boston Museum of Science.

(G. PARKER)

So was recorded the official documentation of the killing of the Wardsboro Panther in the 1875 land records of the town of Wardsboro, Vermont. Wardsboro is approximately twenty-five miles east of the New York-Vermont state line. As we entered the expansive and very modern Museum of Science in downtown Boston, we passed among orderly but enthusiastic throngs of school children here to see and experience the educational exhibits of natural science. Carolyn Kirdahy, Curator of Objects, met us in the front lobby and led us through the public display area and to the back room working area of the museum. In a small storage room and under cover on a wheeled dolly, stood the infamous Wardsboro Panther. Missing part of its left front paw, presumably to a trap, this was a fine specimen, sporting a dark rufous on the back, flanks and tail with a lighter tawny on the shoulders, neck and sides. A prominent tuft, more exaggerated than on other panther specimens, embellished the end of the tail. Like the Rhode Island specimen, this was a large panther, measuring 6 feet 8 inches from nose to end of tail and standing 22 1/2 inches at the shoulders, somewhat less than the measurements given by Mr. Dexter, the Town Clerk for Wardsboro, in 1875.

A somewhat more colorful tale of the last days of the Wardsboro Panther appeared in the January 17, 1971 edition of the *Boston Sunday Globe*:

"Supposedly killed by a band of Wardsboro men set upon tracking down a large and frightening beast in November, 1875, the penultimate panther died somewhat less gloriously than at the hands of village yeoman out to protect their wives and children. Two lime-stone burners saw a bear on a sunny November Saturday morning, and returned to West Wardsboro to borrow a musket. They ended up, as you might imagine, with a half-dozen village boys in tow, and one recalled later how the bear hunt turned more exciting, and then bittersweet. Tracking their bear, armed with a muzzle loader, and a town dandy's five-shot nickel-plated .22 revolver, they came upon the mountain lion skulking in a tree. The musket shot only knocked it down (no one knew how to reload the borrowed muzzleloader), and all five shots from the nickel-plated special did not kill the catamount. At last, one of the boys, not remembered now, out of pride or pity ended the lion's life with a pocket knife."

A news release from the Boston Museum of Science dated January 30, 1964, states: "The controversy continues. Witnesses still insist that they see panthers; skeptics still take an 'I'm-from-Missouri; you've-got-to-show-me' attitude and demand proof. A fence-sitter in the argument, Boston's Museum of Science, is offering $100 for definite proof that panthers do, indeed, exist in New England. It will pay the money to the first person bringing in a specimen certified by a local game warden as having been legally taken within the six-state region. This is not a bounty, just an enthusiastic desire to know the truth. Mounted, it would become a companion piece to the Wardsboro Panther, which meanwhile still just grins and waits."

It is interesting that, a few years later, after Bruce Wright convincingly argued that panthers from New Brunswick were moving south and repopulating parts of former range in New

England, the museum retracted its offer. A column in the *Boston Globe* [date unknown] stated: "Dr. Bradford Washburn, the mountaineer-photographer-scientist president of Boston Museum of Science, withdrew the museum's standing offer for cougar pelts. He said that with the mountain lion returning to New England, he did not want to be responsible for sending mercenaries to wipe out the vanguard of a pussycat with gelignite temper."

Our holiday, and our search for eastern panthers, was drawing to a close. We fought the snarl of traffic back onto Interstate 95 and fled north out of Boston. As we distanced ourselves from the congestion of the city and moved north towards Maine, I retraced the events of the past two weeks—the places visited, eastern panthers seen and, above all else, the people we met and shared stories with. We all held a common concern: if eastern panthers do still roam through wilderness sanctuaries of the Appalachians, they should be recognized and fully protected. I wondered what evidence it will take to convince the skeptics that panthers are still with us. What I am saying? Did I not include myself as one of those skeptics only a few short weeks ago, an acknowledged fence-sitter of long repute? Had personal encounters with the tattered feline remnants in the basements, attics and back rooms of assorted museums, universities and other institutions dislodge the dogmatic impression of eastern panthers imprinted on my mind through the years?

These stuffed trophies had once been feared and revered wild beasts of the eastern forests. The sounds and smells of the Green Mountain Tavern in Bennington, the excitement of the small band of villagers that gathered at Panther Rock as George Walker prodded the snarling Weathersfield Panther in his rocky retreat, the feeling of triumph by Alexander Crowell as he paraded the trophy panther on his wagon before the townspeople of Barnard—these and other tales describe the chase and capture of the American lion by the folks of rural America in a more innocent age. Had this nostalgia permeated the trained and disciplined thought processes of a trained scientist?

THE NEHASANE PANTHER

Our trip uncovered several specimens of eastern panther unknown to me prior to our departure. One of these was the Lycoming County specimen in Pennsylvania referred to earlier.

Reference to the location of another was found in a manuscript prepared by Ranier Brocke of Syracuse University and which I perused during my visit to the New York State Museum in Albany. I have named this specimen after the lodge on Lake Lila in the Adirondack Mountains where it was displayed over the fireplace for many years. The Nehasane Panther was apparently killed by Mark Smith after being treed by dogs in Lewis County, New York, in the year 1876. While at the lodge, the panther was the property of a Dr. Webb. After Mr. Webb's death, William Verner, then curator at the Adirondack Museum at Blue Mountain Lake, secured it for their collection there, where it resides to this day.

THE LAKE PLACID PANTHER

A specimen of an "Adirondack Cougar" sits on display at the North Elbe Historical Society in Lake Placid, New York. Information is lacking, other than that it was donated to the museum by the Brewster family in 1972.

THE ST. LAWRENCE PANTHER

The whereabouts of a mounted specimen of eastern panther shot near Canton, New York, in 1843 and referred to in earlier literature remains a mystery. The following is from Stoner's 1950 paper on Adirondack cougars:

"A mounted specimen of a panther is deposited in the Geology Department Museum of St. Lawrence University in Canton, New York. It found its way to the university in a rather round-about way. It appears to be the same animal reported on in the following news story which appeared on the editorial page in the Monday, January 2, 1843, edition of *The Northern Cabinet* published in Canton, New York.

PANTHER KILLED

"A full grown panther was slain in this town not long since, by three of our leading citizens.... In the morning a farmer came into this village and stated that the track of some large animal had crossed the southern road, and they immediately sallied forth with their rifles in pursuit. After following the track for some three or four miles, they started the animal, and a small dog which accompanied them soon drove him into a tree, where the pursuers, after several deliberate shots, soon brought him to the ground. The "trophies of victory" can be seen over Mr. Clark's store."[12]

The above account was in most part confirmed in a 1937 interview by the weekly newspaper of Canton with a Mr. Cyrus Clark, the son of J.E. Clark, one of the three leading citizens of that town who dispatched the panther in 1843. His account is as follows: "This is the story as told to me many times by my father, but I do not remember his telling me the date when the panther was killed. All fall, the farmers had been losing sheep, and after a snowfall Lester White found the body of one, and he saw the tracks of the animal that had done the killing in the snow, and three men, Mr. White, my father, Edmond Clark Jr., and an uncle of mine, Austin Clark, started to follow them.

"They followed the tracks to a brush fence back of the barn, but after getting through the fence they could find no tracks, so they began circling around, when suddenly the panther jumped from the brush and started toward Lester White, but then the animal turned and ran. They put a shepherd dog they had on his trail and the dog would follow the trail a little way and then run back to the men and they gave it up. They wanted a dog that would chase the panther up a tree, when they could overtake it. And so they sent a man to Canton to get Elijah Clark and his hound.... My father told me there were six in the party [when the panther was killed]. They could have been the three North Russell boys ... and the three from Canton ... and they had a hound with them. My father used to say that they were armed with everything from guns to pitchforks....

"They took up the track where the panther had broken out of the brush and the dog followed it three or four miles, from North Russell to Martyn's Corners, a couple miles out of Canton, where you turn from the Canton-Russell road to Pyrites. The dog treed him right there, and he was up the tree when the hunters arrived. My father told Elijah to take a good aim, and Elijah shot and never hit the animal, which jumped from the tree and after running about 20 rods, then jumped into another tree. My father said that this leap carried him 15 feet up the tree before he hit it.

"Then father said he handed Elijah his own rifle to use, and Elijah shot the panther, which fell across a branch and they had to climb the tree to get him down. The body measured six feet 10 inches from tip to tip. They took it to the Smith school house where a meeting was being held, and the whole crowd boiled out to see what they had."[13]

The panther was purchased by a local merchant of Canton, mounted and displayed in his store window. It subsequently landed in the chemical laboratory at St. Lawrence University. Numerous contacts with present and former professors of St. Lawrence University have failed to find a trace of this panther. No one seems to know anything of it, and, like its present-day descendants, it now remains part of the lore of the Adirondack wilderness.

THE MCGILL PANTHER

A letter to Dr. Stoner from J.D. Cleghorn, Associate Curator of Zoology at the Peter Redpath Museum of McGill University in Montreal, Quebec, dated January 17, 1939, says in part:

"[when] the defunct Montreal Natural History Society ... closed its museum in 1906 c., all of the zoological materials came to the Peter Redpath Museum, and amongst it, a cougar. The original museum label which is still attached, reads as follows: 'The Puma or American Panther (*Felis concolor*) is, still, found (1896) in British Columbia. It used, also, to inhabit Eastern Canada and this specimen was killed at Russelltown, about 30 miles south of Montreal, and was presented to the Museum, by the late John Leeming, in 1859.' I understand that when this specimen came to McGill it was in very poor condition, but it has since been remounted, and its measurements are as follows: Length 74 inches. Tail 28 inches. Hind foot 11 3/4 inches."[14]

THE LITTLE ST. JEAN PANTHER

The Little St. Jean Panther is the only known mounted specimen from the state of Maine, and today resides at the New Brunswick Museum in Saint John. It was trapped by Rosarie Morin of St. Zacharie, Quebec, east of Little St. John Lake in Somerset County, Maine, in January, 1938. Mr. Morin returned to his home in St. Zacharie with the skin of the panther. It was soon acquired by the village priest, who sent it to Quebec City to be mounted. The priest's heir subsequently sold it to Bruce Wright of the Northeastern Wildlife Station at Fredericton, New Brunswick. The fact that a raw panther skin was delivered to the taxidermist in Quebec City is strong supporting evidence of its local origin.

Bruce Wright with the Little St. Jean Panther, trapped by Rosarie Morin of St. Zacharie, Quebec, in Somerset County, Maine, in January 1938. This is the most recent specimen of a panther believed to be of the eastern race.

(WRIGHT, 1972)

The specimen measured, from tip to tip, 7 feet 1 inch, and was estimated to have weighed about 100 pounds.

"There was some fading but no sign of the usual black and white facial markings or eye stripe.... The animal was of the red color phase—a uniform red–brown, darker dorsally and lighter ventrally, with a black tip to the tail."[15]

THE WISCONSIN PANTHER

Because intact specimens of eastern panthers are so rare I include here the tale of a panther killed in the state of Wisconsin. There appears to be some confusion as to just when and by whom this panther was killed. The following is a summary of the available information on this specimen collected by A. W. Schorger of Madison, Wisconsin:

"*The Neenah and Menasha Conservator*, December 17, 1857, stated that Samuel B. Hart of Appleton killed a 'huge panther' on November 22. *The Appleton Crescent*, December 12, 1857, carried a circumstantial account of the event. Samuel P. Hart, with a neighbor, was searching for a colt when his dog treed the cougar. The animal measured 7 feet 2 inches in length. 'Two of his tusks, one of the upper and the other of the lower jaw, were broken off, and had apparently been gone for several years. The other two tusks were very large but much worn.' The specimen was mounted by 'Prof. Mason and Dr. Beach.' An accompanying article in the *Lawrence University Cabinet*, stated: 'As you enter the room the first object that attracts attention is the Panther recently transferred from a savage roaming life, to one more congenial to the wishes of the people.'"[16]

A card on the specimen, however, reads as follows: "Killed by Mr. Reese in 1848 on the Randall Farm, two miles north east of Appleton. He was searching for a lost horse in the snow, and found panther tracks. The following day he went on horseback, tracking the animal through the snow, finally killing him near the Ballard Road."[17] This is believed to have been the only mounted specimen of eastern panther from the state of Wisconsin. Originally preserved as a mounted exhibit, it was taken down in the 1950s and the skin was properly tanned. It is now stored as Specimen UWZ 13464 in the Zoological Museum at the University of Wisconsin in Madison.[18]

Conclusion

This concludes our review of the tattered remnants of that proud and feared race of eastern panther that once ruled with unchallenged supremacy the length and breadth of the Appalachian Mountains—twenty-two unflinching reminders of the legions which fell before them—a roll call, of sorts, for this wild beast which gave source to verse and tale, and became a symbol for much of what was wild and untamed, feared and revered, in early pioneer America. Are these "ludicrously stuffed effigies," as Henry Shoemaker referred to them in his tribute to the Dorman Panther, all that we have left? If so, it is both pity and shame that we feel when we reflect on these words left to us by that early Pennsylvanian historian: "When the last panther falls, then woe betide, nature's retributive cataclysm is at our side."

CHAPTER FIVE

Pushed to the Edge: The Final Years

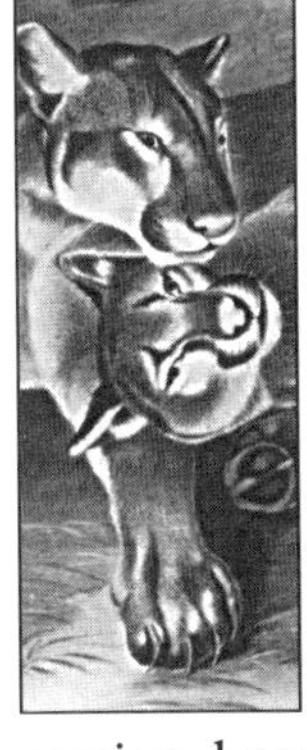

"**IN NORTHEASTERN** Susquehanna County [Pennsylvania] … there lies an undefined section known as the Highlands. Though most of the virgin timber in the country had been cut by 1860, this section had hardly been touched. Settlement here was sparse and the country was rugged and wild. In the very early days of settlement, before the Highlands were settled, a road had been cut through them, and is known as the 'Old Harmony Road.' Sometime in the winter, between 1857 and 1859, two small boys were walking down the abandoned section of the Old Harmony Road on their way to the small settlement at Brushville. They came upon some tracks in the snow which puzzled them. Definitely they were tracks of a cat. The boys knew that there were bobcats in this section and had seen many of their tracks, but these tracks were much too large for any bobcat of which they had ever heard of or dreamed. They sensed that there was something here beyond their comprehension and felt a warning tingle of fear. Without much hesitation, they scurried on down the road to Brushville to look for Sam Brush, who could answer their anxious questions.

"Samuel Brush was a prosperous lumberman and businessman. He was also known throughout the section for his skill as a hunter. Sam was born in Connecticut and in 1820, at the age of twelve, migrated with his parents to that section of northeastern Susquehanna County which was to become known as Brushville. When the boys found him, Sam was probably amused by their excited tale. But his sporting blood was aroused and he said that he would go up with them and take a look at the tracks. He took up his trusty old muzzle-loader, unchained his dogs and set off up the valley.

"Sam was surprised when he saw the tracks. He had little time to ponder though, as the dogs picked up the tracks and soon gave voice. The tempo of the dog's baying changed and Sam knew that they had jumped the animal. The beast stood momentarily at bay against a ledge on the southeast side of the valley. Sam could hear the dog's excited baying mingled with their yelps of pain and he knew that this was no ordinary animal. The animal broke and, with the dogs in hot pursuit, came down across the valley in front of Sam. Any questions Sam might have had were answered, suddenly. For here was an actual, live, extra large, adult mountain lion. We can only imagine the thoughts that raced through Sam's mind in those brief seconds.

"As the lion came across in front of him, Sam shot and knew not whether he hit or missed. In a short distance the lion treed and the dogs clamored at the tree trunk. In the tall tree the lion was not an easy target, but at least it was a still one. How many times Sam shot and reloaded the old muzzle-loader gun, we'll never know. One version says that the seventh and fatal shot hit beneath the lion's ear and that the lion fell from the tree dead. Another says that on the third shot the lion fell from the tree mortally wounded and that in its death throes tore one of the dogs to pieces. Regardless of the detail, we know for sure that there and then the last known mountain lion of Susquehanna County was killed."[1]

Was this, indeed, written testimony to the final slaying of this noble wild beast in yet another pocket of Pennsylvanian wilderness? The mounted specimen of the "Brush Panther" now resides at the Forest Resources Building at Pennsylvania State University. Although the American lion was once distributed throughout most of North America south of the boreal forest, the length and breadth of its range shifted with that of its main prey—white-tailed deer in the east, and mule deer and black-tailed deer in the west. Changes in the distribution of deer were often associated with changes in patterns of regional and continental climate. In the northeast, for instance, archaeological digs of Native encampments have shown that white-tailed deer were once common in the eastern Canadian provinces of Nova Scotia and New Brunswick until about 1100 A.D. At that time a general cooling trend caused the northern limit of this species to shift further to the south, probably well into southern Maine. When the first settlers arrived in the extreme northeast, therefore, deer were relatively scarce or absent, and we can only assume that panthers were as well. Early records suggest that was so. At that time, the northeastern limit of panther range was probably northern New Hampshire and central Maine, extending west into the southern St. Lawrence and Ottawa river valleys. To the south, early records suggest that panthers were found most everywhere east of the Mississippi River to the Gulf of Mexico.

Like most wild animals, especially predators, panthers were not distributed evenly throughout this vast range. They appeared to be most common within the rugged hills and valleys of the Appalachian Mountains. The core areas of exceptional panther abundance seem to have been the Great Smoky Mountains of western North Carolina, north along the border of West Virginia and Virginia, through northwestern Maryland and into the Alleghany Mountains of Pennsylvania. Further to the north, early records suggest that panthers were most common, and survived the longest, in the ruggedness of the Catskill and Adirondack mountains of New York, the Green Mountains of Vermont and the White Mountains of New Hampshire. How common were they? It is very difficult to guess, but there are some tempting clues which might be pursued.

Henry Shoemaker believed that in the early 1800s panthers were as numerous as lions of the African plains. "The woods fairly teemed with them. Yet they made no inroads on the myriads of elk, deer, hares, heath-cocks, wild turkeys, grouse, quails, wild pigeons, rabbits and hares which shared the forest covers with them."[2] Shoemaker had a flair for embellishing some of his stories from the early years, and his interviews and writings were done in the early 1900s, well after most panthers had vanished from their former haunts. But he did speak with many former panther hunters, and even with the tendency of old-timers to glorify the past and magnify personal accomplishments, this feared creature was apparently once quite common throughout much of Pennsylvania. As we have seen earlier, however, a certain amount of fraud was associated with most early bounty programs, and inferences of numbers from bounty records may tend to exaggerate the early abundance of panthers.

Perhaps one of the more credible accounts of the early distribution of panthers in New England in the mid-1800s was left to us by J. A. Allen, an early curator at the American Museum of Natural History: "The woods are often spoken of as filled with wild animals, among which the most numerous were beavers, foxes, wolves, bears, moose, deer, raccoons and martens; lynxes were common, as was also that 'most insidious and deadly foe of human kind, the catamount.' The range of the catamount or panther, extends, as is well known, from Northern New England southward not only to the Gulf of Mexico, but throughout the greater part of South America. It long since, however, disappeared from the southern half of New England, as well as from most of the more settled parts of the United States everywhere; the capture during the last ten years [1866-76] of an occasional individual in the Green Mountains and in the forest region of Northern New Hampshire and Maine shows that it still lingers in Northern New England, where it is slowly but surely becoming extirpated."[3]

Is there any way to obtain an estimate of the early densities of panthers in parts of their ranges? Very risky, but there have been some "guesstimates." In 1979, David Lee of the North Carolina State Museum examined records of some of the early circle hunts and from those made a rough estimate of the density of panthers in Pennsylvania at that time.[4] Circle hunting appeared to be most popular in that state during the ninety-year period from 1760 to 1850. The sparse records from several of those hunts allowed Lee to speculate that the density of panthers must have been around one individual per seventeen square miles, certainly within the range of more recent estimates of home ranges of western mountain lions which vary from five to thirty or more square miles.

So let us now review accounts and narratives of early panther abundance throughout its former range in eastern North America, from the cold spruce-fir thickets of New Brunswick to the sweltering swamps of southern Florida. We will begin in the south, where panthers are still found for certain, and work our way north. The only confirmed population of wild panthers breeding east of the Mississippi River is in the state of Florida. Early explorers and settlers were aware of the Florida panther and left many early references to it. Perhaps the first was that of Cabeza de Vaca, who in 1513 reported seeing "lions" in the Florida Everglades. His was the first report of panthers in North America. Later, explorers such as the English sea captain Sir John Hawkins in 1565, and René Laudonnierre in 1598, reported seeing "tigers" and "lions" during their explorations in parts of Florida.[5] Near the close of the last century one early naturalist reported that the panther was "not uncommon in the unsettled portions of the state."[6] About the same time, another naturalist confirmed that while it was restricted to the more thinly settled parts of the state, he thought it was extinct in northern Florida, and in those states to the northeast.[7]

THE FLORIDA PANTHER

The Florida panther is recognized as being a different subspecies than the eastern panther to the north. It has been described as being more rufous or reddish brown in color, and having longer legs and smaller feet than its northern cousin. The small foot of the Florida panther seems particularly characteristic of the subspecies, being at least a full inch less in diameter than panthers further to the north.[8] The color of the Florida panther, like most other members of the species, is quite uniform throughout its range: tawny above and a lighter color beneath. The tip of the tail and the back of the ears are either dark brown or brownish black. The lower chest, belly and inside of the legs of adult Florida panthers are typically creamy white to brownish white.[9]

The early distribution of the Florida panther included Florida, Georgia, South Carolina, Alabama, Mississippi, Louisiana and as far west as eastern Texas. East of the Mississippi, the Florida panther probably met and interbred with eastern panthers at the southern limit of their range. The Florida panther is presently confined to the southern third of Florida in the Big Cypress National Preserve, Collier Seminole Park, Fakahatchee Strand, Everglades National Park, and the Big Cypress Indian Reservation.[10] Today the panther is recognized by Florida and federal law as endangered, and is fully protected. However, the Florida panther has been the focus of intensive research, media attention and controversy over the past twenty years and today teeters on the brink of extinction. Although as recently as the early 1970s there was some doubt as to its continued existence, a few panthers in Florida did manage to survive centuries of persecution by humans. They did so by remaining deep in the insect-infested swamps, as far away from their human tormentors as possible. The burning question became how many, and exactly where. Until the 1950s the only reason for asking that question had been to better seek out and destroy them.

Panthers had a reputation for occasionally killing livestock, and with agriculture gaining popularity in the state during the early 1900s, this real or imagined threat to the industry was dealt with. Bounties had been paid on Florida panthers during several periods in the nineteenth century. As if added fuel for the fire was needed, more panthers turned to killing livestock, following deer eradication programs to control the fever tick during the 1930s. In 1935 a Florida sportsman brought the Lee brothers, two professional cougar hunters from Arizona, to Collier County to demonstrate that panthers could still be found in significant numbers. Within five weeks the hunters and their dogs had killed eight panthers in the Big Cypress Swamp![11]

A Florida panther, ***Felis concolor coryi***. This race of panther would have been quite similar to the eastern panther to the north. (RUSSELL KAYE)

Fortunately, the mid-twentieth century ushered in a time of personal and spiritual reflection, a time when past sins were recognized and acknowledged, and when consideration and compassion for creatures other than humans were gaining favor. Many predators received a reprieve—not all, but some. One of the lucky ones was the Florida panther. In 1950 the state of Florida took the panther off the most wanted list and afforded it official recognition as a game animal. This acknowledgment provided the panther protection except during the open hunting season for deer. Panthers which killed livestock could still be removed by special permit throughout the year. In 1958 the panther was given complete protection by the Florida Game and Fresh Water Fish Commission. The United States Fish and Wildlife Service listed the Florida panther as endangered on March 11, 1967. This act of benevolence stemmed the threat from gun and trap, but did little to stop the accelerating loss of wilderness habitat so important to this secretive predator. By the early 1970s, little attention had been given this feline recluse. The World Wildlife Fund took the initiative and called in Ronald Nowak and west Texas rancher and mountain lion hunter Roy McBride. McBride and his hounds treed their first, but certainly not their last, Florida panther in 1973 and established for certain that wild panthers were still in the state. It was not until 1976, however, that the Florida Game and Fresh Water Fish Commission began a study to locate and describe at least one population of Florida panthers. Robert Belden, a biologist with the commission was asked to carry out the appropriate studies.[12] At that time, small numbers of panthers were found to be breeding in south Florida from Lake Okeechobee southward, primarily in the Big Cypress region. By 1987 the number of Florida panthers was estimated to be only thirty to fifty animals, and this isolated subspecies appeared to be heading towards extinction. Only one-half of the known animals were on public lands. All factors contributing to the decline of the Florida panther, whether hunting or loss of habitat, can be traced back to an increasing human population.[13]

A Florida panther treed by dogs, just prior to being immobilized by researchers with a tranquilizer gun and dart. This endangered species is being studied intensively in hopes of preventing extinction. (RUSSELL KAYE)

The continued survival of the Florida panther was attributed to the impenetrable wilds of one of their last strongholds—the Big Cypress Swamp/Everglades region. With the construction in 1966-67 of State Highway 84, otherwise known as Alligator Alley, which cut through the heart of these swamplands, the last refuge of the Florida panther was threatened. That threat grew even larger with a proliferation of access roads off this major highway, and the increased use of off-road vehicles, both factors opening up greater access to the potential panther range.

Another threat to the integrity of the endangered Florida panther was the very real possibility of "genetic contamination" from release or escape of some of the estimated one thousand non-Florida panthers (western or southern origin) kept in captivity in that state. In 1986 various state and federal agencies combined forces to provide guidance and coordination on research and management activities involved in the implementation of a

Florida panther recovery plan. The issue rapidly attracted state and national attention, and an assortment of well-intentioned public and private conservation organizations sought to be heard and to join in saving this high-profile symbol of threatened and endangered species throughout the nation. In 1982, after a poll of nearly 600,000 Florida school children, the panther was officially declared Florida's state animal. Following a feasibility study in 1981, a full-scale program of capturing, radio-instrumenting, and tracking panthers was begun in 1982. By 1988, twenty-three panthers had been collared, of which fourteen remained alive. These studies of radio-marked panthers provided new and important information on many aspects of habitat use, daily activities, home range characteristics, social interactions, population dynamics and health of this endangered subspecies. Continued research in the 1980s and 1990s has included studies of reproduction and general health, home ranges, food habits and the effects of deer hunting on panther survival. Florida also accelerated its program of land acquisition and created the 32,000-acre Florida Panther National Wildlife Refuge.

The final phase of the Florida Panther Recovery Plan called for efforts by the Florida Game and Fresh Water Fish Commission to reintroduce panthers into suitable areas within the state. It was felt that introduced panthers would add to the genetic vitality of the population. This would hopefully reduce the risk of extinction from diminished population viability through inbreeding. A captive- breeding facility was constructed at White Oak Plantation near Yulee, Florida, and by 1987 this facility housed one male and one female Florida panther. In addition, three wild-caught Texas female cougars were brought to the facility for initial breeding trials with the Florida male. The plan called for subsequent offspring of these matings to be surgically sterilized and used in the reintroduction feasibility phase of the project.[14] Through all these developments and actions towards saving this threatened predator, however, the general prognosis was that "It is probable that the Florida panther is involved in a slow but rather certain extinction process and that genetically the population numbers are critically low."[15]

This concern, expressed by Robert Belden, for the survival of the Florida panther was verified by a group of specialists assembled by the U.S. Fish and Wildlife Service in 1989. Population data on the Florida panther was fed into a computer and subjected to what biologists call a "population viability analysis." What this means is that the future of a particular population or subspecies is predicted based upon the best available information. In the case of the Florida panther, the computer model predicted that the subspecies would become extinct in twenty-five to forty years!

The live-capture and radiotelemetry study of panthers continued. By 1992 the number of panthers collared and monitored had reached forty-five. Information on home-range sizes, rates of mortality, feeding habits, habitat use and other aspects of natural history and ecology were accumulating. David Maehr, a biologist with the Florida Game and Fresh Water Fish Commission at the time, had assumed responsibility for most of the field studies by the Florida Panther Recovery Project. A team of veterinarians, led by Melody Roelke, examined the captured panthers for general health and took blood, sperm and tissue samples for further analyses.

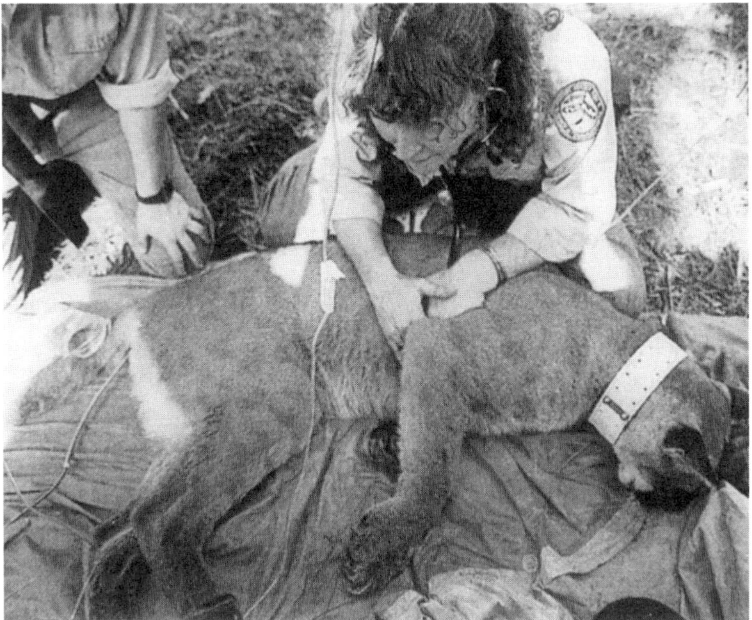

Veterinarian Melody Roelke examines a tranquilized Florida panther. This panther has been fitted with a collar and radio transmitter so researchers can monitor its activities.

(RUSSELL KAYE)

Examination of the live-captured panthers revealed some disturbing trends. Inbreeding had led to physical deformities, such as a hereditary kink at the end of the cats' long tails and a cowlick in the fur on their backs. Most males were born with only one testicle descended into the scrotum and most had reduced and abnormal sperm. Heart defects and reduced immune systems were also related to severe inbreeding. As well, unacceptably high levels of mercury were detected in panthers from the Everglades National Park.[16] Although some have suggested that mercury may have contributed to the virtual extinction of this subpopulation, others, such as David Maehr, believe the latter came most likely from a general lack of forest cover in the park, and a very low prey base.

To stem the predicted path to extinction, breeding facilities were established at the White Oak Plantation in northern Florida. This five hundred-acre conservation center for endangered species, close to the Florida-Georgia border, is the private property of New York paper magnate Howard Gilman. The original purpose of the facility, as envisioned by Maehr, Roelke and others, was to be a center where young Florida panthers could be assembled. Then, after controlled breeding to assure maximum genetic diversity of subsequent offspring, genetically superior Florida panthers were to be released back into the wild. The original goal was to establish a colony of 130 panthers by the year 2000 and 500 by 2010. The live-capture program of young Florida panthers with which to stock the White Oak facility was planned to cause minimum disruption of the existing wild population. The original plan called for establishing panther populations in other parts of Florida and the Okeefenokee Wildlife Refuge in Georgia. This would increase genetic diversity and reduce health risks from inbreeding.

However, nothing ever works exactly as planned. So it is with planned panther re-introductions. In 1988 seven sterilized, radio-collared cougars from Texas were released north of the Osceola National Forest in northern Florida.[17] This release was an experiment, a dry run, to evaluate the feasibility of future releases of fertile Florida panthers. Would released panthers quickly adapt to life in the wild, establish territories, find a mate and successfully reproduce? If not, the breeding facilities at the White Oak Conservation Center might be futile. The Texas experiment proved somewhat less than encouraging. Three wandered beyond the National Forest—one to a nearby exotic-game compound; another to the outskirts of Jacksonville, fifty miles away, and one to a goat farm over the Georgia border. Two others were killed by hunters. All surviving cougars were recaptured and shipped back to Texas.[18]

In the early years the Florida panther recovery plan was also getting some bad press. People were questioning the wisdom of sending men with dart guns and dogs out to chase down, immobilize, collar and release these last remaining panthers. However, through better public relations, and a greater understanding of the issues, the program became generally accepted and endorsed by the public. However, more problems developed from animal rights activists. A legal challenge to the removal of wild panthers by the U.S. Fish and Wildlife Service for the breeding program at the White Oak Conservation Center was threatened unless an environmental impact statement was filed. This well-intentioned but perhaps unjustified confrontation created a messy debate, which was soon followed by a threatened lawsuit from the Fund for Animals. An out-of-court settlement was reached when the proposed capture-breeding program was modified to accommodate certain of the groups' objections. The first six Florida panther kittens were captured and brought to the conservation center in early 1991.

Objections by the Fund for Animals group to the breeding and release program may not be entirely unfounded. As Holly Jensen, a local animal-rights activist from Gainesville in partnership with the Fund for Animals, explains, " 'The point is that there has been all this attention placed on one particular area of recovery, genetics, and captive breeding. I think it's because baby kittens are appealing. They provide great pictures for public relations. But what about saving the habitat? What about mercury contamination? If this kind of stuff is not addressed, there's no reason to spend millions of dollars on captive breeding. What you'll end up with are caged cats and nowhere to put them.' " [19]

Perhaps, but without a captive breeding stock of Florida panthers to ensure their continued genetic viability, none of these threatened creatures may be left in a few years. What is the logic of sentencing wild Florida panthers to almost certain extinction while waiting for habitat to be secured and for the time-consuming process of removing toxins from the environment to begin? There must be panthers available to be put back into a secured and cleaner habitat. A more logical approach is to ensure a genetically improved stock of captive panthers while securing suitably toxin-free habitat and, through regulations and education, to protect those few panthers remaining in the wild.

While the captive breeding program at the White Oak Conservation Center was put on hold, scientific interest turned to the feasibility of introducing cougars of non-Florida stock to restore physical and reproductive fitness to Florida panthers by an injection of outside genetic material. A meeting of scientists at the 1994 workshop on the Florida panther recommended that eight young, nonpregnant female Texas cougars be captured and moved into Florida panther range as soon as possible.[20] These scientists reasoned that before European colonization, a much larger Florida panther population was contiguous with other subspecies to the north and west, assuring a slow but continued ingression of outside genetic material. This was both healthy and natural. By the middle of the nineteenth century, however, rapidly expanding urban and agricultural development of the landscape and continued persecution by humans created the isolation of the Florida panther that has continued for the past 150 years or more. This is an unnatural situation, and one where the outcome is both predictable and conclusive—the extinction of the subspecies. What the scientists at the workshop were recommending was nothing more than a restoration of the natural interchange of genetic substances between closely related but geographically distant subspecies.

Others saw it differently. One of those was David Maehr. Maehr, as an employee of the Florida Game and Fresh Water Fish Commission, had been the driving force behind the live capture and radiotelemetry studies of the Florida panther through the mid- and late 1980s and early 1990s. He had expressed his concerns about the possibility of translocating western cougars into Florida when it was first discussed in the 1980s. However, as an employee of one of the sponsoring agencies, he had kept his concerns to himself. Leaving the FGFWFC in 1993 to pursue a Ph.D. with the Department of Wildlife Ecology and Conservation at the University of Florida allowed Maehr the liberty to objectively criticize the proposal. He questioned the scientific merits of releasing western cougars into Florida in the scientific journal *Conservation Biology*.[21] By the time his article appeared in print, however, western cougars were prowling the swamps of the Big Cypress Swamp/Everglades region, the last stronghold of the Florida panther. Eight female cougars from Texas had been released into south Florida between March and July 1995. Maehr is no irrational animal rights activist. He is a trained scientist with more experience with Florida panthers than most others. His argument against the translocation of western cougars was as convincing as those extolling its virtues. He basically questioned whether there was sufficient evidence to support the contention that such drastic action was necessary.

He argued that the population characteristics of Florida panthers compared favorably with those of secure populations of western cougars, and that demographic stability was at least a defensible hypothesis. He also suggested, completely contrary to the fears of the scientists on the recovery program, that inbreeding, rather than being detrimental to population health, can result in population enhancement by exposing deleterious recessives and selecting them out of the population. And here the argument starts to get complicated. Basically, Maehr's position was that those same models used to predict extinction, when fed more optimistic information on populations of past and present Florida panthers—information which Maehr believes to be more realistic—actually predict population growth! So it was a disagreement among scientists about which population data to feed into the computer model. Maehr suggests that controlled experimental breeding trials between Florida panthers and western cougars would have been prudent before introductions were made—perhaps a salient point now. However, there is a precedent from which to draw conclusions. There is reason to believe that a few panthers from South or Central America, a different subspecies from the Florida panther, were illegally introduced to the Everglades National Park sometime in the 1950s or 1960s. These relocated "pumas" were physically and reproductively different, some would say superior, to the genetically introgressed Florida panther. However, they have now disappeared, and whether they interbred with the few Florida panthers which may have resided in the Evergaldes National Park at that time is uncertain. Why these few released animals of apparent superior genetics disappeared is not known. Some suggest it was from mercury poisoning. Maehr, however, suggests that this may be an example of outbreeding depression, that is, the interchange of genetic matter between the two subspecies of panther caused even greater genetic deterioration and eventual extinction. Whether such a conjecture is justified or not, Maehr uses that possibility as a further reason that prudence should be key when considering further introductions of non-indigenous cougars into the Florida panther range. He concludes his argument with the following words of caution: "The only known wild population of Florida panthers should be considered too valuable to gamble with current genetic theory."[22]

It was a young Ronald Nowak who accompanied Roy McBride and his cat hounds on the first organized attempt to document the continued survival of Florida panthers back in 1973. In 1993, Nowak looked back on the events which had transpired over the previous twenty years:

"When Roy McBride and I began an investigation of the Florida panther in early 1973 ... we could not have imagined the management, scientific, political, and financial developments that would follow. Indeed, we were looking for an almost mythical animal, one that some authorities thought was already extinct.... We received a $1,700 grant and spent about a month in Florida.... Despite our success in Florida [one panther treed and the tracks of several others found], we generally were pessimistic about the panther's situation.... [Since then] ecological and physiological research [has] proliferated, millions of dollars were spent for land purchase and roadway modifications, and the panther became Florida's official State Animal. However, controversy also followed about stress to the cats, the possible long-term effects of removing wild animals for captive-breeding purposes, and even whether the panther population was a fully native component of the south Florida ecosystem.

Some people say that researchers should never have begun chasing, marking, and analyzing panthers, but should have left them behind their veil of mystery and simply done what was possible to protect their habitat. On the other hand, could the immense public and scientific support for panther conservation have developed without gaining some familiarity with the animal?

Looking back, I am not certain that what we did two decades ago was for the best. Yet the fact that we still have wild Florida panthers, together with many people prepared to support their continued survival and well-being, gives cause for hope."[23]

What has happened in Florida may give us reason to reflect on the controversial issue of panthers in regions to the north. First, persons involved with field studies on Florida panthers have little trouble in finding tangible evidence of their presence. And there may be as few as fifty panthers in the state! Talk of hundreds and even thousands of eastern panthers roaming the wilds of the Appalachians, with virtually no substantive evidence of their presence, is certainly wishful thinking. In most years, one or more panthers in Florida is killed on the highways or, in one manner or another, runs afoul of humans. But yet, in the past eighty years or more, only a handful of panthers have been recovered to the north, and evidence suggests that all or most of those were probably escaped or released captive animals brought there from South America, western North America or Florida.

Second, the panther issue in Florida has created mistrust and accusations of wrongdoing among intelligent and well-intentioned conservationists, the media and government scientists and bureaucrats. A similar mood of mistrust towards the government is evident among citizenry concerned with panthers to the north. An attitude of "them versus us" is both counterproductive and unhealthy. With some it borders on paranoia, and allegations of government-sponsored re-introductions of panthers with subsequent disclaimers and cover-ups are not uncommon. To my knowledge, there has never been an attempt by any state, provincial or federal wildlife agency to reestablish panthers into any area east of the Mississippi River, either in Canada or the United States—except Florida, of course, where the introduction of Texas cougars to improve genetic stock and, hopefully, the survival of the Florida panther was an openly debated issue. I know of no such "authorized" government initiative elsewhere. There are, however, more than a few incidences of captive western or Florida panthers being released or having escaped in many eastern states. But government-sponsored covert operations to reintroduce panthers back into unoccupied eastern ranges, with the intention of controlling expanding deer populations, I don't think so.

History of Eastern Panthers to the North

One might expect that some panthers from Florida would occasionally wander into adjacent states. It is apparent that at one time panthers did occur throughout all of the wilder sections of western Georgia. In the late spring of 1773, while traveling north and west of Augusta, one early traveler remarked that "Bears, tygers, wolves, and wild cats are numerous enough.… This creature is called in Pennsylvania and the northern States 'panther,' but in Carolina, and the southern States, is called 'Tyger'; it is very strong, much larger than any dog, of a yellowish brown, or clay color, having a very long tail; it is a mischievous animal, and preys on calves, young colts, etc."[24]

The panther was known to occur in the Okeefenokee Swamp of southeast Georgia as late as the 1920s.[25] The decline of deer populations combined with the loss of large areas of forested habitat during the 1800s and early 1900s, and unregulated hunting probably contributed to its decline to virtual extinction by the turn of the century.

To the west, in the state of Alabama, early records suggest that panthers there, as throughout most of Georgia, were very rare by the turn of the century. "The cougar, or 'panther,' as this animal is usually called, doubtless in early times occupied the greater part of the State; it is now [1921] nearly, if not quite, exterminated.... Recent reports, although rather indefinite, indicate that a very few still remain in the big swamps of the southern counties."[26]

Alabama has no official position on whether panthers continue to exist in that state. Staff members are about evenly divided. Keith Guyse, Assistant Chief, Wildlife Section, Alabama Department of Conservation and Natural Resources in Montgomery, is of the opinion that the state no longer has any panthers that have lived all their lives in the wild and were born to parents that lived all their lives in the wild.[27] Officially referred to as mountain lions in Alabama they have been listed as game animals with the hunting season closed for many years.

On March 16, 1948, however, a panther was shot by a farmer in St. Clair County. Although there had been reports of several panthers being killed in the state a few years earlier, this one was both confirmed and highly publicized. The following story of the event, with a photograph of the farmer and his panther, appeared in the April 1948 issue of the *Alabama Conservation Magazine*.

"Add another variety to the list of Alabama big game species, the mountain lion. While one has been reported from time to time in the William B. Bankhead National Forest, game authorities have been loath to place credence in their existence in this state. That is, until A.D. Hare, a 29-year-old farmer of Route 2, Ashville, drove into Birmingham with a 109-pounder he killed in his St. Clair County pasture on March 16. The big cat, a rare inhabitant of Alabama more common to the mountainous regions of the Far West, stood more than two feet tall. From its head to the tip of its tail it measured over five feet long. With claws exceeding two inches in length and fangs an inch long, it was judged by amateur wildlife enthusiasts who saw it to be about two years old. It was a male. Farmer Hare was taking down a pasture fence March 16 on his farm slightly more than a mile west of Ashville. His hound dog Queen began baying at something in the grass. Thinking it was a calf, Hare went over to investigate. Without warning, the big cat jumped high in the air, snarled, and struck out for a pine thicket 200 yards away. Courageous black and tan Queen started in pursuit. Farmer Hare split the wind for his house, half a mile away, and his 12-gauge shotgun.

"Running back to the pine thicket, he found Queen had the mountain lion or cougar treed. A limb snapped as the cougar ran out on it and he hit a lower limb. Then, it leaped for the ground. Twice did Hare fire at the animal and he believes his birdshot took effect. The big mountain lion made tracks toward a creek half a mile distant with Queen on his trail. Following it to the creek, Hare found the oversized animal backed up against the bank. It was slashing at the dog and once it looked like he had whacked Queen. Circling around the crouching lion, Hare shot it in the back of its head. Queen followed up by running in on the animal and it responded by leaping out at the hound. Twice again the young farmer shot it in the head. The battle was over. Hare dragged the dead animal up on the bank. Hauling his rare animal into Ashville on a mule drawn wagon, Hare drew much attention."[28]

Other reports as recent as the 1960s and early 1970s were probably authentic but written records were not made of any of them. The Department of Conservation and Natural Resources continues to receive approximately one hundred reports of panthers each year, and personnel investigate those that have physical evidence, such as tracks. None of these investigations, however, have led to more recent confirmations of panthers in the state. As approximately one hundred cougars are held captive at various locations throughout Alabama, escapes and intentional releases may occasionally occur.

In their 1946 review of the species in North America, Young and Goldman referred to several explorers who described the early distribution of panthers in Mississippi. "DuPratz was probably one of the first individuals to comment on the occurrence of the animal in this State, indicating it was not very abundant even at that early date, as he wrote [in 1758]: 'I have seen two at different times about my habitation' [near Natchez].... Audubon, in 1851, remarked on its occurrence in the low swampy sections. A few years following Audubon's observations, Wailes wrote: 'The Panther is now rarely met with, except in dense and extensive swamps and canebrakes.' "[29]

J. J. Audubon described panthers in Mississippi during the

early 1800s and even told of hunting a panther in the Coldwater and Yazoo rivers area.[30] Ronald Nowak, however, found little mention of panthers in most early records for the state. Although there have been no confirmed kills in the past one hundred years, unverified sightings of panthers continue to be reported, especially from the southwestern part of the state.[31]

The central coastal plains of the southeastern United States are an extension of the Atlantic Gulf Coast lowlands. These lowlands extend from the northeastern limit of North Carolina back through eastern South Carolina, southern Georgia and west to the Mississippi River and beyond. This area is unique as it may have represented the southern limit of eastern panther range. As well, it may have been here that ranges of the eastern and Florida panthers met and overlapped and interbreeding between the two races occurred. It also has some unique panther history.

As early as 1819 it was noted that the panther, along with several other larger mammals, had become scarce, if not completely extinct in much of the central coastal plains region.[32] However, Audubon and Bachman record the "cougar" as being present in South Carolina as late as 1851.[33] After that, however, there are few substantiated reports of panthers in the state, although, as noted in Mississippi, reasonably reliable sightings of this large cat persisted, especially near swamps of the larger rivers.[34] South Carolina Wildlife carried a letter which reported a surprisingly late panther kill in the Camden region:

"Mr. Thomas Ancrum wrote 'About 1916, the late Wardlaw Russell killed one in Taylor Field, just this side of Mulberry Plantation.... Beckham Russell said he and his brother Charlie were with his father when he killed the panther. The panther ran out of the deep grass and up a small tree nearby and Beckham said it was about fifteen feet up the tree when his father killed it. The panther was brought to Camden, where it was displayed in the business section. I was one of many who saw the animal.... Beckham said, as he remembers, it was not skinned or photographed.' If this species has persisted to the present time, it is astonishing, as almost every report in a farming region elicits an extreme reaction on the part of hunters. During the past five years, there have been a number of newspaper reports of 'black panthers' in northern Georgia and adjacent regions. These reports have caused local agencies to muster packs of hunting dogs and to stake out goats to attract the panthers. But all to no avail!"[35]

The presence of the panther in the coastal lowlands of North Carolina was noted as early as 1718 although not in a particularly friendly manner. "This beast is the greatest Enemy to the Planter, of any Vermine in Carolina."[36] As humans expanded their sphere of influence throughout the Atlantic coast, the panther, like so many other wild creatures, became fewer in number, and probably disappeared altogether by the mid-1800s. In 1851 Audubon reported that the panther was close to extinction in all the eastern states.[37] But sightings and reports of panthers being killed in the Carolinas continued through the late 1800s and well into the early 1900s. The *Wilmington Morning Star* carried a number of reports through the years of large cats, probably panthers, in the state of North Carolina. The following are a few:

"Gaston County, N.C. 'A panther, measuring seven feet, was killed in Gaston County, a few days ago. Attention was first called to its presence by the fact that it killed a faithful dog accompanying some children to school in the neighborhood of Craig's Ford.' *Wilmington Morning Star*, January 31, 1868; Alexander County, N.C. 'About four years ago a venerable citizen of Alexander County gave origin to the report that a Catamount or North American tiger inhabited the cliffs of Davis Mountain, near Bethel Church. He also stated, with great earnestness, that this or some kindred animal was visiting his flock of sheep and geese, and that the track of the largest was about the size of that of a Newfoundland dog. All speculation and conjecture in reference to the correctness of Mr. Davis' statement was settled a few days ago by the chasing with hounds and shooting of a large animal, supposed to be a North American tiger.' *Wilmington Morning Star*, December, 17, 1878; Wrightsville area, New Hanover County. 'An immense wild cat, or catamount, was killed by the Wilmington Fox Club yesterday afternoon, on an oak ridge back of Wrightsville. The animal gave the dogs a long chase and a terrible fight, in which several of the pack were severely cut. The hunters, Messrs. Thomas, Wiggins and Heide, brought their trophy to the city and exhibited it at the STAR office. It measures fifty-seven inches in length and weighs thirty-seven pounds and is truly a most ferocious looking "varmint." *Wilmington Weekly Star*, January 18, 1884; Buncombe County, N.C. 'There is a large and ferocious panther ranging in the neighborhood of Dryman's mountains,' said a reliable man who was here yesterday from the country. The man was asked if the panther was really dangerous. He expressed astonishment at the question. "Why, of course," he said. "He eats chickens, sheep, hogs and children." The latter statement sounded rather formidable and the man was asked how many children the panther had eaten. He replied that he could not say that the panther had actually eaten any children as yet, but would do if he got a chance. A number of people have seen the panther at a distance and all agree that he is a big beast. At any rate the children in the neighborhood are not allowed to go in the woods alone or out after dark. Dryman's mountain is only three miles from Asheville. It is five by the road but the panther doesn't use the road.' *Wilmington Messenger*, January 10, 1906."[38]

This young female panther was shot in 1967 by John Gallant in Crawford County, Pennsylvania. The source of this panther is uncertain, but some authorities believe it may have escaped from a game park in Ohio. Others disagree.

(WRIGHT, 1972)

In many rural areas the term "catamount" was used in reference to the bobcat; in other areas it was used to describe the panther. Such regional colloquialisms are reason for caution when reviewing early references to "large wild cats." However, several of the measurements and descriptions of the animals killed leave little doubt that what they were referring to was indeed a panther.

The Appalachian Mountains begin in northern Georgia and stretch northeast to Atlantic Canada. This vast range of geologic faults and uplifts presented a formidable challenge to the early pioneers and settlers who, with families and worldly possessions in tow, pushed westward towards the rich farming lands of the Mississippi and beyond in the late 1700s and early 1800s. These same mountains provided final sanctuary for many of the large game animals and predators that were pursued by their human tormentors. The imposing Allegheny and Blue Ridge ranges extend north from eastern Tennessee and western North Carolina through eastern Kentucky, western Virginia and West Virginia. This rugged chain extends into Pennsylvania, where the mountains give way to a broad expanse of rolling hills drained by such mighty rivers as the Susquehanna and the Delaware. North of the Catskills, the Hudson River has gouged a fertile swath which isolates the Adirondacks of northern New York from the Green Mountains of Vermont and the White Mountains of New Hampshire to the east. These distinctive mountain formations also influenced distributions of wildlife.

The southern Appalachians include the Blue Ridge and Allegheny mountain ranges and extend north to Pennsylvania. Some early naturalists felt that these ranges provided convenient travelways for panthers, and occasional panthers killed in Pennsylvania and Maryland in the late 1800s were thought to have come from West Virginia. If the panther is alive and well anywhere in the east, it is probably somewhere within this great tract of mountainous wilderness. Here, the eight-hundred-square mile Great Smoky Mountains National Park straddles the Tennessee and North Carolina border. Surrounding the park are the Cherokee, Nantahala and Pisgah national forests, together forming an unbroken mountainous chain extending some three hundred miles from northern Georgia to southern Virginia.

The severe decline in white-tailed deer throughout most of this region by the late 1800s removed the major food source for panthers, and the few that may have survived the continued human persecution were dealt yet another blow to their continued survival. There is, however, evidence that some panthers probably did survive this critical period of food shortage. In the Great Smoky Mountains of North Carolina their former presence is obvious from state and county bounty records of the 1700s and 1800s, and from the thirty-seven places named for them which are scattered throughout the state.[39]

According to the publication, *The Wildlife Met by Tennessee's First Settlers*, the last of Tennessee's native panthers were probably extirpated prior to the year 1900, though unconfirmed reports came in later. The National Parks management report, *Status and History of the Mountain Lion in the Great Smoky Mountains National Park*, states that the last mountain lion in the Great Smoky Mountain region was reportedly killed in 1920 near Fontana Village, North Carolina. Several years later, lions were pronounced extinct in this area.[40]

The hills of Kentucky were certainly home to panthers prior to extensive land clearing and uncontrolled hunting of the wildlife by early settlers in the late 1700s and early 1800s. One was killed south of Louisville in 1784, one in Allen County in 1815, and one, believed to be the last of the species in the state, was killed in 1863 a short distance from Lexington.[41] However, there is no specimen of an eastern panther from Kentucky in any formal museum collection. Barbour and Davis, in their reference book on the mammals of Kentucky, state that "At one time it was common in Kentucky, but there have been no valid records for some 75 years. Although one occasionally reads newspaper accounts of this animal in Kentucky, unfortunately these are probably based on escaped animals or a vivid imagination."[42]

John Smith may have been the first to make note of panthers in Virginia when he referred to "lions" sometime around 1609-16. Young and Goldman also refer to early references on the occurrence of the panther in this state. "In the Blue Ridge and Alleghany Mountains in earlier times, with their large numbers of game, particularly deer, affording a plentiful food supply, and other conditions making for ideal habitat, the animal was found in good numbers at the time of the State's settlement. Nevertheless the Dismal Swamp area appears to have been the section where the animal held out longest.... An early Virginia historian lists it among the animals killed in the so-called 'vermin hunts' conducted by the hard-riding young Virginia aristocrats during the latter part of the 17th and the early 18th centuries. It is now extinct in the State, but when it finally disappeared is difficult to determine."[43]

The Central Appalachian Mountains include some of the most historic panther ranges in eastern North America: the state of Pennsylvania and southern New York. It was from the rolling hills and mountains of Clinton, Lycoming, Potter and Tioga counties of central Pennsylvania that Henry Shoemaker left us tales of the wild animals and early settlers of the Juniata and the Susquehanna. It was here, in the early 1800s, that Philip Tome, after a lifetime of travel and hunting the wilds of Pine Creek Valley and the Allegany and Clarion rivers, left us his stories in *Pioneer Life, or Thirty Years a Hunter*. And just to the south, across the border in the state of western Maryland, Meschach Browning, born in 1781, hunted and trapped the wilds of the Youghiogheny and Castleman rivers, and recorded those thrilling adventures in his classic book, *Forty-four Years of the Life of a Hunter*. Surely, if the eastern panther is to be found anywhere in the Appalachians, it is here among the forested wilderness recesses of its early historic range, here among the rocks and the laurel where the likes of Tome and Browning pursued their quarry with dog and gun.

William Penn was perhaps the first to make mention of panthers in Pennsylvania when in 1683 he described it as one of the "creatures for profit only, by skin or fur, and which are natural to these parts."[44] Other records near the turn of the century give the animal a wide distribution throughout the state in the early 1800s. One naturalist recorded that there had been no substantiated kill of a panther in Pennsylvania since 1871, although rumors circulated of several being killed in Clinton or Clearfield counties in 1891.[45] A 1985 paper described the early distribution of this predator and its relationship with the early settlers in the state of Pennsylvania:

"During the 18th and 19th centuries, the mountain lion was viewed with a great deal of fear by many inhabitants of the Commonwealth [Pennsylvania]. Newspaper accounts fueled these fears by attributing attacks on man and domestic animals to this species. Thus, the killing of a mountain lion was a matter of pride that was remembered by many hunters for years after a small record had been placed in the local newspaper. Such accounts were popular and were frequently telegraphed to other newspapers in the Commonwealth. The bounty system which was initiated throughout Pennsylvania in 1807 provided additional incentive for hunting mountain lions.... The last known mountain lion to be killed from the northeastern region of the Commonwealth was taken in Susquehanna County in 1874."[46]

The northern Appalachians include the Adirondack and Catskill mountains of New York, the Green Mountains of Vermont and the White Mountains of New Hampshire, and they extend north into western Maine. Along with the remote wilderness of Pennsylvania, many people believe these rugged mountains and forested valleys of the northeast have provided sanctuary for small, isolated breeding populations of eastern panthers. Others disagree. There can be no argument, however, that panthers once roamed these remote regions and many were killed by early settlers. Exactly when, if ever, these mighty predators finally lost their battle to survive here remains the subject of heated debate.

Young and Goldman left us the following description of the early occurrence of panthers in New York. "Formerly abundant throughout most of New York, and particularly in the forested regions of the Adirondacks, the animal was so reduced in numbers by the variety of attacks upon it that by the close of the last century it was nearly extinct. A bounty of $20 was placed on it by the State in 1871, and between that date and 1882 a total of 46 were killed for bounty.... The bounty was $10 less than that set for the wolf at the time, and continued in effect for approximately a quarter of a century. An early account of it ... in 1823 ... states: 'Panthers ... are occasionally seen in the southern section of the Catskill Mountains, but are not so numerous as in the middle region. A panther measuring in length about 9 feet was recently killed in the southern range; this animal is rarely seen; but from its strength, size, and ferocity it is regarded with terror, and considered the most formidable beast of the forest; their color is grey, the head small in proportion, the general form indicating agility; they have been known in ascending a ledge or tree to rise at a leap twenty feet from the ground.' " [47]

These authors quote another early reference to the size of some of these panthers of the Adirondacks: " 'Full grown Panthers killed in northern New York have been known to measure over eleven feet from the nose to the tip of the tail, being about twenty-eight inches high, and weighing near two hundred pounds. Their color is a reddish brown above, shading into a lighter color underneath.'"[48]

The panther appeared often in the early folklore of Vermont. It was included in the list of thirty-six animals occurring in that state during the early 1800s. On the occurrence of the panther in the state by 1853, one early naturalist commented that they had formerly been much more common and had at times done much injury by destroying sheep and young cattle.[49] By the 1930s, however, it was considered extinct. To settle the matter once and for all, one Vermont newspaper offered a $100 reward for a Vermont panther "dead or alive."[50] There were no takers and the offer was retracted.

But the early history of Vermont is filled with descriptions of predators and of the settlers who fought and feared them. The following account of settlement in the state of Vermont and the subsequent changes to the forested landscape and the native animals there serves as an example of what happened throughout much of eastern North America in the late 1700s and early 1800s:

"At the commencement of settlement of Vermont, wolves, panthers, bears and wildcats abounded in the state. To some extent, these animals were feared by the early settlers and undoubtedly did considerable damage to their livestock. Only the wolf was trapped and hunted for fur, but panthers and bears were much hunted for sport in the early days. 'The Panther ... has never been abundant, but they were formerly much more common in Vermont than at present day and have at times done much injury by destroying sheep and young cattle.... When the country was new, much precaution was considered necessary when traveling in the woods in this state. In order to be secure from the attacks of this ferocious beast, travelers usually went well armed, and at night built a large fire, which served to keep this cautious animal at a distance. Under such circumstances a Catamount will approach within a few rods of the fire, and they have thus been shot in this state by aiming between the glaring eyeballs, when nothing else was visible. There are authentic stories of the fierceness of this animal and proof that when hungry it has pursued and attacked men on horseback. One instance of this kind occurred in Mt. Holly, another in Wallingford.... I find no record of a person having been killed by a panther, although they attack and kill horses.' "[51]

In the lobby of the Vermont Historical Society at Montpelier stands the famous Barnard Panther, felled by a shotgun in 1881. Was this indeed the last panther to roam the hills of Vermont? Two other mounted specimens from the Green Mountain State were shot a few years earlier: the Weathersfield Panther in 1867, and the Wardsboro Panther in 1875. But stories of panthers in an earlier Vermont abound, as well as a history of their persecution. Thomas Altherr provided a thorough review of the panther legacy in Vermont at the 1994 Eastern Cougar Conference in Erie, Pennsylvania.[52] Similar to other New England colonies, a bounty on panthers was established early in Vermont. In February 1779, a bounty of eight pounds for an adult and four pounds for a whelp was passed in the legislature. The bounty remained at $20 throughout the 1800s.

A Dr. Samuel Williams left us the following panther tale in his 1793 *Natural and Civil History of Vermont*: "This seems to be the most fierce and ravenous of any animal which we have in Vermont. Some years ago, one of these animals was killed at Bennington. It took a large calf out of a pen, where the fence was four feet high, and carried it off on its back. With this load, it ascended a ledge of rocks, where one of the leaps was fifteen feet in height. Two hunters found the cat upon a high tree.

Discharging his musket, one of them wounded it in the leg. It descended with the greatest agility, and fury; did not attack the men, but seized their dog by one of his ribs, broke it off in the middle, and instantly leaped up to the tree again with astonishing swiftness and dexterity. The other hunter shot him through the head, but his fury did not cease but with all the last remains of life. These animals have been often seen in Vermont; but they were never very numerous, or easily to be taken.... On account of their fierceness, activity, and carnivorous disposition, the hunters esteem them the most dangerous of any of our animals."[53]

The many stories of early encounters between panthers and settlers of Vermont, as compiled by Altherr from books, journals and newspapers of the time, provide a most entertaining review of the awe held for this mightiest of predators, and of the intensity of the settlers' fears and campaigns against it. Stories are filled with testaments to its strength and tenacity—exceedingly vicious, savage disposition, dreaded animals—such epithets are liberally strewn among stirring accounts of battles with this beast. But as the stories became more frequent and perhaps more colorful around the evening campfires of the northeast, the battles were becoming fewer. Ol' Painter was losing ground. Even by 1850 an article in the *Burlington Free Press* remarked that "in the last 40 years, the whole number killed within the state [Vermont] has not, probably, exceeded half a dozen."[54]

Although panthers were probably never common in the adjacent state of New Hampshire, the old Chapman specimen now at the Woodman Institute in Dover is evidence that they were seen on occasion and infrequently shot. Some believe a few panthers survived until the late 1800s, but there are few reports of any of these big cats being killed after the Chapman specimen was felled in the township of Lee in 1853. One 1902 account of mammals in the northeastern states, however, did refer to occasional hearsay of panthers in the northern part of New Hampshire and suggested that their presence might be due to the increase in white-tailed deer.[55] Although rumors had it that a pair of panthers prowled parts of the state as recently as the 1920s,[56] the old Chapman panther remains the last specimen to be killed in New Hampshire in the past 150 years.

As we move further to the north and into the spruce-pine forests of Maine, the trail of the panther continues, but records of its historical occurrence, similar to New Hampshire, are not common. This is probably because of historical low numbers of white-tailed deer. Young and Goldman suggested that panthers were always rare in Maine[57] and refer to a 1930 study of mammals in the Portland area which considered the panther to be "never more than a straggler."[58] One was reported to have been killed about the year 1845 in the town of Sebago, Cumberland County, about thirty-five miles northwest of Portland, and another was said to be killed in 1891 near Andover.[59] There are no mounted specimens of any of these panthers. But Bruce Wright did track down the Little St. Jean specimen which was trapped in the northern section of the state as recently as 1938. A mount of this panther now resides at the New Brunswick Museum in Saint John.

Densely populated states such as Massachusetts, New Jersey and Connecticut are not particularly noted as wilderness retreats where panthers might find seclusion, but they do continue to produce sightings of mysterious long-tailed cats. And history shows that in earlier times, before the forests were laid bare by the lumberman's axe and saw, they were home to a great abundance and variety of wildlife. As recently as 1842 a noted naturalist reported on panthers in Connecticut: "I saw a fine specimen, said to have been killed in the northern part of the State, exhibited in Mix's Museum some years since. Dr. Emmons says they are still found in St. Lawrence County, New York, where one man killed five with his dog and gun not many years since."[60]

The panther was also found throughout the state of Massachusetts at the beginning of colonization, but battle lines were soon drawn between it and the early settlers who lived in fear of this great predator. "It was early outlawed, however, and persistent warfare on the part of everyone who carried a musket, dug pits, or set traps, gradually brought about its complete extinction, so that by the middle of the 19th century it was doubtful that a single individual remained."[61]

Paul Rego, a wildlife biologist for the Connecticut Department of Environmental Protection, told me that although panthers are currently classified as extirpated in that state, they do have protected status, i.e., they cannot be hunted or trapped.[62] Similar "legislative safety nets" for protection of panthers, even though they are generally recognized as long disappeared, are found in most other eastern states.

James Cardoza, a wildlife biologist for the Massachusetts Division of Fisheries and Wildlife in Westborough, agrees that the panther did occur in Massachusetts during the historical period, but its status is somewhat blurred because it was apparently extirpated at an early date. He believes the animal was virtually eliminated from the state by 1800, although small numbers may have persisted a little longer. The last panther known to have been killed in Massachusetts was shot near Amherst in 1858, a mount of which is now on display at the Arcadia Wildlife Refuge in Easthampton. Even though it was shot in Massachusetts, Cardoza considers it to have been a vagrant rather than a "lone survivor." The land-use history of the state between 1820 and 1850 was such that up to 80 percent of the area in some counties was cleared, with consequent disastrous effects on those species requiring forested habitat. Deer were virtually extirpated from most of the state by this time, remaining only in the rugged areas of the northern Berkshires, on Cape Cod and in a few pockets elsewhere. Consequently, it would have been unusual for resident panthers to persist.[63]

In Rhode Island, similar to Delaware, references to the early distribution of panthers are exceedingly rare. But Rhode Island undoubtedly harbored the species, and it was included in a turn-of-the-century list as one of the wild animals known to have inhabited the state during the historic period.[64] The last to be killed and preserved was shot by the "James Boys" in 1847 or 1848 in West Greenwich and now resides in the Museum of Comparative Zoology at Harvard University. A 1968 publication on the mammals of Rhode Island stated that although the panther was once found there, it was considered by most authorities to be extinct.[65]

As we saw earlier, Meshach Browning left us detailed stories of panther hunts in the western portions of Maryland among the rolling hills of the Appalachian Mountains in the early 1800s. And Audubon and Bachman include it among the mammals of that state in 1851. Elsewhere, especially near the coast, it likely disappeared before 1800.

Early accounts suggest that at the time of colonization by Europeans, panthers occurred throughout New Jersey. Officially, panthers are believed to have become extinct in the state by the early 1800s. In his 1903 reference book on the mammals of Pennsylvania and adjacent states, Samuel Nicholson Rhoads commented on early occurrences of panthers in New Jersey. "So far as can be ascertained by meager and unsatisfactory returns from my correspondents, the last New Jersey panther was destroyed about the third or fourth decade of the 19th century (1830 to 1840). It is probable that the last specimens lingered in the swamps of Cape May, Ocean and Atlantic Counties. The only other part of the state where they may have lingered so late would be Warren and Sussex Counties, along the upper Delaware Valley, opposite Pike County, Pennsylvania."[66] He suggested that some stragglers may have entered the northwestern part of the state in Sussex and Warren counties from Pennsylvania after these dates.

Although our interest here is mainly in and around the ranges of the Appalachian Mountains, those states east of the Mississippi which lie to the northwest of the Ohio River also fall within the early range of the panther (officially, panthers of this region are considered to have been a separate race, *Felis concolor schorgeri*). Roland Baker, in his book *Michigan Mammals*, believed that in early settlement days the panther was apparently distributed statewide, becoming rare by the 1830s. Although sightings continue to be reported, he conceded that although the large cats are secretive, if present, they would not escape detection for long, and suggested that one would certainly have been shot, treed by hounds or trapped if actually present.[67]

A 1994 book on endangered and threatened wildlife in Michigan, however, is more sympathetic to the possibility that panthers are still found in that state: "Historically, the [panther] occurred throughout the state. Following European settlement, the [panther] declined due to lower prey abundance, unrelenting hunting pressure, and general human persecution. By the turn of the century, the [panther] was considered extirpated in Michigan, although there are a few documented Upper Peninsula records several years afterward. In recent years, reports of [panthers] have become increasingly more frequent and believable in Michigan and the upper Great Lakes region. This upward trend may be partially attributed to public awareness and understanding, increasing favorable habitat conditions for prey, lessening human persecution, and small, outlying populations reestablishing their former range in Michigan."[68]

Adrian Wydeven, Mammalian Ecologist for the Wisconsin Department of Natural Resources in Park Falls, presented a paper at the 1994 Eastern Cougar Conference held in Erie, Pennsylvania. Wydeven could find reference to twenty-six authentic observations of panthers in Wisconsin, eleven of which were of animals actually killed. Only one of those reported kills, however, has been preserved as a biological specimen, that of a male killed near Appleton in 1857. That specimen was used to describe a new subspecies, the Wisconsin puma, or *Felis concolor schorgeri.* The last native panther known to be killed in Wisconsin was shot near Manly, Douglas County, in 1908, although one was observed a year later near Kremlin, Marinette County. It was thirty years before the next reports of panthers in the state, when four were reported from Oneida County in 1939. Wydeven suggested the return of white-tailed deer to the state in the 1930s and 1940s may not have been coincidental with the return of sightings of panthers.[69]

In his 1936 book *Mammals of Indiana*, Marcus Ward Lyon, Jr. chronicled early reports of panthers in that state and found references to their former occurrence to be rare. He believed them to be gone from southwestern Indiana by 1832-33, although a few may have remained in the north for a few more years. He spoke with an eighty-five-year-old woman who remembered her grandfather killing panthers in Wells County. But in a list of furs purchased at Noblesville in 1859 there was no mention of panthers.[70] In a 1969 monograph on the distribution of mammals in Indiana, Russell E. Mumford suggested that panthers had been most common in the hilly and well-forested portions, but the last of them probably fell to the gun by 1850.[71]

The last eastern panthers in Illinois were probably killed in the early 1800s. Donald Hoffmeister searched out early records of panthers for his 1989 book, *Mammals of Illinois*. Citing an 1882 reference to the history of Madison County, Hoffmeister reports that " 'The neighbors said of him that he killed several bears and panthers in this neighborhood [Saline Township], and the three pointed out to me where he shot the last panther, in 1818.' This same account recorded that in Alhambra Township, Madison County, one man killed seven panthers in the winter of 1817."[72]

Edward Heske, Curator of Wildlife Ecology for the Illinois Natural History Survey, summed up his department's position on panthers in Illinois by stating that there have been no verified sightings of panthers in the state for over one hundred years and that "[I would] have to look somewhere other than Illinois if I wanted a panther!"[73] Milton Trautman provides us with a summary on the natural history of Ohio for the period 1750 to 1977, with many early observations on the wildlife of the region, including the historic distribution of panthers. He believed that panthers became extirpated in Ohio around 1850 and were uncommon as early as 1800.[74] The following panther anecdote is taken from the *Centennial History of Licking County, Ohio*, published at Newark, Ohio, by Isaac Smucker: "In the autumn of 1805 Jacob Wilson, living within a mile of Newark, was suddenly called to the door of his cabin by the commotion among his swine and pigs. A huge panther had just seized a pig, and when in the act of making off with it was pursued and treed by the dogs not far from the cabin. The pioneer at once seized his trusty rifle and brought it to bear upon the ferocious beast, which at the first fire fell at the root of the tree among the dogs."[75] Denis Case, Assistant Administrator of Wildlife Management and Research with the Ohio Department of Natural Resources, believes that panthers in that state were uncommon as early as 1750 and probably were lost altogether shortly thereafter.[76]

Eastern Canada

Eastern Canada has frequently been referred to as the last wilderness sanctuary for panthers in the east. Some believe that it was here, in the vast expanse of forests in New Brunswick and Ontario, that panthers sought refuge and rode out the tide of persecution to the south. It was from here, they believe, that panthers have recently migrated, moving south to reoccupy former ranges throughout the Appalachians Mountains. Some people suggest that this has been made possible through legal protection from hunting, reforestation of much of the eastern landscape and growing populations of white-tailed deer, the preferred food of the eastern panther. This sounds logical, but how realistic is it? Let us look at what history tells us of the former occurrence of panthers in eastern Canada. Let us examine what evidence there is that panthers have survived here through the past century and successfully reproduced in numbers that would allow colonization of lands to the south.

The province of Ontario contains enormous tracts of wilderness, much of which appears quite capable of supporting breeding populations of panthers. One of the most promising is the Lake of the Woods region in the extreme western portion of the province and immediately north of Minnesota. Before drastic changes to the lands from forestry and agriculture, the panther was apparently quite common throughout much of southern Ontario. Early records on the abundance of panthers there, however, are confusing. Some were quite convinced that the panther was never abundant in the province, having been mainly restricted to the southern border region, and was eliminated entirely by 1908.[77] Others suggested panthers had been much more common and widespread[78] and that they "were the most persistent and relentless foes against which new settlers had to contend. A pig, or a sheep, and occasionally a large animal, easily fell a prey to one of them."[79]

Dr. C. H. D. Clarke was a scientist in Ontario for many years and served as director of the provincial Wildlife Branch. He believed that panthers had survived in the northern forests of Ontario, and further east in the province of New Brunswick. "Because of uncertainties of name and description, it was never recorded properly in Ontario until the settlers came. In 1894 the old records were brought together, along with some rather fanciful stuff, in *The Biological Review of Ontario*. Something similar was done by Ernest Thompson Seton and others. We learn that Charles Fothgill, the pioneer naturalist, had a specimen in his museum in Toronto, destroyed by fire shortly after his death. It was killed in Scarborough Township around 1820. It measured 6 feet, 10 inches, of which the tail was 2 feet, 3 inches. It is evident from Fothergill's diary that several, probably skins, were exhibited at some kind of show or fair in Whitby in 1835.... [W. P. Lett of Ottawa] refers to a specimen shot near Farran's Point on the St. Lawrence as seven and a half feet long. It is still extant in poor shape, and I question that it even went six feet. It was killed, incidentally, on U.S. soil, so it is a New York specimen. It looks very puny alongside an Alberta lion, and one feels that few indeed were the eastern animals that went 100 pounds. Most of them would be short of full size, little more than twice the weight of a big bobcat. Nevertheless, the most recent dated killing of a [panther] in Ontario, from the *Evening Telegram* of January 4, 1884, describes one killed by T.W. White of Creemore as 'measuring nine feet from tip to tip.' Even in Alberta that would be stretching things. There were never all that many killed in Ontario. What happened was, that when settlement came the habitat was destroyed, but it may have been able to follow the deer a little farther north than either had ever lived before. There it still is—we think."[80]

Early records suggest that the eastern panther was also found in parts of Quebec south of the St. Lawrence River. There is a newspaper account of a panther killed about 25 miles southwest of Montreal in 1836, and in 1887 one early naturalist was of the opinion that the panther at one time had abounded in the Ottawa Valley.[81] The last Quebec records left to us by Ernest Thompson Seton in 1929 are of one killed near Sherbrooke about 1840, and another near Sorel on October 3, 1863. Apparently the latter specimen is that mentioned as killed near St. Francis, on the St. Lawrence River, on October 3, 1863.[82] Bruce Wright researched early documents for mention of panthers in Quebec and found that records of panthers ended about 1880. He also refers to Seton who, in 1929, "quoted Thomas Anderson of the Hudson's Bay Company to the effect that an Indian hunter shot a panther on South Bay of Lac des Quinze, which is fifteen miles northeast of Lake Timiskaming on the Quebec-Ontario border, in March 1880. The writer has not seen this record used before, probably because the exact location was not clear."[83]

Like Ontario, the province of New Brunswick has been considered by many as a refuge for eastern panthers. Most of this enthusiasm over a great northern reserve of panthers in Canada has been generated by the writings of Bruce Wright. Bruce was a firm believer that New Brunswick and several other areas of the northeast continued to support small breeding colonies of eastern panthers long after the last of the panther slayers had gone to their graves. For all his determination and good intentions, Bruce uncovered little evidence in support of his case other than many reports of panther sightings which, as we know today, are easily collected from every state and province, especially if such reports are solicited. First, how common historically was the panther in New Brunswick? The answer is, not very. Young and Goldman searched out the early records and could find only one reference to a panther in the province.

"The only record we have been able to find of the [panther] in this part of Canada is that given by Adams. His information was derived from Dr. Robb, at the time professor of Natural History in the provincial Museum, who mentioned an attack by a [panther] on a man 'near the capital of the province in 1841.' As the animal once occurred in Maine, and as New Brunswick harbored an abundance of its favorite food—deer—the [panther] may have ranged into the province from the southward in earlier days."[84]

But stories and tales of early hunting and fishing trips through the backwoods of New Brunswick often made reference to the elusive panther. Such as this account of a trip in 1862-63 by the Honorable Arthur Hamilton Gordon, Lieutenant

Governor of the province at the time. While camped near the forks of the Tobique River, he refers to the nickname given a young companion by the Maliseet Indian guides as " 'Lhoks,' the American panther, or 'Indian devil,' the roughest, ugliest, and most dangerous of the wild beasts of the New Brunswick forest."[85]

Bruce Wright first became interested in reports of panthers in New Brunswick when stationed there with the Dominion Forest Service in 1938. He compiled reports of panther sightings and tracks from the files of the New Brunswick Game Division and through correspondence and personal interviews with the eyewitnesses concerned. He also made an exhaustive search of the literature but could still find only several historical references to panthers in New Brunswick.

"The presence of the panther during the early period of settlement in New Brunswick has always been doubtful, although references to it appear in many early works on the fauna of the region. In 1708, Diereville wrote of 'chats et loup cerviers, chat sauvage' which may, or may not, have included the panther. In 1832, Cooney described an animal which appears to have been part wolf, part wolverine, and part panther, but Gesner, in 1847, was more explicit. He listed '*Felis concolor*—cougar; catamount—very rare,' again he said, 'The panther, painter, or catamount—better known in the province as the Indian Devil—although small, is a very dangerous animal: they are very rare, yet sometimes a single skin is brought into the market' at Saint John. In 1884, the Natural History Society of New Brunswick listed in their catalogue of New Brunswick mammals '1. Panther. (*Felis concolor.*) In 1847 Dr. Gesner records this species as 'rare'. No recent instances of its occurrence are known.' In 1873 Adams recorded an incident of a large cat attacking and nearly killing a man in the vicinity of Fredericton in 1841 [and referred to by Young and Goldman]. He received this report from Dr. Robb, Professor of Natural History at the University of New Brunswick. In 1894, Allen, referring to the Tobique region, said that it 'is said to occur but no satisfactory evidence of its present existence in the region was obtained.' In 1903 Boardman listed it as 'well authenticated,' but Ganong, in 1903, went to considerable pains to contradict two gentlemen who fired at and wounded an animal, in the Canaan region, which they identified as a panther. He concluded: 'Summarizing now the entire subject, we are brought to the conclusion that there is not a solitary authentic record, or any other authentic evidence, of either the present or former occurrence of panther within the limits of New Brunswick.' The latest publication referring to the species is by Squires (1946) who concluded: 'Reports concerning the former presence of the cougar or panther in New Brunswick are so numerous that it would seem very probable that it was found here in the early days of settlement.' This, then, is the early history of the species in New Brunswick."[86]

But Wright and others produced additional seemingly authentic reports of panthers in the province, such as this newspaper article which appeared in the *Saint John Telegraph Journal* for November 24, 1923: "Shoots a Panther in New Brunswick: Animal rarely found in the province killed in Northumberland [County]: Newcastle, November 22:

"While superintending the work in the lumber woods on the headwaters of the Sevogle River last week, Collingwood Fraser, foreman for William M. Sullivan Ltd., saw a large animal which he thought was a wildcat. Procuring a rifle Mr. Fraser fired and wounded the animal, whereupon it charged him, but a second shot fired when the beast was less than five feet away killed the animal which upon examination proved to be a panther or cougar. Persons who saw it say it measured about four feet in length and had a tail almost as long as its body."

A more tangible piece of evidence which Wright uncovered was a photograph of a man holding what appears to be a cased skin of a panther. In March 1932 the track of a panther was followed in the snow by Havelock Robertson of Mundleville, Kent County, New Brunswick, and Mr. Roy Grant of Halifax, Nova Scotia. The panther was soon found sitting in a large pine tree and was promptly dispatched by two shots from Mr. Robertson's Lee-Enfield .303 rifle. The carcass, which measured 7 feet 3 inches from tip to tip, was disposed of, but the cased skin remained in Mr. Robertson's house until it became full of moths and was also thrown out. Wright considered this to be the only photograph ever taken of a New Brunswick panther.[87] Or was it? In the course of my search for panthers in Atlantic Canada, I also had the opportunity to uncover a photograph of what was alleged to be a panther shot in southeastern New Brunswick in the winter of 1941. A deeper search of the history of this picture, and the location where it was taken, suggested that it was rather of a western cougar, one which had hung on the wall of the cabin in the background for many years. The cabin and cougar sub-

sequently burnt to the ground. Without further investigation, this "photographic evidence" of a New Brunswick panther would have lived on. I do not know whether the 1932 photograph uncovered by Bruce Wright was authentic or not; it probably was. But hasty endorsement of such apparent proof of panthers, or any other rare creature, can be risky.

Although sightings of panthers continue to pour in from the province of Nova Scotia, there has never been any confirmed evidence to verify their presence. The province is a peninsula and panthers would have had to emigrate there through southeastern New Brunswick. This would have occurred after white-tailed deer had become established in the province at the turn of the century. Before the presence of deer it is doubtful that panthers could have survived. There is no mention of panthers in the early historical literature from the province. Even so, several naturalists in the 1940s suggested that panthers were probably once found in small numbers in Nova Scotia, although they had no evidence to support that suggestion.

A panther reported to have been shot in southern New Brunswick in 1941. Further inquiry suggested that the animal was shot in western Canada. (HUGH RILEY)

Nor has there ever been a report of a panther on the small island province of Prince Edward Island. I describe elsewhere the story of an illegal introduction of three western cougars on the island of Newfoundland in eastern Canada. As well, there have been panther sightings following the supposed Newfoundland release and one report of a panther being struck by a vehicle.

Conclusion

In summary, then, the pattern of early panther extirpation throughout eastern North America pretty much followed that of early human settlement and clearing of the forests. Land was cleared, crops planted, domestic animals pastured and large predators pursued and killed. Unrelenting persecution from humans and drastic declines in white-tailed deer populations through the mid- and late 1800s spelled the end for this magnificent American lion throughout most of its former eastern range.

But what is it, then, that people are seeing? As reviewed earlier, many common animals could be mistaken for a panther, and perhaps some sightings might even be of released or escaped cougars from western parts of the continent, panthers from Florida or pumas from Central or South America. But whatever their identity or source, more people are seeing what they believe to be Klandagi, the Lord of the Forest, than ever before. Thousands of sightings are reported the length and breadth of the Appalachians every year. So to gain an appreciation of who is seeing what and where, let's review a small selection of those sightings.

CHAPTER SIX

I Saw A Panther—Really!

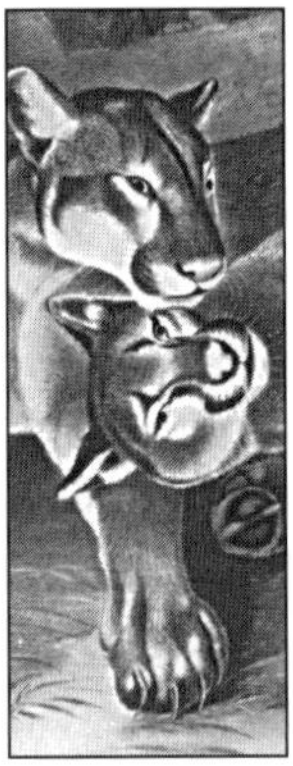

TO THOSE with a curiosity for, and even a vague familiarity with the mysterious long-tailed cat of the northeast, the word panther and Bruce Wright are synonymous. Bruce was born in the province of Quebec in 1912. His study at the University of New Brunswick towards a forestry degree, however, appears to have instilled a love for the Maritimes, and most of his career as a professional biologist was spent there. He distinguished himself well during service in the Second World War, after which he earned a graduate degree in science at the University of Wisconsin under the tutelage of Aldo Leopold, often referred to as the father of wildlife management. In 1947 he returned to live permanently in New Brunswick as director of the newly formed Northeastern Wildlife Station. Bruce was a great speaker and writer on behalf of wildlife and its conservation. He published extensively, and one of his great passions in life was the eastern panther.

Bruce first heard of panthers in the wilds of New Brunswick in 1938 as a member of the Fire Hazard Research Division of the Dominion Forest Service. He was watching a forest fire with a senior forester of the New Brunswick International Paper Company. When casually asking about any wildlife seen, he was surprised to hear that the foreman had spotted a panther moving ahead of the fire that morning. That lit a flame of interest in Bruce that was to burn until his death in 1975. He was convinced that in certain regions of eastern North America the panther had survived the loss of habitat and persecution by humans and continued to maintain viable, though small breeding populations. He pursued this belief with great energy, especially in his home province of New Brunswick. He wrote numerous scientific and popular articles espousing his theory and called for legislation to ensure its protection and continued survival. Just months before his death, the panther was included as an endangered species under the New Brunswick Endangered Species Act. Bruce wrote seven books, two of which, *The Ghost of North America*[1] and *The Eastern Panther*[2] remain the most authoritative sources of reference on panthers in the northeast. Another of his books was called *The Monarch of Mularchy Mountain.*

Mularchy Mountain stands majestic among the rugged forested wilderness of the headwaters of the Keswick River in central New Brunswick. It was this place that Bruce chose as the setting for his fascinating stories of the interactions of farmers, hunters and biologists with wild animals. He cleverly intertwined the lives and events of moose, deer, black bear, bobcat and panthers to provide the reader with new insight into the fascinating world of predator and prey, and to explain the science of wildlife management to the average person. This world of which Bruce wrote included man as only one player in a complex system, but a player who was exerting an ever-threatening influence on the other animals around him. Bruce wrote these stories in the early 1960s, a time when the Province of New Brunswick still held some of the finest hunting and fishing grounds to be found in northeastern North America. The sparkling waters of many lakes could only be reached by airplane or several days travel by canoe and backpack. Bruce looked upon these unbroken stretches of wilderness as perhaps the last refuge for the great wild cat of eastern North America. I would like to share with the reader an abridged version of Bruce's story of the panthers of Mularchy Mountain:

"When the panther left the valleys behind Mularchy Mountain where the deer wintered it wandered on toward the west. The great five-inch tracks in the snow were seen where it crossed a road and a man came to look at them. 'Must be a bear,' he muttered, not knowing that a panther's track shows only four toes and a bear's five. He followed the track for some distance and he noticed how straight it was. 'This fellow sure seems to know where he's going. No messing about for him.' He came to a place where the panther had broken stride to stalk a short distance and pounce. There the snow was red with blood and the skin of a porcupine lay neatly on its back nearby with every scrap of flesh and bone eaten out of it. 'Well I'm blowed! That's some trick for a bear!'

"He went back and examined the track where the panther had crouched and started its stalk. This time he noticed a long shallow drag mark in the snow at intervals among the paw prints. He stood staring at these marks for a long time. 'Bears can't drag a long tail—and that's a tail mark if I ever saw one. From here on this is a job for the warden—not for me.'

"He retraced his steps to the road and went home and telephoned the game warden. 'Bob, there's something up here you better come and have a look at. Did you ever hear tell of a long-tailed bear that eats porcupines? Well, we got one now. Pick me up at the house.'

"The warden needed but one glance at the great track. 'That's no bear, Jim. That's a panther—and a big one too! He'll be just passing through, but I'll trail him until he's well clear of the settlement.' 'Panther, eh? Is he dangerous? How about the kids going to school?' 'He's not dangerous to man. There's plenty of deer in this country so he's not starving, and nobody has stock out in the fields at this time of year anyway. Do me a favour, Jim, and don't talk about this for a few days until he's moved on. You know how easy it is to start a panic. The very mention of a panther makes so many people's hair rise—and I don't want him shot. He's been around for a number of years and he comes through here once or twice every winter. He's never done any damage, and he's the rarest animal we have. The mail driver tells me he's seen him a couple of times and that he's a magnificent animal. Judging from his tracks he's a full-grown male and probably weighs close to two hundred pounds. The driver swears he's all of seven feet from tip to tip, and I wouldn't doubt it. If you're nervous about him and you see him, stand still. He'll do all the running for both of you.'

"The panther opened his eyes and stretched to the full seven feet of his length and flexed his mighty muscles. He lay in the shelter of a boulder on a hillside looking over a valley with a farm in the bottom along the stream. He had been sleeping all day and the sun was just setting behind the far hills. As the shadows lengthened he rose and stretched again, and walked over to a nearby tree. He rose on his hind legs and reached as far up the tree as he could and set his claws in the bark. With a mighty backward surge he raked his claws down the trunk, gouging channels through the bark with each claw. This cleared out the accumulation of old dried blood and scraps of flesh in the deep grooves behind his claws that were the remnants of his last meal. He raked the tree several times until his claws were clean and fresh, and then he started up the hill. Half-way up he found an old pile of sawdust and bark from a woods operation of bygone years. Here he made his first scrape. He stopped and looked carefully up and down the trail and then he crouched down and began to dig with his forepaws. He dug a shallow hole and heaped up the loose sawdust in a pile under his chin, then he stepped forward and deposited a few drops of urine on the pile. As he moved off his hind foot stepped into the hole he had dug.

"When he left the hill he had renewed all his scent posts and found no sign of any intruders on his range. He descended the hill and crossed into the frozen cedar swamp beyond the brook. Here he found a few old deer tracks but nothing new. The place was alive with rabbits, and he had not gone far when he came to the track of a bobcat. Here was a meal more his size, and immediately he turned to follow it. The bobcat had been hunting rabbits in the swamp all that winter and it had lived well. It never left the swamp after the snow came and the bouncing rabbits supplied all its needs. The thick foliage of the cedars was ample protection against storms. Snug in its little world, the bobcat had lived secure within two hundred yards of the farm without the farmer ever having occasion to know it was there.

"When the panther found its trail it had finished its night's hunt and climbed into an old dead elm that had broken off many years before. The broken crotch provided a snug punk-filled nest where it could drowse away the days. It saw the panther coming and its ears lay back and a prudently silent snarl curled its lips. The panther followed the tracks to the base of the tree and looked up. Their eyes met for a second and then the bobcat was off in a flying leap to the ground. It dashed madly through the swamp with the great tawny shape bounding behind. Several times it darted under logs and windfalls but the panther was not to be shaken off. Finally it did what all hard-pressed cats do. It climbed a tree. The tree was tall, but the night was young. The panther had not eaten for two days and his appetite was keen. He had seen his next meal and he was not to be distracted. When the bobcat went up the tree it chose a large limb to run out on. This was its undoing as the panther was almost as agile in a tree as a bobcat. He followed fast on the heels of his prey, and in the fork he caught it.

"The next day the warden trailing the panther reached the hill where the scrapes were made. He carefully noted the location of each pile and he stuck a small stick upright in the center of each. When he returned he would only have to glance at the piles to tell which were the new ones and how often the panther had been back since his last visit.

" 'That's a help. Now at last I'll have a place to come and see if he has come back. Just the same I'll keep this to myself. I don't suppose old Amos Story down there would be too happy if he knew a panther regularly visited the hill above his farm.' He descended the hill and crossed the valley to the farm. 'Mornin', Amos. Pretty good winter so far. How many head o'stock you got this year?' 'Twenty-two cows and twelve sheep. Why?' 'Just wonderin'. Ever have any trouble with bears or cats botherin' them?' 'Nope. Never did—but one day last fall all the cattle came runnin' back to the barn and wouldn't go near the back pasture for two days. Somethin' scared 'em, but I never seen nothin'.' 'Well, let me know if you have any trouble and we'll look after it for you. Bye now.'

"He crossed the brook and headed into the cedar swamp. He had not gone far before he found the tracks of the panther following the bobcat. He knelt on his snowshoes and observed the tracks very closely. Each print had a ridge of snow around it and loose crystals lay about on the unbroken surface. Very carefully he reached over and tried to pick up one of these loose crystals. It was frozen down. Then he reached over and touched the track itself. It was soft and not yet frozen. 'Made before sunrise or the loose crystals would have melted, not frozen,' he muttered. 'The track is just beginning to freeze now.'

"He followed until he came to the base of the tree where the final act of the drama had taken place. There he stood and stared long and thoughtfully. The small bobcat track led to the tree in ten–foot bounds and the great panther prints followed in twenty-foot leaps. Around the base of the tree were tufts and clumps of bobcat hair, and a few drops of blood dotted the white surface. Caught on a bush at the level of his eyes was the largest and heaviest piece. He walked over and lifted it off. It was a patch of skin as big as his hand and attached to it was the complete stub-tail of the bobcat. Quietly he gathered up all the fragments he could find. Later in the Game Office he spread them on the biologist's desk.

" 'That was a big cat, Bill. He chased it around the swamp until it treed, then he went up after it and caught it and ate it in the fork of the tree!' 'That would have been something to see and photograph! What a one-in-a-million shot that would have made! He probably did old Story's chickens a good turn by removing that bobcat. Once the rabbit concentration broke up this spring and Story turned his hens loose that cat might have relished a change of diet. Then there would be another howl for the return of the bounty. Keep moving, oldtimer, and we'll wish you well!'

"One bright moonlight night the panther sat on top of a great boulder on a ridge overlooking the valley. His ears were tilted alertly forward and he was all attention. Then again he heard it. Faint and far away he heard a sound that sounded for all the world like a baby crying. He left his boulder and started down the hill in great bounds. At intervals the sound came again, and whatever was making it seemed to be crossing the base of the hill opposite. He paused to listen and the strange cry came from directly in front of him and half a mile ahead. The next time he paused the sound was very close, and now he caught the strong warm scent. It was a female panther in heat seeking a mate, and she called softly from the shoulder of the ridge until he joined her.

"There is nothing delicate about the courtship of the cats, and that night the valley heard caterwauling and babies crying as the pair chased each other about the ridge. The wife of the farmer in the valley woke him at 4 o'clock in the morning. 'Amos, wake up! There's a child lost over on the hill! It's crying somethin' awful!' He grumbled but got up and they both stood shivering at the open window. Then it came. An almost human sound that started with a low sobbing note and ended with a high-pitched scream. The wife turned wide-eyed to her husband. 'It's O.K. dear. Them's cats. I heard a bobcat once that made that sound—but not near as loud as that. I'll call the warden in the morning.'

"When the biologist got the news he asked the warden to go and look for tracks to make sure it was the panthers. Later he reported in. 'It's them all right, Bill. The male's track is as big as the palm of my hand and the female is about half the size.' 'Well done. Mated on March 10th, gestation period say 96 days, so by

June 14 there'll be a litter somewhere around here,' and he pushed a red pin into the wall map.

"The panthers stayed together for several days and the male made his scrapes all over the hill. He was staking his claim to this female and giving fair warning to others that he would fight to protect his rights. The little female killed a deer by the creek and they consumed it in three meals down to bone fragments and tufts of hair. They carefully buried it between each meal until there was nothing left to bury. Then she left him. He hung about inspecting his scrapes for a few days, but as he found nothing had visited them he moved away on another of his endless wanderings. The female did not move far. She crossed the hill and established a hunting territory in the next valley where there were several bands of deer, many fat porcupines, and a beaver colony. Her food supply was assured and she settled in comfortably to await the birth of her cubs.

"High on the hill above her a great pine had stood for over two hundred years. It had seen the Indians in their birch canoes moving swiftly and easily down the streams and lakes, and the first shot ever fired in the valley had echoed from its trunk. Then came the settlers. They cut a small clearing in the forest and piled the slain trees in heaps. On a fine day with a good wind they set the piles alight. Soon the raging flames had passed far beyond the small clearing and the whole hillside was ablaze. When the fire reached the great pine it baked the bark and killed the living wood beneath, and then it ran up the tree. The crown exploded in a sheet of flame that could be seen for miles, and when it died down there was nothing left but the blackened skeleton of the great tree. For many years it was a bonanza for the woodpeckers as the insects gathered to devour it, and then one winter's day a great storm howled down from the north and felled it. It had been hollow for a long time now, and when it fell the great hollow trunk lay stretched along the hillside beside the blackened stump.

"In the fall before the panthers mated on the hill an old male black bear had glutted himself on the blueberries and raspberries on the hillside, and when the snow came he began exploring the upper reaches of the hill. It was not long before he found the hollow log. He sniffed around and forced his way in as far as he could get. A few swipes of his great paws cleared out the dead wood from the far end, and he settled himself comfortably in his new-found den. As the snow deepened and blew off the crest it drifted over the log and buried the bear and his den below the reach of the fierce gales that howled down from the northern barrens.

"When spring came back to the valley the bear awoke lean and hungry, and fierce of temper. His first call was to the bottom of the valley where he visited the cedar swamp where the deer had wintered. As he expected it was not long before he found the carcass of a long dead deer that had starved during the winter. He reveled in a great gorge on the putrid meat and lay down and slept beside the carcass.

"He awoke to see a great brown cat surveying him suspiciously. He snarled and the cat spat and bared its gleaming teeth, but they both went their separate ways. Several times he met this cat in his rambles, and once she barred his way and snarled and lashed her long tail when he attempted to pass to investigate a tangle of blowdowns behind her. She blocked the path and looked so savage and determined that he gave way and wandered off in another direction. The cat turned and crawled into the depths of the tangle where four tiny cubs greeted her with hungry whimpers.

"One day the bear was again in the vicinity of the blowdowns, but this time no angry cat barred his way. He wandered close snuffling, and then his keen nose caught the scent. His ears went forward and he began to swing his massive head from side to side. Quickly he burrowed into the pile, heaving aside logs that got in his way. There before him lay the den with the still blind kittens mewing piteously for their mother.

"The panther was returning to her den and lazy after a good meal when she caught the bear's scent. Immediately she came alert, and crouching close to the ground, she followed quickly. When she reached the blowdowns she saw where a great body had forced itself to the den. All that was left of her family were tufts of hair and a few drops of blood. She ranged the hills in discomfort for a week until her milk dried up, and then she left the country.

"The warden searched the hill several times but he found no fresh panther sign. 'Something got that litter, Bill. It could only be the bear, but I never did find the den.' 'They have no enemies beside man once they're full-grown, but something must get the cubs quite often or they would be much more numerous then they are. Apparently it's quite a job for a panther to raise a litter successfully in this country. I wonder why. They've been so close to extinction for so long that there can't be many females around and each litter counts.'

" 'It's too bad, but maybe one of his other girlfriends will be luckier.' 'I hope so. We can use a few more deer-cullers on parts of this range.' 'I'd give anything to see the big boy, Bill.' 'You might as well forget it. It's a one-in-a-million chance. Good fieldmen have lived all their lives in country like Vancouver Island where there is a hundred for every one we have here and have never seen one that wasn't treed by dogs. It'll be pure chance if he gets careless enough for you to catch a glimpse of him, and he didn't get to live this long by being careless.' 'I know, but there's always a hope. A few years ago a female and two well-grown cubs wandered into the suburbs of Montreal. She got careless.' 'She got careless all right, but still she didn't get caught, if you'll remember.' 'I don't want the body like some people. I'll settle for a good hard look and a photograph as a dividend. That would satisfy me.' 'Well, good luck to you. I suppose you always have a camera with you?' 'I do—you can bet. But the chances of getting it into action are pretty slim.'

"The big male panther stretched along a log and watched the quiet surface of the pond in front of him. A form floated silently to the surface and the beaver lay motionless watching for any movement on shore. It rested there until all ripples had died away and its head and back were a dark blotch on the silver surface. The moon shone brilliantly and a whip-poor-will called continuously from the forest beyond the dam.

"The dark object in the middle of the pond began to move and silver ripples spread from its nose. The beaver reached the shore and turned into one of the shallow hauling canals that led off into the dark woods. The panther, motionless as a graven image, followed only with his eyes. The beaver reached the end of the canal and hauled out onto dry land. Again it stood motionless for long minutes listening, and then satisfied it moved noisily over the dry leaves to the trunk of a large poplar that was already half cut through. The noise of its chisel teeth at work soon sounded around the pond.

"Not until the beaver had been at work for a good five minutes did the panther move. Then it slid from the log noiseless as a shadow. Flat to the ground it flowed toward the beaver ever so slowly. Then, twenty feet behind the industrious carpenter intent only on his work, the motion ceased and the great hind quarters gathered under it for the spring. The tip of the tail twitched ecstatically twice—and it sprang.

"The next morning the warden stepped up on the dam and

sat down to examine the pond. 'Two occupied houses this year. They're building up—and there's no place for them to go down stream without getting into somebody's woodlot where they won't be welcome. We may have to move this lot out of here.'

"He got up and circled the pond, and when he came to the bloody patch at the base of the half-cut poplar he examined it long and carefully. He followed a dim drag mark on the leaves until it stopped. Then a few drops of blood led to where the panther had cleaned out the carcass of a forty-pound beaver. Nearby was about half the carcass covered by a pile of leaves that had been scraped over it. At the first telephone in the settlement he called the Game Office.

" 'The big boy's back, Bill. He took a forty-pound buck beaver up at Burns' pond last night. Ate half of it and buried the rest. He'll be back.' 'Not only will he be back—but he's not far off right now sleeping. Oh for a pack of trained dogs! We'd get our picture sure.' 'Well, what do you want me to do?' 'Nothing. But keep an eye on the settlement livestock. He's never touched them yet, and with plenty of deer and beaver he probably won't now, but you never can tell. I want you there to handle any complaint right away. Keep me posted!'

"The panther took one more beaver from the colony and then moved on. This time he wandered far from the settlements into the great forest beyond. He was heading for the territory of a female that he had mated with a year before. When he entered her valley he found her scent easily enough and he crisscrossed the valley until he found her. She was lying on a boulder with three well-grown cubs playing below her when he arrived, and her ears lay back and a snarl curled her lips as she saw him.

She walked toward him snarling and lashing her great tail—and there was no mistaking the lack of warmth in her welcome. She was plainly telling him to go. He was not wanted there. Disappointed, he hung around for a few days, but the female would not leave the cubs and she would not permit him to come close to them. She trusted no one, not even their own father, with her young—and she may have had good cause.

"When the male realized that the female would not leave her family to hunt with him he soon lost interest and left the valley. She watched him go with relief and turned to her three kittens. They were two months old and small replicas of their mother except in their color. Two of them were densely spotted with rings on their tails like a raccoon—but the third was jet black.

The spotted cubs were the normal color for young panthers but the black one was a very rare freak. However, his mother seemed to notice nothing unusual about him and he played and wrestled with his brother and sister.

"Later that year the big male returned to the valley in the deep forest. This time the female greeted him and they went off to hunt together. The family had left the den months before and now the cubs found the female was indifferent to them. They still wanted to be with her and followed her about, but when her mate returned they made themselves scarce. The venturesome black male wandered off by himself and was seen no more in the lands of his great father."[3]

As we have seen, as early as the mid-1800s the killing of an eastern panther was a rare occasion, and one which generated considerable local gossip and attracted much attention in county newspapers. The crudely mounted effigies of these trophies were proudly displayed at county fairs, often to be seen for a small fee. But yet, even then, rumors and stories flourished about strange and mysterious cats being seen and heard prowling near the neighborhood and clearly full of bad intentions. Occasionally a panther was killed, but the source of most such rare specimens was left in doubt. Most were discarded, misplaced or lost and only the story of the event lingered on. But the sightings of pantherlike creatures have continued, from Mississippi to Ontario, and their numbers are increasing every year.

Most state and provincial wildlife agencies, and many museums, act as centers where sightings can be reported and filed in some sort of systematic fashion. Some agencies have actively solicited such reports in hopes of identifying areas of especially frequent sightings. This would help, it was thought, in assessing the situation and to focus efforts when searching for further evidence of panthers. Most such initiatives have been discouraged, however, after wall maps became literally cluttered with sightings with no obvious pattern to their distribution. There have also been private efforts to collect and sort through eastern panther sightings, and several newsletters circulated to members and subscribers.

So who are seeing these mysterious long-tailed cats of the Appalachians? How credible are these sightings? Are they being seen by people who wouldn't know a panther from a bobcat or house cat? Some, perhaps. But the vast majority of the thousands of sightings which have been compiled by government and private organizations in every eastern state and province over the past several decades are reported by the average citizen who, by and large, is firmly convinced that what he or she saw was a large cat which could be nothing else but a panther. Although a few reports, for some reason or another, may be intentional hoaxes, most are by honest persons who only wish to ensure that those responsible for such matters are aware of what they saw. Many sightings are by trained professional outdoors persons: biologists; park wardens and rangers; experienced naturalists. Others are by hunters, trappers and fishermen who are quite aware of the differences between panthers and other similar-looking wildlife.

A set of tracks photographed by Bruce Wright in southern New Brunswick in 1947. Bruce was convinced that the tracks were those of a panther. He believed that the impression between tracks was a tail drag, while others believe it was the scuff mark of a paw, probably from a lynx. The small track is that of an otter. (WRIGHT, 1972)

What is most surprising about these reports of panther sightings throughout eastern North America is their consistency. Most are of a large, tawny, long-tailed cat ranging from forty to one hundred pounds, characteristics typical of a panther. Also, approximately 15-20 percent of sightings from most regions are reported to be black. Of course most of us know what a panther should look like, so when we see something that we think is a panther, those are the characteristics which are reported. All panthers have long tails, so a long tail must accompany every sighting. Any large cat with a short tail would immediately be identified as a bobcat, an animal common in most of eastern North America. All panthers are larger than house cats, so a relatively large body size must also be included. But what about the black cats? This is very interesting, and I will address the issue later.

It would be impossible, of course, and certainly impractical, to attempt to compile all such reports in one volume. There have been literally thousands of panther sightings through the years, and that is not the intention of this book.[4] But I do wish to give the reader a selected few of these sightings so that he or she might appreciate how such sightings originate and who is seeing these strange animals. The few presented here are in no way special. They were selected only to give the reader an appreciation of the great variety and wide geographical distribution of panther observations throughout the east. They are a few of the many submitted to district wildlife offices, federal, state and provincial park headquarters, museums and private organizations each day throughout eastern North America.

We begin with an early sighting in the Great Smoky Mountains National Park, a remote mountainous section which lies in the southern Appalachians, and an area where, if panthers do exist in the east, may well be one of their last retreats.

Sitting on the front porch of their bunkhouse following an evening meal in a wilderness region of the Great Smoky Mountains National Park in North Carolina, five park employees were watching a doe and two yearling white–tailed deer as they fed in a valley next to the Cataloochee River. The men, all of nearby Bryson City, had been working in this remote section of the park for over a week and enjoyed chatting and watching the deer as the evening shadows lengthened and darkness approached. It was July 23, 1975, and all was peaceful and quiet, as it usually was in this mountainous retreat, except for the odd behavior of the three deer below.

Horace Cunningham, one of the men on the porch that day, remembers the incident. "At first, we thought they were just playing. But then, the more we watched them the more we could see that something was bothering them." The deer were obviously nervous. They were feeding in the meadow but their tails were twitching; their heads jerked anxiously as they scanned the adjacent woods. Suddenly they darted towards the woods one way, then another. Finally splitting up, the doe and one yearling dashed off one way, the lone yearling another. Walter Laws left the porch and stepped towards the meadow to search for the startled deer. At that moment a park service truck rambled by the cabin and proceeded down the road, its red tail-lights dancing in the approaching darkness. Then, from the direction of the meadow, a dark long-tailed animal leaped across the road between the men and the truck.

The five men watched in disbelief as the large catlike animal bounded across the field and on towards the woods. They shone lights where the cat was last seen but saw nothing. That night, several horses in a nearby barn were unusually skittish. Horace Cunningham, another of the men, remembers that the horses snorted and blew all night long. This was particularly unusual for these park horses which were normally calm and well-behaved. A search of the road the next morning found round clawless tracks which were a little smaller than a man's palm. The next time the men saw the deer in the meadow, the doe was with only one of the yearlings. Had this been a mountain lion? Had it killed one of the young deer that night?

Because of the credibility of this sighting the park released a press report describing the incident. This was picked up by the media throughout the southeast and given prominent coverage, especially as many considered this incident proof that mountain lions still roamed the southern Appalachians. The five park employees were given celebrity status and sought out and hounded by reporters.[5]

A few years later the Great Smoky Mountains became the focus of an intensive government sponsored search for eastern panthers. In 1977, Robert Downing worked as a research biologist with the United States Fish and Wildlife Service (USF&WS) in Clemson, North Carolina. At that time certain environmental groups were protesting the harvesting of timber in the Nantahala National Forest. One of the reasons by which they justified their disapproval was the importance of those wilderness areas as eastern panther range. They rationalized their actions based upon several recent sightings of panthers in the area. A law suit was pending. Following an initial assessment of the issue, and an unsuccessful search for panthers by a professional cougar hunter from Colorado, the USF&WS and the United States Forest Service assigned Downing the task of organizing a study to pursue the matter further. Downing spent the next three years searching for evidence of panthers in the southern Appalachians, especially in his home state of North Carolina. He developed a network of fellow panther enthusiasts and circulated a newsletter with current stories and information on panthers throughout the east. He explained his study at public meetings, through the press and at scientific conferences and symposia. After three years devoted to the search of eastern panthers, however, Downing concluded that panthers were either absent or extremely rare. "Despite several years of intensive effort funded by the U.S. government, the author has been unable to positively confirm that there are self-sustaining populations of cougars in the eastern

United States north of Florida."[6] Although his efforts may not have confirmed the presence of panthers, they certainly served to focus renewed interest in the issue throughout the east.

More recently, in the spring of 1990, and far to the north of the Great Smokies in the province of New Brunswick, Roger Noble saw, and recorded on videotape, a large cat near his home at Waasis, not far from the city of Fredericton. Not experienced in using a video camera, and obviously excited at the time, the pictures are far from clear, but the animal photographed was most certainly a large, long-tailed cat. Just how large remains in

Robert Downing, standing right, and Ranier Brocke, standing left, search for panther signs somewhere in the southern Appalachians.

(AUDOBON, MARCH 1981)

question, and although the pictures were thoroughly studied, and the site searched for traces of the cat, not everyone agrees on just what it was that John Noble photographed. But John Noble has no doubt what it was that crossed his path—only ol' Painter could have aroused such a rush of excitement and touch of fear.

Two years later, and some seventy miles north of Waasis, Rod Cumberland, at that time furbearer biologist for the province of New Brunswick, was hot on a trail left in the snow by a very large catlike animal. Cumberland, a knowledgeable and experienced woodsman, certainly knows a large cat track when he sees one. Alerted to the fresh track by J.D. Irving Ltd. forest technician Tom O'Blenis, Rod and wildlife technician Jeff Dempsey picked up the trail early in the morning of November 19, 1992, near Juniper in the central part of the province.

The tracks were certainly impressive, yet they could have been made by a large coyote, an animal new to the region which can often reach fifty pounds in weight. The two men followed the trail for several kilometers until they found a scat on a rock. They collected this piece of evidence and continued on. The fresh tracks averaged four inches in diameter; the stride of the animal was measured at forty-four inches. The animal that made these tracks must have approached four feet in length! Certainly no bobcat, and probably not a coyote. Could it have been a panther? As they went along, Dempsey was making detailed measurements and taking notes. Later, Rod recalled the excitement as the two experienced outdoorsmen and wildlife professionals continued on the trail. "Jeff kept hollering: 'What do you think?' I was still skeptical. The more we followed the track, the more I couldn't believe it. I've investigated about a dozen reports of cougar sightings, and in each case we found it hadn't been a cougar."[7]

The animal had leaped onto some logs three feet off the snow and bounded twenty-five feet, clearing a small tree, in pursuit of a snowshoe hare. The tracks showed typical cat characteristics, a lead toe with the weight on the front of the pad, a greater width than length, and no claw marks, a distinct trait of cats which retract their claws when walking. Members of the dog family do not have retractile claws and their nail or claw impressions are clearly visible in fresh tracks.

All measurements and observations suggested that the animal which made these tracks was a large cat, and certainly a cat much larger than the largest of bobcats. The two men returned to their office in Fredericton and examined the final thread of evidence, the frozen scat. Cats spend considerable time grooming themselves and in the process ingest some of their own hair. Thus, most cat scats contain traces of the cat's hair. Perhaps hairs in this scat would provide the final bit of evidence as to the identity of this mystery animal. The scat was shipped off to experts at the Canadian Museum of Nature in Ottawa for analysis. On February 25, 1993, Rod received word back from Dr. Stan van Zyll de Jong, the Curator of Mammals at the museum. Besides remnants of hair and bone from a snowshoe hare, the scat also contained hairs from the feet and legs of a panther, apparently ingested while grooming after feeding. This was proof beyond a doubt, irrefutable evidence that a panther had passed by Juniper, New Brunswick, on that cold day of November 18, 1992. But the nagging question remained. Was it an eastern panther? If so, could it have been the one seen earlier at Waasis? Perhaps it was a released or escaped captive panther, cougar or puma brought here from some other part of the world. Although the provincial Wildlife Branch issued a press release proclaiming evidence of a panther, the exact origin of this animal was left in doubt.

The trail in the snow followed by Rod Cumberland in central New Brunswick in November 1992. Hairs found in a scat left by the animal were identified as those of a panther. The source of this panther is unknown. (ROD CUMBERLAND)

There have been other wildlife biologists and game officers who have seen what they believed were panthers. Robert Hatcher, Coordinator of Nongame and Endangered Species for the Tennessee Wildlife Resources Agency in Nashville, told me that several personnel in his agency have reported seeing panthers. In midsummer of 1975, fishery biologist Eugene Cobb saw a cougarlike animal crossing a highway thirty to forty yards in front of him in Hardeman County, southwestern Tennessee. "The animal appeared dark in color, had a long tail, a catlike appearance and glided across the road in a very graceful way. If it indeed was a cougar, it was, according to size, about two-thirds grown or possibly a small adult female."[8]

One night around 1980, Wildlife Biologist Jay Story of Oak Ridge National Laboratories of Oak Ridge, Tennessee, was conducting a study of bobcat and deer. He shone his flashlight for about seven seconds on the side of a cougar, with tan color and long tail, before it ran away. About the same time, fishery biologist Ged Petit and photographer (without camera) Aubrey Watson were fishing from a boat in the Big Sandy River embayment of Kentucky Lake, Tennessee, when a cougar took a drink at the shoreline. And in the mid-1980s, wildlife officer George Gregory of Hickman County, Tennessee, shot and killed a cougar that had been 'stalking' a child. The cougar had been declawed, indicating former captivity.[9]

Other apparent sightings make the headlines of local papers. One such sighting near Caratunk, Maine, with an accompanying photograph of a live panther in the company of two hunting dogs, appeared in an outdoor column of the February 6, 1994, edition of the *Maine Sunday Telegram*.[10] After closer study of trees in the picture, which appear to be pinyon pine, state wildlife officials believe that it was most likely taken in the western United States, possibly Colorado, where pinyon pines are quite common. Although not confirmed, this supposed eastern panther sighting might best be considered a prank. Others are less easily explained, such as this incident of a mysterious black cat near Bridgeton, New Jersey, which made the June 25, 1992, edition of the *Bridgeton Evening News*:

"Just when you thought it was safe to go in the woods, it's back. At least the stories are back. Whether there is—or ever was—a large black cat loose in the woods of the North Vineland-Pittsgrove Township area is something still being debated. In 1987, stories started circulating of mutilated household pets, an ungodly roaring in the woods and 'something' that reportedly tried to claw its way into a home. Some said it was a black leopard, either deliberately set loose by a demented person or an escaped cat kept illegally as a pet whose owner stayed quiet because of the liability if the animal injured or killed someone. Both local and state police and the state Division of Fish, Game and Wildlife searched the woods and left baited traps. Nothing ever was caught and the stories eventually ceased."[11]

In 1987, John DiOrio, a resident of Haddon Heights, New Jersey, was only vaguely aware of the South Jersey reports. He bought an old home on twenty-two acres in Heislerville in 1989 and began to renovate it. A correctional officer, he is intensely interested in the flora and fauna of the area. In early June 1992, he came face-to-face with a legend. Shortly after midnight,

DiOrio was driving south on Route 55 when a black cat crossed the road in front of his van and went up a sandbank into the woods. DiOrio knew immediately that this was no ordinary cat and later estimated that it weighed as much as 125 pounds. It also seemed to have an injured right hind leg, which caused it to limp. DiOrio said he has absolutely no doubt about what he saw. The next day, having made careful note of the spot, he went back, found the animal's tracks and took several photographs, which he said proves it was a cat. The tracks were about 3.5 inches across and too round for a dog print.

Harold Hitchcock was born in Hartford, Connecticut, on June 23, 1903, and died in his ninety-second year on September 13, 1995, in Middlebury, Vermont. His interest in panthers began in 1944 and continued unabated for the next fifty years. Dr. Hitchcock taught biology for twenty-five years at Middlebury College. Although his main research interest was in the study of cave bats in the northeast, he also pursued his passion of learning more about the mystery cat of the Appalachians. After retirement from Middlebury College in 1968, he continued teaching as visiting professor at Boston University, Norwich University, University of Hawaii and Bates College. Dr. Hitchcock published and lectured extensively on this mysterious cat of the northeast. Through his personal curiosity and interest in the mystery, Dr. Hitchcock collected many accounts of people seeing what they identified as eastern panthers. The most obvious reason for denying its presence has been the absence of physical evidence. But Dr. Hitchcock, among others, insist that panthers have been killed and reported. Read the following report by Kevin Corkins, a high school teacher in Rutland, Vermont, which was given to Dr. Hitchcock in December 1992:

"On approximately September 15, 1992, I was driving south on Route 7 at about 6:20 in the morning. I had driven across the long straightway in Salisbury over the river and just past the large pull-off area for parking on the right. I was travelling at about 65 or 70 miles per hour. Just as I had passed the parking area to the right a large cat jumped out in front of me, travelling west to the east. I missed it. However, a second cat following right behind it hit the middle of my car. I pulled my car over, as did a man driving a dump truck behind me, to take a look-see. It was a cat, solid brown in color with a thick tail about 15 to 18 inches long. It weighed about 40 to 50 pounds. I know this because I picked the cat up by his tail to move him out of the middle of the road.

I used a rag out of my trunk because I was concerned about the recent rabies outbreak in Vermont. Finally, when I draped the cat over the metal guardrail its paws touched the ground on either side."[12] The incident was reported to the Vermont Fish and Game Department on the morning of the killing, but there was apparently no further investigation of the matter. Dr. Hitchcock searched the area after he heard of the event several months later but found no evidence of a panther.

Not all reports of panthers appear in local newspapers. The respected *Journal of Mammalogy* carried a paper on reports of panther sightings, and of a panther killed in Louisiana in 1965. The question of panthers in Louisiana is as contentious as it is in Mississippi or Alabama to the east, and is worth including here. By 1950 some authorities estimated that perhaps as few as ten of these large cats may have still lived in the entire state of Louisiana.

"At 12:15, a.m. 30 November 1965, Deputies Frank M. Normand and Ray V. Lindsay of Caddo Parish saw a [panther] on the old Mansfield Road about 2 miles N of the DeSoto Parish line, directly behind the KV Bar near Keithville. Deputy Normand explained that the animal was shot as it stood near the road in the glare of headlights. We examined this animal approximately 12 hr after death at the Independent Ice and Storage Company of Shreveport. At this time, the [panther] weighed 114 lb.; its maximum weight was probably between 115 and 120 lb. before death."[13]

And we have already mentioned the panther killed in St. Clair County of Alabama in 1948.

Many people look to the wilderness areas of western Ontario and New Brunswick as reserves where eastern panthers have escaped past persecution by humans and managed to breed and maintain eastern panther lineages. Others disagree, but an article in the scientific journal, *Canadian Field-Naturalist*, reviewed several very interesting sightings in Ontario during the 1950s.

On July 23, 1953, two employees of the Great Lakes Paper Company were driving on the Trans-Canada Highway near Martin, about thirty miles west of present-day Thunder Bay when they saw by the side of the road what they were convinced was a mountain lion. They drove past, turned round and drove back again. As the animal was still there, they were able to get a good view of it. They state that it was of the cat family, of a tawny color and with a long tail. They estimated it to be about 5 1/2 feet

Reported sightings of eastern panthers often make the headlines of local papers, but not all are treated in a serious manner. "UFOs" has sometimes referred to "Unidentified Furry Objects." *(FUR-FISH-GAME, MAY 1993)*

long and to stand about 30 inches high. The sighting was reported to the chief Fish and Wildlife Officer of the Ontario Department of Lands and Forests in Port Arthur.

On April 13, 1954, Charles Seal, engineer, and Glen Chisamore, fireman, were on a run on the Canadian National Railway between Port Arthur and Atikokan when they both saw a cougar about forty-three miles west of Port Arthur. The brown five-foot-long cat cut across the tracks in front of the train and leaped up on a rock-cut, about six feet high, without any trouble. At one point it was not more than twenty-five feet from them. It headed up a rocky hillside into the timber as the train passed. Both men had seen cougars while working in British Columbia and had no doubt of what they saw. As one of the two men exclaimed, "we saw it right there, on the hoof, and there was no mistake about it."[14]

One of the most well-publicized panther incidents was the killing of one in Pennsylvania in 1967. The story of that event was considered noteworthy enough to be published in the *American Midland Naturalist* by Dr. Kenneth J. Doutt, former Curator of Mammals for the Carnegie Museum in Pittsburg, Pennsylvania:

"The last panther in Pennsylvania was supposedly killed in 1871 (or possibly as late as 1891).... However, since that time there have been persistent reports of others having been seen, heard, or tracked. On 28 October 1967, Mr. John D. Gallant of R.D. 3, Edinboro, Crawford Co., Pennsylvania, killed a panther ... 1.5 mi. SE of Edinboro. It was a young female, a little less than half-grown. Some of the kitten spots were still faintly visible on its sides and flanks [see photo on page 27].... Mr. Gallant said it weighed 48 pounds when killed. It was accompanied by a larger cat (possibly its mother), which Gallant thought he wounded, but which got away; this larger one was seen again the following day. Sometime later, two panthers were seen together. According to one story, both were caught in traps, but escaped.

"Opinions are divided concerning the source of these cats. Some people think that a few mountain lions have always been in the forests of northeastern North America. Others believe they have been extinct since at least the turn of the century, and are skeptical of all reports of panthers in Pennsylvania. They consider that the animal killed had escaped from captivity. Lending credence to this argument are stories of wrecked circus cars, from which the animals escaped; stories of captive animals escaping from their cages; and even a rumor that 'someone' had actually released a pair or so of panthers. I have no evidence to offer which would either confirm or deny these tales. Neither do I have any proof that panthers have been present in Pennsylvania since 1900. However, I find it hard to discredit some of the observations which people have reported. The present specimen is positive proof that a panther was killed in Pennsylvania in 1967, and we have Mr. Gallant's word for the fact that a larger one escaped.

"No concrete evidence in the form of photographs or actual specimens was available until the specimen was killed by Mr. Gallant. However, in dealing with an animal as elusive as the panther, it may be just as unscientific to ignore all of these reports as it is to accept every one of them. In a letter to Roger Latham, Outdoor Editor, *Pittsburg Press*, 13 November 1967, Mr. Charles McCrory, who is a reporter on the *News Herald*, Conneaut, Ohio, in speaking of the panther killed by Mr. Gallant and the other which escaped, wrote as follows [in part]: 'Speculation in the Conneaut area is that they, or at least one of them may have come from cages of a former circus performer, C.R. Bordonelli (Prince Muhammed as he called himself), who lived on a farm near Pierpont, Ohio, about 40 miles west of Edinboro.' Jim Kelley, Game Protector, R.D. 2, Jefferson, Ohio, investigated the case. According to his report, it seems unlikely that Bordonelli had more than two panthers, one of which was a male and was killed. The other was a four-month-old female. If it could have been the one that Gallant killed we still have to account for the other one which Gallant saw at the time he killed his specimen, and if we accept the fact that two panthers were seen after Gallant killed his, we must account for a total of three cats."[15]

Dr. Doutt concluded his research of the Gallant panther, and evidence of panthers in the state since 1900, by stating, "I think the evidence is ... very convincing that there may be several more [other than the Gallant cats] in the wilder parts of the State, and that this evidence is sufficient to justify further serious investigation of the matter."[16]

Helen McGinnis is a professional wildlife biologist now working with the United States Fish and Wildlife Service out of Vicksburg, Mississippi. In the 1980s she studied coyotes and collected reports of panther sightings in Pennsylvania. She reviewed the information available on the Crawford County panther and concluded that the animal shot was probably a subadult. Also, abnormalities in the postcranial skeleton (neck area) indicated that it was raised in captivity. Based on its coloration and small size, she suggested that it was derived from Central or South American stock.[17] Arnold Hayden of the Pennsylvania Game Commission told me another interesting story of a panther encounter in Pennsylvania. In the 1960s a conservation officer saw a panther on a back road in Forest County. He drove up to it, gave it a sandwich and it jumped into his car. This panther had been declawed and defanged, obviously an escaped or released captive.[18]

And there have been other panthers killed more recently in eastern states, such as the three-month-old specimen shot by a hunter on December 31, 1993, in Saratoga County, New York.[19] This emaciated 7.5-pound kitten was most likely a captive animal of western origin, or from Florida, which escaped or was released by well-meaning but misdirected owners.

Bruce Wright did not limit his search for eastern panthers to the province of New Brunswick. Among the many sightings of mysterious cats collected by Bruce was the following credible observation of an eastern panther in the Quabbin Reservation of Massachusetts in 1968: "On October 12, 1968, Jack Swedberg, now Senior Wildlife Photographer for the Massachusetts Division of Fisheries and Game, was in the Quabbin Reservation. It was 9:30 in the morning and he had a friend, Dick Smith, of West Sutton, with him. A panther crossed the road in front of them at a distance of twenty yards. It was the color of a buck deer in wintertime and it was about six feet overall. On the way out they met four students from the Massachusetts Cooperative Wildlife Research Unit who were trapping beaver.

When setting their traps the night before they had heard a very loud half-scream half-roar noise that they were unable to identify and they asked Swedberg what it might be. He then told them about seeing the panther."[20]

A year later, on August 25, 1969, Harry Hodgdon, a wildlife graduate student at the University of Massachusetts at the time, was also in the Quabbin Reservation. At 6:41 p.m. he had an experience which he taped at the scene. Here is what the tape says:

Bruce Wright spent thirty years searching for panthers in the northeast, especially in the province of New Brunswick. Here Bruce is shown with a plaster cast of a track identified as that of a panther. The cast was made from tracks left in the mud somewhere in southern New Brunswick in the summer of 1948. (WRIGHT, 1972)

"I just saw an animal out here that I'm still not sure whether to believe it or not. As I drove in Gate 17 (about two hundred or three hundred yards inside the gate), I rounded a small curve and there in the road about two hundred feet ahead of me was this animal walking toward the truck, down the middle of it between the wheel tracks. It spotted me about as I spotted it, because it stopped, still facing me with the rest of its body still behind its head—directly away from me.... It was a cat—a definite cat. It turned around broadside, then started walking back up the road (going directly away from me). I still don't believe it. It was light tan, long, deep-bodied (back to stomach), big, biggest cat I've ever seen, and had a long tail. Mountain lions aren't supposed to be around here, but that sure wasn't any bobcat. That was one big cat; it's a cat, no question in my mind, and must be close to eighty to ninety pounds, maybe more, but I sort of doubt that 'cause it was low [to the ground]."[21]

Wright left us several other accounts of panther sightings in Massachusetts.

"On May 4, 1971, a housewife in Granville, Massachusetts, noticed the unusual actions of the family horse in the corral. It was rearing on its hind legs and attempting to break down the fence. She took the family dog and went to investigate. Her dog weighed about 75 pounds. She found an animal the size of a large dog in the corral. It had a cat's face, was tawny and had a long tail. When the dog attempted to attack it, it knocked the dog sprawling three times with swipes of its paw and escaped into a nearby swamp. A passing motorist witnessed the action."[22]

On November 15, 1960, an animal identified as a panther was struck by a car on the Massachusetts Turnpike in Hampden County. Two couples were en route from Albany to Westfield, Massachusetts. Due in Westfield at 8:00 p.m., the party, already late and with light traffic, was making good time. Suddenly, an animal identified as a panther bounded down the embankment between the westbound and eastbound lanes, and out onto the pavement. The animal was struck directly by the oncoming vehicle. Although a fairly large animal, it was thrown under the vehicle and, in the opinion of the driver, could not have survived the impact. The party continued on and reported the incident to an attendant on duty at the toll booth. Other than a broken license-plate frame, the car sustained no noticeable damage. The driver requested that a maintenance crew be dispatched to remove the carcass, which he felt represented a hazard to other vehicles. He did not know at the time of the rarity or importance of such an event or he would have stopped and examined the carcass himself. There is no further record of this incident.

The driver had seen three mountain lions during two years in Arizona. One of the three he had shot about fifty miles east of Kingman while working on a ranch during the summer. The animal that he had struck on the highway in Massachusetts was tawny-colored and carried its tail straight out behind. The tail had a marked upward turn at the end. The shoulders were muscular, and the hindquarters more tapered. It appeared to be all the same color. He concluded his letter to Bruce Wright with "All I can say is I know what I saw, and regret that I did not stop to pick it up."[23]

Further to the northeast, the Green Mountains of Vermont have long been thought to provide sanctuary to those last few surviving remnants of the original eastern panther. In fact, as we have seen, it was at Barnard, Vermont, on Thanksgiving Day of 1881 that one of the last of these mighty predators was shot. Even in those early days the killing of a panther was not common, and when one did happen to be brought into town it was an event of no small significance. The hunter was toasted for his good fortune and marksmanship, while the county newspapers quickly dispersed the entertaining and often highly embellished details. Mounts of these prized trophies were proudly displayed in taverns and hotels. We can only imagine the stories traded across the tables beneath the frozen stare and sneer of those feared beasts of the darkened forests. As the country moved into the twentieth century, specimens of panthers were replaced by tales of their continued presence "back in the hills." Although scattered stories of panthers being killed were heard on occasion, actual specimens were rare to nonexistent.

The Reverend William J. Ballou moved to Vermont from Wyoming, where he had spent his youth and where he had become familiar with the western cougar. Stories of the continued survival of the panther in Vermont intrigued him and he became one of the first of others to follow who spent much of their energy in the pursuit of evidence to prove the presence of this great predator in the Green Mountain State. Then, in December 1934, while leading a troop of Boy Scouts on a hike a few miles from his home in Chester, Reverend Ballou made a cast of what he thought was a panther track. He had the foresight to send the cast to scientists at the American Museum of Natural History who confirmed that the track had, indeed, been made by a panther. However, the identification was returned with the qualifier that because panthers had long since passed from the living in the northeast, the track must have been made by an animal brought into the region (a response still heard from professionals to explain evidence of panthers in eastern North America). The Ballou cast is now deposited with the Bennington Museum.

Encouraged to know that he had established that at least one panther was still to be found in Vermont, Reverend Ballou continued his quest for more evidence to confirm that a breeding population of panthers was present. This irrepressible man of the cloth sounded the call for all those of similar conviction to join him and become "pantherites," true believers in the continued survival of their namesake in Vermont. These feline followers formed the first organization devoted to the study and pursuit of the mystery cat of the Appalachians, and called themselves the Irrepressible and Uncompromising Order of Panthers. The first meeting of this feline assembly met in May 1934 and attracted some one hundred persons, who were rewarded by eyewitness accounts of panther sightings and encounters. They sang specially composed panther songs, and elected a full slate of appropriately feline-labeled officers. The president, none other than the Reverend William Ballou himself, was called the Grand Puma. Others on the executive of this unique group included the treasurer, otherwise referred to as Grand Catamount Keeper of the Catnip, and a songmaster called the Grand Caterwauler. A second meeting was held a year later, but the enthusiasm had dwindled and apparently the Order faded into history. In 1984, however, the Chester Historical Society observed the fiftieth anniversary of the founding of the Order with a banquet at the Chester Hotel, where the first meeting was held.[24]

One of the more recent panther sightings in the northeast, and one widely acclaimed as evidence beyond a reasonable doubt that panthers are still with us, occurred in Vermont in April 1994. It is quite similar to the earlier story from New Brunswick. The following are details of the story as they appeared in the 1994 winter edition of *Vermont Life*. This sighting has received special attention because hairs from a scat collected on the trail of these animals, similar to the scat in New Brunswick, were identified as those from a panther by Bonnie C. Yates, Senior Forensic Scientist (Mammals) with the National Fish and Wildlife Forensics Laboratory in Ashland, Oregon.

On Saturday, April 2, 1994, Mark Walker, thirty-three, up from Massachusetts to visit his mother and grandmother near Craftsbury, Vermont, was on his way through the snow to a cleared spot on the hillside. There he often left seeds and table scraps for the birds which his grandmother, Dorothy Counter, liked to watch from the window. Relaxing and enjoying a cigarette before returning to the house, Walker heard the crunching noise of something moving through the brush and breaking through the crusty spring snow. Assuming that the noise was from deer, which were common in the area, he calmly watched the forms among the trees as they moved toward him.

What emerged from the brush was not a deer. Although not a hunter, Walker was familiar with wildlife, and he immediately identified several large cats which could be none other than mountain lions! A tawny golden color, the largest of the three animals stood at least three feet at the shoulder, with a tail three feet in length. Frightened, he raced back to the house and called a Vermont Fish and Wildlife number. His report received only mild curiosity from the dispatcher, not the enthusiastic response Walker had hoped for. But his report of panthers was picked up on a police scanner and found its way to Wayne Alexander, a sixty-eight-year-old former employee of General Electric with a passion for reports of panthers in the northeast. His son Cedric was a district wildlife biologist for the Vermont Fish and Wildlife Department and was also involved with collecting reports of panthers.

Things began to move into action. Following phone calls to the state police in St. Johnsbury and to Mark Walker for directions, Wayne Alexander, two of his sons and veteran hunter Arthur Ingersoll headed for Craftsbury. The sighting was too fresh to delay. They arrived at Craftsbury by noon, and after a brief talk with Walker, headed for the clearing to search for tracks in the snow. Wayne Alexander remembers the excitement as the group approached the Walker's residence in Craftsbury: "Here we had for the first time a report of the sighting the same day it occurred, and with snow cover. We hoped to find some good tracks. That was really all we were interested in."[25]

The snow was crusty, not good for tracking, but there were signs of animals breaking through and the men picked up the trail. Hard going in the three-foot-deep snow forced the elder Alexander and Arthur Ingersoll to return to Walker's, but the two younger men, with the aid of snowshoes, continued on the trail. There were three sets of tracks, and the men were convinced that they had been made by panthers. Then, similar to the experience of Rod Cumberland in New Brunswick, the two men found a fresh scat. They collected this important bit of evidence and returned to Walker's. The scat was handed over to district Wildlife Biologist Cedric Alexander, who forwarded it on to the U.S. Fish and Wildlife Service forensic lab in Oregon. The results finally arrived back on Alexander's desk—the sample contained hair from the front paws of a panther! Like the scat collected a year earlier in New Brunswick, this was irrefutable evidence of panthers in Vermont.

The Alexanders began to examine other recent panther sightings in the area: two spotted kittens seen in Craftsbury in May 1992, an adult and two younger animals seen ten miles away in Elmore State Park in August 1993. It certainly appeared this "family group" had been seen before. The Vermont Fish and Wildlife Department issued a press release citing "hard evidence of panthers in the wild in Vermont." But the nagging questions remain. Do they represent true surviving remnants of former eastern panthers? Or are they escaped or released captive mountain lions from the west, or panthers brought here from Florida, or pumas from South America? Whatever their origin, these large cats appear to not only be surviving in the northeast but successfully breeding as well.

Mark Walker's feelings on the Craftsbury panther sightings are similar to those felt by many. "I was real scared. It was nice to see 'em but then again you get the other feeling. You get chills coming up your spine. I'm just curious where they're coming from and why they're coming down here."[26]

Cedric Alexander does entertain doubts as to the ability of wild eastern panthers to now reoccupy former ranges in the northeast. "It's pretty interesting. I don't know which is more plausible—that two animals happened to meet and mate, whether they were released, or whether a pregnant animal was released." He finds the idea that wild panthers are reoccupying their former range hard to believe because there's no known source of the animals. There is, however, a known source of non-wild panthers, he said: the pet trade.[27]

Back in Ontario, near the town of Hearst in the District of Cochrane, an August 1973 sighting of a panther was noteworthy and credible enough to be published in *The Canadian Field-Naturalist.* Sheila Thompson, her husband and three teen-aged children were having a roadside lunch near their parked vehicle, when one of her sons pointed to a large tawny-colored cat which emerged from the brush into a field about one hundred yards away. They watched it move along the edge of the field for about thirty feet. About the size of a German shepherd dog, but with the profile and gait of a cat, the Thompson family was convinced that what they had seen was a panther. A search of the spot where the cat had disappeared back into the woods found one "fist-sized footprint in damp clay, imperfectly registered as the cat had skidded slightly, but it showed a catlike track, with toe-prints fanned across in an arch in front of the central pad. Apart from this one print, we could make out the route the cat had taken through the damp grass, but nothing else."[28]

Helen McGinnis and several of her colleagues have continued to collect and investigate reports of panthers in Mississippi. Several are very interesting. She spoke with one lumberman who since 1977 had seen panthers on several occasions in a remote forested section of eastern Mississippi. One of his closest encounters took place one Saturday evening in August 1986. His son burst into their house at a youth camp and told the lumberman and his wife of a large cat that he had just seen. He thought it was a panther. His father switched on the outside light and walked out the front door. The large cat was standing in the driveway not more than twenty feet away. It squatted down, turned slowly and ran off. The couple saw the cat again the next morning, across the road in a wooded stream valley at a distance of about fifty feet. At first it ignored the car but then looked up at them and jumped across the road. On another occasion, the lumberman and a clergyman from Atlanta were driving down a woods road when they spotted a panther walking down the road ahead of them. It turned and began to run toward them. When it was thirty feet away, they noticed that it was carrying a kitten in its mouth. The kitten was about the size of a half-grown house cat and darker than the mother. At about ten feet from the car, the cat turned off the road and disappeared in the woods.[29]

David Ring was hunting deer near Hardwick, Vermont, in November 1994. Hidden in a blind in a field frequently used by deer to feed, Ring was amazed to see a large long-tailed tawny cat emerge from the woods and amble into the clearing. It is interesting that the field is only several miles from where Mark Walker saw the three large cats only several months earlier. Alerted by a rustle in the leaves, Ring couldn't believe his eyes when the large cat, unaware of his presence, began moving toward his blind. At first mistaking it to be a large bobcat, he was taken back when it turned sideways and he saw the full outline. He focused in with his ten-power binoculars at a distance of sixty-five yards. It had a down-curved two and a half foot long tail, about as long as the body, and a smooth catlike gait. There was no doubt in Ring's mind that he was looking at a panther. He had seen them before in zoos, the western variety. "That long, flowing tail just twitching back and forth. When you see it, you know what it is."[30]

Katheryn Milillow was driving with her seven–year-old son, Benjamin, on a road in Proctor, seventy miles south of Craftsbury. As she rounded a curve she saw "what looked like a good-size dog thirty feet away loping up a rocky outcropping along the break-down lane. It was the color of oak and had the longest tail I'd ever seen on a creature. It just about touched the ground. It was moving slowly with the gait of a cat. He just went in between some boulders and some foliage and disappeared instantly."[31] Frightened at first, she now considers herself fortunate to be one of the few to have seen the ghost cat of the Appalachians. Why all these sightings in the Craftsbury area unless there are, indeed, panthers there to be seen?

During the summer of 1972, naturalist Alex McKay had a close encounter with an animal he believed to be a panther, while birdwatching in the Adirondack Mountains of New York. He not only saw it, he photographed it! McKay was so convinced of what he saw, and recorded on film, that he pursued the panther controversy through libraries, museums and fish and game offices for over a year. This is his story.

While silently watching a Blackburnian warbler in a thick balsam fir tree, McKay became aware of another creature nearby and saw a large cat moving through the brush some twenty yards away. Their eyes met, and the cat, as surprised as McKay at this unexpected encounter, crouched low in the grass. It continued to stare directly at him, obviously uncomfortable at being caught in this embarrassing predicament. But before it could disappear into the darkened forest, McKay was able to capture the moment on film. In the instant it took for McKay to glance down to rewind the film, the cat had vanished. He searched the thick underbrush but saw only his dog, unaware of the close encounter with the mysterious cat. He moved cautiously to a road about thirty yards away. There, bounding from the brush, onto the road and back into the woods on the other side, was the cat. No time to take another picture. The lasting image in his mind, however will never be forgotten: "an olive tan, almost grey body, long thin flanks like a greyhound, the long, thick tail curling behind, the loose, graceful lope and the leap into the woods."[32]

But McKay was successful in capturing that one fleeting feline stare into the camera. Panther? Bobcat? Difficult to tell. But there is one person that needs no further convincing of what it was he shared a moment with among the thick-forested wilderness of the Adirondack Mountains. Those glaring almond eyes seared a lasting memory in the mind of Alex McKay.

The 1974 *Adirondack Life* article by McKay in which he described his encounter with a panther elicited considerable reader response, especially personal accounts of panthers seen in other remote mountainous regions of New York. Ed Blankman, a frequent contributor to *Adirondack Life*, submitted the most bloodcurdling tale, in the form of a newspaper clipping from the *St. Lawrence Plaindealer*, dated March 17, 1925.

"John K. Markill, of Norfolk, had a terrific hand to claw fight with a panther on his farm. The animal sprang at Markill and fastened his teeth in his neck, which was protected by a big fur collar, but his breath was nearly cut off. His big dog, a cross between a bull dog and mastiff, attacked the panther, fastening on his throat, relieving Markill, who secured a pitchfork. The family had been aroused and appeared with a lantern. The panther, with the dog at his throat, sprang for the person carrying the lantern but was hampered by the dog. Markill then ran the animal through with the pitchfork and with aid impaled him on the ground. Another member of the family had secured an axe and the animal was dispatched. He was seven feet five and a half inches long from tip to tip. He had been killing farmer's sheep for some time."[33]

These are only a few of the thousands of reported sightings of panthers throughout the eastern half of the continent; and by only a few of the many people who have spent countless hours, days, even years in the pursuit of this elusive great cat. There are many others. Through all the years of panther controversy, through all the pronouncements, accusations and denials, there have been those few who have made their mark—dedicated persons who have devoted large amounts of their professional and personal lives to searching for this elusive mystery cat of the east. They have, in their own way, legitimatized the issue. Through their determination, they have managed to bring the eastern panther out of the closet and into the public forum. They have given those countless persons who claim to have seen panthers reason to step forward and tell their story. They have added credibility to the issue through rigorous field investigation, patient pursuit of evasive clues and leads, logical and methodical deliberation, and reasoned inference. They have given hope that small numbers of eastern panthers somehow, in some way, have escaped persecution from their tormentors and returned to reclaim those secluded forested wilderness retreats of the Appalachians.

They are a varied and diverse lot. Some have been schooled in the discipline of scientific reason and study. Others have been driven by an innate passion to learn more of this mystery animal that has come to influence their lives in profound and personal ways. School teacher, wildlife researcher, merchant, retired policeman, historian—I have already mentioned a few, but there are others, such as Henry Wharton Shoemaker, one of the great storytellers of early American history, who spent his youth in the rolling hills and valleys of Pennsylvania, generally recognized as one of the last strongholds of the eastern panther. And it was here that Shoemaker learned through spoken tale of the frontier families before him, of their struggles in a harsh wilderness and of the wild beasts with which they lived and upon which they depended for their survival. We have heard from him earlier. In the 1880s and 1890s some of the last remaining reserves of remote wilderness in Pennsylvania had not yet fallen to the onslaught of the lumberman's axe, and it was here that a young Shoemaker became enthralled with stories of "Indians," wild animals, outlaws and ghosts.

A descendant of Dutch immigrants, he was born in New York City on February 24, 1882. His father was a hard-driving businessman who, following service in the Civil War, became head executive of the Cincinnati, Hamilton & Dayton Railway and organized the Hamilton National Bank of New York. The young Shoemaker entered college and later joined his father's railway business, all the while continuing his quest for legends and tales of the mountains so dear to his heart. He was a man of meticulous order, detail and persuasion. So much so, that his talents and worth were apparent to those of political pursuit, and he was convinced in 1904 to serve his country in the European diplomatic theater. He returned to the United States in 1905, and with his brother formed the banking firm of Shoemaker, Bates & Co. That company dissolved in 1911, after which he purchased the *Altoona Tribune*. His publishing acquisitions grew until he became one of the most prominent newspapermen in Pennsylvania. On his return from Europe, he had been appalled by the desolated landscape left by loggers.

"Miles of slashings, fire-swept wastes, emptiness, desolation, ruin met the eye on every side; the lumberman had done their work. Hoping against hope, the writer rode on, but only dreariness was his portion. Gone were the hemlocks, beeches, maples and pines; gone were the sweet singing birds, the balmy breezes, gone even were the lumbermen with their red and blue shirts, the lumber camps, the stemwinder log railways, gone was everything but ruin."[34] In those few short years the last virgin stands of Pennsylvania timber had been ravaged. He surveyed the devastation and was determined that he would record for posterity the fast-disappearing history of the Commonwealth State.

So Shoemaker entered into a personal mission of recording hundreds of stories, legends and songs of early Pennsylvania. His writings were prolific. He also served on numerous commissions, boards and societies devoted to preserving the natural and cultural history of Pennsylvania. Henry Shoemaker died in 1958 at the age of seventy-six. The sheer magnitude of his writings (he is credited with writing over 250 items, including books, pamphlets and articles) suggests that he may not have been as attentive to all the facts as perhaps he should have. And this has been one of his greatest criticisms, that he failed to let the facts get in the way of a good story. He made no apologies for this, however, noting that "doubtless some one could have done this work more thoroughly or better, it deserved more time, but the truth remains that no one else has tried."[35]

That puts it all into perspective rather nicely. If Shoemaker had not devoted his energies to recording stories of early Pennsylvania, they would have been lost forever.[36] In many of Shoemaker's stories are tales of panthers and the men who hunted them. In his classic book *Extinct Pennsylvania Animals*, Shoemaker discusses in great detail the "Pennsylvania Lion" and hunters such as Bill Long, "The King Hunter," and Aaron Hall, the "Lion Hunter of the Juniata."[37]

Ronald Lewis of Brandon, Vermont, has been collecting reports of panthers from northeastern United States over the past fifteen years—well over four hundred from Vermont alone. Lewis has formed an organization called the New England Panther Research Alliance. Similar to several other organizations, it is dedicated to the survival of panthers in the northeast. All sightings of panthers received by the Alliance are reviewed and given a grade based on various attributes of the report.

Perhaps the most active association involved with the collection and analysis of panther sightings in eastern North America is the Eastern Puma Research Network (EPRN). John and Linda Lutz live in Baltimore, Maryland, and are the founders and driving force behind this very proactive organization. The Eastern Puma Research Network publishes the *Eastern Puma Network News*, which the Lutzes claim to be "the first and foremost news dedicated solely to the species' survival."[38] Similar to other associations, this group of panther enthusiasts is "dedicated to the preservation and restoration of the species."

John Lutz first began to collect and study reports of panther sightings in 1963, while working as a Baltimore area radio news reporter. John shared his sightings with the Maryland State Police, many of whom were also interested in this mysterious cat, and directed their sightings to him. In 1983, at the urging of colleagues, the Lutzes officially formed the Eastern Puma Research

Network. They also extended their area of study to include all states east of the Mississippi River. From 1983 to 1995 the network received, evaluated and recorded more than 2,500 sightings in every eastern state except Rhode Island. The Lutzes have struggled to receive credibility from most state wildlife officials but have received considerable support from many other outdoor enthusiasts. "Today, the Eastern Puma Research Network consists of many professionals and lay persons, all with an intense interest in solving the 'extinct' eastern puma mystery. After 30 years of collecting and researching the cats' habits and charac-

Roger Cowburn of Galeton, Pennsylvania, is a member of the Eastern Puma Research Network, a group actively searching for evidence that eastern panthers are still found in parts of eastern North America.

(G. PARKER)

teristics and observing several in the wild, colleagues consider us to be an authority on the subject."[39] The Lutzes maintain a twenty-four-hour Cougar Clearinghouse Informational Hotline (410–254–2517) and are eager to hear from you and about panther sightings throughout the east.

There are many persons, such as Charles Humphreys, who believe that wild eastern panthers continue to be found in certain parts of North Carolina. Born in 1911 in the small town of Wilmington in southeastern North Carolina, Humphreys expressed an early interest in natural history and exploring the out-of-doors, especially the wilderness solitudes where he lived near the Great Green Swamp. There, during the middle and latter part of the 1920s, he met several people who lived on the edge of the swamp. He heard tales of hunting and of the wild creatures that lived in the deep recesses of that foreboding place. One of those mysterious animals was the "pant'a cat." It was mentioned only rarely and the young Humphreys paid it little attention. Following a career as a research chemist, he returned to his hometown in 1972 to pursue his passion for nature.

His interest in panthers began in 1980 when friends who were attending a mutual meeting reported seeing a panther on the road. A scientist by training, Humphreys began to systematically solicit and record panther sightings, analyzing sightings by region, time and other particulars within a forty-mile radius of Wilmington. From these data, Humphreys concluded in his book *Panthers of the Coastal Plain* that from 1952 to 1993 there had been at least 121 cats involved in 210 sightings. He reasons there may have been a minimum of 30 to 35 cats and a maximum of 164 cats in that 2,954-square-mile area per year. Since publishing his book in 1994, Humphreys has expanded his area of search and has accumulated over 350 sightings, half of which are of black panthers.[40]

Ted Reed was a businessman and spent much of his career as proprietor of a heating company, Ted Reed Thermal, Inc., in South Kingston, Rhode Island. Born and raised in the Hampshire and Berkshire hills of western Massachusetts, Reed was an avid hunter and fisherman familiar with the wildlife of New England. While on vacation during the Memorial Day weekend of 1974 in Digby County, Nova Scotia, Reed was astonished to see what he identified to be a very large and very wild panther. He knew that the eastern panther was believed to be extinct, so he reported his sighting to Nova Scotia wildlife officials. He was told that several other sightings of a panther in the same general area had been reported to them over the past few months. Returning to Rhode Island, Ted was intrigued by the possibility of wild eastern panthers remaining in parts of eastern North America, but his business left him little spare time to pursue that challenge further. In 1989 he sold his business and moved to Exeter, New Hampshire.

With this newfound independence, he engaged in his smoldering preoccupation with gusto. He soon read the research on panthers in eastern Canada by Bruce Wright and drove north to meet with this pioneer. He arrived at the University of New Brunswick in Fredericton only to learn that Bruce Wright had died many years earlier. However, Reed met with Bruce's widow, and she entrusted him with much of her late husband's research and correspondence on panthers accumulated over thirty years of study. On careful review of Wright's published books and unpublished notes and correspondence, Reed became more convinced that the evidence for the continued survival of the eastern panther was overwhelming. He was determined not to let the efforts of Bruce Wright be in vain. In September 1989, at his summer cottage in St. Andrews, Reed informally launched an organization known as FOTEP, Friends of the Eastern Panther. This initial meeting was followed by formal organization as a New Hampshire charitable trust in February 1990. Membership in FOTEP grew from a handful to several hundred, and it now has membership from coast to coast and border to border. The initial newsletter of FOTEP contained a statement of objectives, several of which were the following: "The assembly of sufficient, clear evidence to convince the state and provincial wildlife professionals in the Northeast that the Eastern Panther does in fact exist as a viable and stable population, and the reasonable preservation and enhancement of existing habitat, culminating with the establishment of the Bruce S. Wright International Range in New Brunswick and Maine."[41]

There are others who deserve recognition for their efforts in searching for evidence of eastern panthers, among them Bruce Johnson and Rudy Stocek of New Brunswick, Susan Morse of Vermont, Roger Cowburn of Pennsylvania and Jay Tischendorf of Fort Collins, Colorado. We can only hope that their efforts will contribute to the solving of this intriguing mystery of the eastern panther.

How do we account for so many people throughout the east seeing what they think are panthers? Well, it is certain that some of them do see panthers, or animals that are similar to the native eastern panther. Take for example this documented account of the recent slaying of a large, long-tailed tawny cat in Quebec, a province where the previous specimen of eastern panther was reported over 130 years ago! On May 27, 1992, near Abitibi Lake, very close to the Ontario border and some 350 miles northwest of Montreal, a 90-pound male panther was shot. This truly impressive and handsome cat, which measured 7½ feet from tip to tip, was submitted to the Quebec Wildlife Division, where it was skinned, and the carcass was sent to the Canadian Museum of Nature in Ottawa for further study—proof positive of a remnant population of eastern panther in Quebec, or at least that is what the press clippings said. But the curator of mammals at the museum, as is the habit of those trained to question such unnatural events, wasn't convinced. Why was this panther so far north? Surely, if breeding panthers are found in Quebec, they would have been recovered further to the south where the weather is less harsh and deer are more abundant.

So a sliver of flesh from the carcass was sent to Melannie Culvar, a researcher at the National Cancer Institute in Frederick, Maryland. Ms. Culvar was studying the similarities among panthers, cougars and pumas throughout their ranges in North, Central and South America. She was doing this through the advanced technique of genetic fingerprinting. Animals of similar heritage would have the closest genetic match, those the most distant would show the weakest match, and so forth. The results were startling. The closest genetic match to the panther killed in Quebec was genetic material from pumas in Chile, South America! This animal must have been brought to this northern Quebec region from South America. How, and by whom, remains a mystery. If nothing else, this incident serves as a caution to those who hastily choose to proclaim the smallest shred of circumstantial evidence, let alone a carcass, as proof that eastern panthers continue to breed successfully throughout much of the Appalachians. Discretion and prudence are certainly recommended.

Hundreds of reports of panther sightings are meticulously filed by wildlife agencies, and private organizations, in most states and provinces. Although most are legitimate, a few have turned out to be hoaxes. One of the most interesting took place at Richwood, West Virginia, in the fall of 1957. What began as an innocent prank, however, soon got out of hand. Cal Price, an elderly newspaper editor and conservationist, believed that panthers still roamed the nearby mountains, and he had proclaimed his beliefs publicly for years. An anonymous "friend" decided to bring a cougar from Mexico and shoot it near Richwood, giving the old gentleman final vindication that he had been right all those years. The cougar was duly ordered and delivered, during which time Mr. Price passed away. Too late now to return the cougar, the prank proceeded, with a twist. The plan now called for a local sportsman to parade into town with the caged cougar in tow, proclaiming that he had trapped the animal in the nearby hills. Two local newspaper publishers, also in on the hoax, were to take photos and run the story in their papers.

All proceeded to plan, and the local volunteer fire department, a non-profit organization, even raised funds by requesting a twenty-five-cent donation to see the caged beast. But upon further questioning, the story began to fall apart, and tempers began to flare among the misled and now quite irritated townsfolk. But all seems to have been forgiven and, as a consolation of sorts, the Richwood fire department was nominally richer.[42]

There have also been illegal attempts to introduce western cougars into eastern panther range, such as this rather bizarre tale from Newfoundland. The following is a fragmented account of that event, based on scattered facts I was able to bring together from a number of reliable sources. It illustrates the countless ways by which panthers, or cougars, might by chance be seen by unsuspecting citizens of honest intent.

As Jack London so eloquently chronicled in his tales from the Yukon during the years of gold rush, there are indeed strange things done under the midnight sun. Perhaps one of the strangest, and certainly one of the most relevant to our search, was one which spanned the continent, from the western United States to eastern Canada, some forty years ago. It involved money, influence, high drama, intrigue and, of course, cougars. I call it the "Newfoundland Cougar Caper." As the whole affair was a little shady at best, there was a brush with the law, and many of those involved are no longer with us, names have been omitted.

In the 1950s there were, as there are today, people of considerable wealth and political influence and power living and doing business in the northeastern United States. Perhaps nowhere was this more obvious than in the industrial and financial establishment centered in New York City. Here, during the early years of industrial expansion, men of great vision and considerable good fortune accumulated prodigious wealth. The children of these industrialists were left substantial inheritances, a gift of birth which allowed them to indulge in a lifestyle of tending to family business, building political clout, indulging in many of life's pleasures and, frequently, behaving quite eccentrically. We all know of, or have read about, some of these jet-setters and highrollers, and our story begins with one of those families.

This family company was centered in New York and presided over by one of two brothers, both of whom combined a flair for entrepreneurship and high society with a love for the out-of-doors and adventure. Their passion for adventure led them, and other friends of prominence, on safaris around the world, many using their own company plane. Hunting and fishing trips to remote parts of Canada were among their excursions, and it was on one of these fishing trips to western Newfoundland, nestled among the mountains near Gros Morne National Park, that one of the brothers was struck with an ingenious idea. Tossed about among the group before the evening fire, it generated considerable discussion and, in principle, received general endorsement.

Here, among the remote mountains and wilderness forests of Canada's most eastern province were large herds of caribou. Moose brought to the island from New Brunswick fifty years earlier had exploded in number and were common throughout that vast interior of spruce-fir forests and lakes, streams and bogs. On their global safaris, these men had seen great herds of antelope and wildebeest on the African plains, and the lions, leopards and wild dogs that fed on them. But here, in the northwoods of Newfoundland, where caribou and moose were abundant, there was no natural predator. The timber wolf, the only large canine predator once common on the island, and the natural predator of caribou and moose in most northern regions, was now absent, a casualty of human persecution. These wild animals, they reasoned, required a predator other than man to maintain healthy populations by weeding out the old and the sick, like in Africa. The concept that predators contribute to viable and healthy populations, although not new, was certainly valid, but we can only imagine the ebb and flow of discussion in that remote fishing camp on Newfoundland so many years ago. How could these men of influence and wealth contribute to the health and natural state of these wild northern populations of moose and caribou? The rugged nature of this mountainous terrain was not dissimilar to parts of the Rocky Mountains of the western United States, an area they were also quite familiar with from earlier excursions. And they were familiar with the most proficient large predator in those mountains, the western cougar, or mountain lion. Here was a predator, they thought, that could survive in this rugged forested wilderness, where moose and caribou would supply an abundant and reliable source of food. And the caribou and moose populations would benefit, they also believed, from a natural and healthy culling.

Well, at least it sounded reasonable to these urban adventurers. Remember, this was the late 1950s, before most provinces and many states had developed wildlife research and management bureaucracies, before rare and endangered species legislation and before the criminal element was heavily involved in international transport of wildlife. The private introduction of a non-indigenous species of wildlife to Newfoundland, without the sanction of the provincial government, however, was certainly illegal and a matter of no small significance, certainly understood by our company of adventurers. But this was only a minor hindrance to these people of influence, men who had, most likely, bent certain rules before in their ambitious pursuits. So the idea was discussed and agreed upon, that cougars would be brought to this island under the banner of conservation, for the long-term benefit of moose, caribou and Newfoundlanders.

We can only imagine the planning which went into this scheme once the party returned to New York. What we do know is that in the spring of 1960, the company plane flew to Idaho and there, with the help of persons unknown, succeeded in the capture of one male and two female mountain lions. The party, with cougars in tow, then flew across the continent to Newfoundland, returning to the isolated camp where the idea had been endorsed so enthusiastically the previous year. The cougars, they reasoned, might be confused and have difficulty adapting when first released in these strange lands amongst strange prey. Deer, the preferred food of cougars, were absent here on Newfoundland (thank goodness they didn't introduce deer to the island!) and it would require improvisation if the cougars were to survive on caribou and moose. So the party shot a moose near camp to feed the cats after the plane had departed. Well, shooting moose in the spring in Newfoundland was definitely illegal, and somehow word of this reached the provincial game warden's office before the party had left the island. Word has it that they were apprehended at Gander airport. A search of provincial files failed to uncover documentation of this apprehension; either charges were never laid or charges were laid and subsequently dismissed. What we do know, from several eyewitness accounts, is that three western cougars were released. The fact that two were females did provide for potential population growth. It is interesting that in the 1980s there were several reports of cougars from within Gros Morne National Park and from communities not far from the source of release. Although far to the east of the apparent source, the following is an example of one such report.

"In July of 1986 Fred Ploughman and Frank Lander, both from Port Rexton, were passing by the community pasture on the highway between Port Rexton and Melrose in Trinity Bay. A passing car struck the head of an animal immediately in front of them as the animal was climbing up a steep bank and just coming out on to the road. The car which hit the creature continued driving but Fred Ploughman, a keen naturalist and now a tour guide with Wildland Tours, pulled over to examine the large cat-like animal. Ploughman originally thought that a large lynx had been struck but when he examined the animal he noted that it was much larger than a lynx and possessed a long tail. He estimates that the animal weighed 35-40 kilograms (75-90 pounds) with the tail measuring close to a meter (3 feet) in length.

"The two gentlemen, who were in dress clothes, were on their way to a dance. The animal was clearly dead with blood coming from the ears, nose, and mouth. The two men pulled the heavy animal off the road and back down the steep bank by the tail. The blood and their dress clothing discouraged them from lifting the animal into the car trunk, so they left it below the bank and marked the site on the road with rocks. They then proceeded on to the dance.

"That night, following the dance, the two men again stopped at the site of the incident, but other than bloodstains there was no sign of the animal. The incident was reported to the nearest Wildlife Division office, but there was no investigation. No fur samples were collected. To date there have been no reports of anybody else finding or hearing about the animal."[43]

Did one or more of these western cougars survive all the years following release, or did one or both of the females successfully mate with the lone male and establish a viable breeding population of Idaho cougars on Newfoundland? Unless further sightings are reported, or a cougar is actually killed and examined, we may never know the fate of these three players in the Newfoundland Cougar Caper.

But the debate continues. What is it that people are seeing, these mysterious long-tailed cats which are unexpectedly and ever more frequently entering peoples' lives only to vanish, leaving them puzzled, perplexed and frustrated by bureaucratic indifference?

CHAPTER SEVEN

The Great Debate

TODAY, most extreme advocates of environmental rights are also self-professed "non-consumptive users of wildlife," a polite way of saying "non-hunter." This was not always the case. In fact, many early naturalists and conservationists were avid consumptive users of wildlife, and hunting and fishing played important roles in their lives. The American President Theodore Roosevelt did much to promote the importance of conservation in early America, a time when the nation was losing many species of wildlife and wilderness areas were being ravaged. But "Teddy" Roosevelt was also one of the most notorious hunters of big game, and many a trophy was bagged by this statesman, from one corner of the earth to the other. Another naturalist with a passion for hunting was also one of the most accomplished and acclaimed wildlife artists of the nineteenth century, John James Audubon. In fact, Audubon was so respected for his artistic contributions to our understanding and appreciation of a great variety of animal and bird species that one of the greatest conservation institutions was named after him—the National Audubon Society.

Audubon arrived from France at his father's country estate in Pennsylvania in 1803 at the age of eighteen. It is said he was brought there to avoid the draft into Napoleon's army. A failure at business, due most likely to his preoccupation with the natural world around him, he and his family moved to New Orleans, where Audubon painted and taught while his wife worked as a governess and teacher. A prolific painter, Audubon amassed a sizeable portfolio of North American birds and mammals and he traveled to Europe to pursue the possibility of publication. This effort produced what has become known as one of the earliest and best-known portfolios of North American bird pictures.

On his return to the United States, Audubon traveled the wilds of the Missouri River, collecting specimens and painting pictures of mammals, or quadrupeds, as he called them. His second portfolio on the mammals was completed by 1848, three years before he died at the age of sixty–five. What is less known of this early American painter was his fondness for hunting, a passion which earned him a reputation as a naturalist with a gun. Among his many hunting excursions was the following encounter with a panther, sometime in the late 1820s, among the swamps and bayous in Choctaw territory in the state of Mississippi:

"In the course of one of my rambles, I chanced to meet with a squatter's cabin on the banks of the Cold Water River. In the owner of this hut, like most of those adventurous settlers in the uncultivated tracts of our frontier districts, I found a person well versed in the chase, and acquainted with the habits of some of the larger species of quadrupeds and birds. As he who is desirous of instruction ought not to disdain listening to anyone who has knowledge to communicate, however humble may be his lot, or however limited his talents, I entered the squatter's cabin, and immediately opened a conversation with him respecting the situation of the swamp, and its natural productions. He told me he thought it the very place I ought to visit, spoke of the game which it contained, and pointed to some Bear and Deer skins, adding that the individuals to which they had belonged formed but a small portion of the number of those animals which he had shot within it. My heart swelled with delight, and on asking if he would accompany me through the great morass, and allow me to become an inmate of his humble but hospitable mansion, I was gratified to find that he cordially assented to all my proposals. So I immediately unstrapped my drawing materials, laid up my gun, and sat down to partake of the homely but wholesome fare intended for the supper of the squatter, his wife, and his two sons.

"The quietness of the evening seemed in perfect accordance with the gentle demeanor of the family. The wife and children, I more than once thought, seemed to look upon me as a strange sort of person, going about, as I told them I was, in search of birds and plants; and were I here to relate the many questions which they put to me in return for those I addressed to them, the catalogue would occupy several pages. The husband, a native of Connecticut, had heard of the existence of such men as myself, both in our own country and abroad, and seemed greatly pleased to have me under his roof. Supper over, I asked my kind host what had induced him to remove to this wild and solitary spot. 'The people are growing too numerous now to thrive in New England,' was his answer. I thought of the state of some parts of Europe, and calculating the denseness of their population compared with that of New England, exclaimed to myself, 'How much more difficult must it be for men to thrive in those populous countries!' The conversation then changed, and the squatter, his sons and myself, spoke of hunting and fishing until at length, tired, we laid ourselves down on pallets of Bear skins, and reposed in peace on the floor of the only apartment of which the hut consisted.

"Day dawned, and the squatter's call to his hogs, which, being almost in a wild state, were suffered to seek the greater portion of their food in the woods, awakened me. Being ready dressed I was not long in joining him. The hogs and their young came grunting at the well-known call of their owner, who threw them a few ears of corn, and counted them, but told me that for some weeks their number had been greatly diminished by the ravages committed upon them by a large Panther, by which name the Cougar is designated in America, and that the ravenous animal did not content himself with the flesh of his pigs, but now and then carried off one of his calves, notwithstanding the many attempts he had made to shoot it. The Painter, as he sometimes called it, had on several occasions robbed him of a dead Deer; and to these exploits the squatter added several remarkable feats of audacity which it had performed, to give me an idea of the formidable character of the beast. Delighted by his description, I offered to assist him in destroying the enemy, at which he was highly pleased, but assured me that unless some of his neighbors should join us with their dogs and his own, the attempt would prove fruitless. Soon after, mounting a horse, he went off to his neighbors, several of whom lived at a distance of some miles, and appointed a day of meeting.

"The hunters, accordingly, made their appearance, one fine morning, at the door of the cabin, just as the sun was emerging from beneath the horizon. They were five in number, and fully equipped for the chase, being mounted on horses which in some parts of Europe might appear sorry nags, but which in strength, speed, and bottom, are better fitted for pursuing a Cougar or a Bear through woods and morasses than any in that country. A pack of large, ugly curs were already engaged in making acquaintance with those of the squatter. He and myself mounted his two best horses, whilst his sons were bestriding others of inferior quality.

"Few words were uttered by the party until we had reached the edge of the swamp, where it was agreed that all should disperse and seek for the fresh track of the Painter, it being previously settled that the discoverer should blow his horn, and remain on the spot, until the rest should join him. In less than an hour, the sound of the horn was clearly heard, and, sticking close to the squatter, off we went through the thick woods, guided by the now and then repeated call of the distant huntsmen. We soon reached the spot, and in a short time the rest of the party came up. The best dog was sent forward to track the Cougar, and in a few moments the whole pack were observed diligently trailing, and bearing in their course for the interior of the Swamp. The rifles were immediately put in trim, and the party followed the dogs, at separate distances, but in sight of each other, determined to shoot at no other game than the Panther.

"The dogs soon began to mouth, and suddenly quickened their pace. My companion concluded that the beast was on the ground, and putting our horses to a gentle gallop, we followed the curs, guided by their voices. The noise of the dogs increased, when, all of a sudden their mode of barking became altered, and the squatter, urging me to push on, told me that the beast was treed, by which he meant that it had got upon some low branch of a large tree to rest for a few minutes, and that should we not succeed in shooting him when thus situated, we might expect a long chase of it. As we approached the spot, we all by degrees united into a body, but on seeing the dogs at the foot of a large tree, separated again, and galloped off to surround it.

"Each hunter now moved with caution, holding his gun ready, and allowing the bridle to dangle on the neck of his horse, as it advanced slowly towards the dogs. A shot from one of the party was heard, on which the Cougar was seen to leap to the ground, and bound off with such velocity as to show that he was very unwilling to stand our fire longer. The dogs set off in pursuit with great eagerness and a deafening cry. The hunter who had fired came up and said that his ball had hit the monster, and had probably broken one of his fore–legs near the shoulder, the only place at which he could aim. A slight trail of blood was discovered on the ground, but the curs proceeded at such a rate that we merely noticed this, and put the spurs to our horses, which galloped on towards the center of the Swamp. One bayou was crossed, then another still larger and more muddy; but the dogs were brushing forward, and as the horses began to pant at a furious rate, we judged it expedient to leave them and advance on foot. These determined hunters knew that the Cougar being wounded, would shortly ascend another tree, where in all probability he would remain for a considerable time, and that it would be easy to follow the tracks of the dogs. We dismounted, took off the saddles and bridles, set the bells attached to the horses' necks at liberty to jingle, hoppled the animals, and left them to shift for themselves.

"Now, kind reader, follow the group marching through the swamp, crossing muddy pools, and making the best of their way over fallen trees and amongst the tangled rushes that now and then covered acres of ground. If you are a hunter yourself, all this will appear nothing to you; but if crowded assemblies of 'beauty and fashion,' or the quiet enjoyment of your 'pleasure grounds' alone delight you, I must mend my pen before I attempt to give you an idea of the pleasure felt on such an expedition.

"After marching for a couple of hours, we again heard the dogs. Each of us pressed forward, elated at the thought of terminating the career of the Cougar. Some of the dogs were heard whining, although the greater number barked vehemently. We felt assured that the Cougar was treed, and that he would rest for some time to recover from his fatigue. As we came up to the dogs, we discovered the ferocious animal lying across a large branch, close to the trunk of a cottonwood tree. His broad breast lay towards us; his eyes were at one time bent on us and again on the dogs beneath and around him; one of his fore-legs hung loosely by his side, and he lay crouched, with his ears lowered close to his head, as if he thought he might remain undiscovered. Three balls were fired at him, at a given signal, on which he sprang a few feet from the branch, and tumbled headlong to the ground. Attacked on all sides by the enraged curs, the infuriated Cougar fought with desperate valor; but the squatter, advancing in front of the party, and almost in the midst of the dogs, shot him immediately behind and beneath the left shoulder. The

Cougar writhed for a moment in agony, and in another lay dead.

"The sun was now sinking in the west. Two of the hunters separated from the rest to procure venison, whilst the squatter's sons were ordered to make the best of their way home, to be ready to feed the hogs in the morning. The rest of the party agreed to camp on the spot. The Cougar was despoiled of its skin, and its carcass left to the hungry dogs. Whilst engaged in preparing our camp, we heard the report of a gun, and soon after one of our hunters returned with a small Deer. A fire was lighted, and each hunter displayed his pone of bread, along with a flask of whiskey. The deer was skinned in a trice, and slices placed on sticks before the fire. These materials afforded us an excellent meal, and as the night grew darker, stories and songs went round, until my companions, fatigued, laid themselves down, close under the smoke of the fire, and soon fell asleep.

"I walked for some minutes around the camp, to contemplate the beauties of that nature from which I have certainly derived my greatest pleasures. I thought of the occurrences of the day, and glancing my eye around, remarked the singular effects produced by the phosphorescent qualities of the large decayed trunks which lay in all directions around me. How easy, I thought, would it be for the confused and agitated mind of a person in a swamp like this to imagine in each of these luminous masses some wondrous and fearful being, the very sight of which might make the hair stand erect on his head. The thought of myself being placed in such a predicament burst over my mind, and I hastened to join my companions, beside whom I laid me down and slept, assured that no enemy could approach us without first rousing the dogs, which were growling in fierce dispute over the remains of the Cougar.

"At daybreak we left our camp, the squatter bearing on his shoulder the skin of the late destroyer of his stock, and retraced our steps until we found our horses, which had not strayed far from the place where we had left them. These we soon saddled, and jogging along, in a direct course, guided by the sun, congratulating each other in the destruction of so formidable a neighbor as the Panther had been, we soon arrived at my host's cabin. The five neighbors partook of such refreshment as the house could afford, and dispersing, returned to their homes, leaving me to follow my favorite pursuits."[1]

The sport of hunting was well developed and accepted by most levels of European and American society in the nineteenth century. Remember, there were few other outlets for those who enjoyed the pleasures of the out-of-doors in that early and very different era. There were no national parks to provide the luxuries and amenities demanded by today's "urban outdoorspersons" as they stroll the well-groomed hiking paths and breathe in the solitudes of nature, no ski slopes within commuting distance of office and home for holiday "wilderness" retreats. In an earlier era, retreats to the wilderness were to hunting and fishing camps and lodges. Although the pursuit of game was ostensibly the reason for being there, their appreciation of nature was probably no less than ours. What they lacked was an appreciation of the delicate balance of nature through which they trod, an appreciation that was to develop later. Although many of us now profess to a new environmental enlightenment, this in no way justifies unwarranted criticism of an earlier society. We would do well to heed the expression "Never judge a man until you walk a mile in his shoes."

So the evidence appears strong that the last of the race of eastern panthers fell to the hunter's gun a century or so ago. It appears equally certain that, in scattered parts of the Appalachians, panthers are again with us today. The evidence from such widespread locations as New York, Vermont, Pennsylvania, New Brunswick and Quebec, where panthers have been shot, or tracks and hairs identified, is irrefutable. If we accept the previous two assumptions, then it is clear that those untethered panthers with us today are not descendants of original eastern stock. Many of us would like to think differently, but there comes a time to acknowledge and accept the statistical improbability of an event. But whether you choose to believe that the panthers which now appear to occupy parts of eastern North America are of original eastern bloodline, or choose not to, does it really matter? Some will quickly point to the real or potential threat to these animals if they are not recognized as true "endangered" eastern panthers. Western cougars, or South American pumas, or whatever they might be, do not receive the benefit of protection afforded by the U.S. federal endangered species legislation, but most states have their own endangered species legislation and/or wildlife laws that protect panthers by simply not permitting the killing or trapping of same. Personally, I do not consider this potential loophole a threat of any great significance. The presence of panthers in the east, when accepted and officially acknowledged, such as in New Brunswick and Vermont, will quickly lead to appropriate amendments to existing laws and regulations, if such are not already in place.

But does it really matter if DNA analysis of material from panthers recently killed in the east establishes that they, or their parents, came from the west, the south or even another continent? Remember, the subspecific designation of the eastern panther was proposed a half a century ago and was based on very few specimens. There has been a recent flurry of interest to change the present classification system of *Felis concolor*. Most people recognize that there are too many subspecies based on too few distinct characteristics. They also recognize that a large predator like the panther, which can travel hundreds of kilometers, would certainly ensure dispersion of genetic material far and wide. There may be small regional variations, perhaps, which reflect adaptations to specific habitats and climates, but there are no obvious contrasts in physical characteristics that justifies the proliferation of subspecies we have now. Most are based on statistically significant differences in certain skull measurements, differences certainly not obvious to most people. The Florida panther was once common throughout much of the Gulf States. This southern panther, now restricted to a small part of Florida, would have interbred with cougars to the west and eastern panthers to the north. There would have been no clear line somewhere north of which was the distinct eastern race and south of which was the equally distinct Florida race. Differences would have been subtle or non-existent throughout the broad zone of frequent interbreeding. It was really one and the same animal, one with perhaps small modifications in the south for survival in the tropics, and in the north for survival in the cold and snow of a New England winter. Slightly smaller feet here, longer fur there, but nothing dramatic and obvious which would set one immediately apart from the other. Physical modifications to address different environmental stresses only, probably not sufficient to justify subspecific status.

The point is a panther is a cougar is a puma is a mountain lion. All are basically one and the same animal, and to quibble about the distinctiveness of one from the other becomes irrelevant and meaningless. Most important is that panthers, for all intents and purposes, similar to the ones first spotted by early European explorers and colonists several hundred years ago, are evidently with us again. Was the panther killed in Maine in 1938 and brought to the University of New Brunswick by Bruce Wright really an eastern panther? The panther shot in Quebec in 1992 was apparently imported from Chile. Why should we think that the 1938 specimen was any more likely to be of the eastern race? There were many traveling wildlife shows on the road and rail at that time, and with virtually no control over interstate or international transport of wildlife, many would have had cougars, pumas and Florida panthers. Certainly there would have been occasional opportunities for such captive animals to escape, or to be left behind intentionally. Whether or not this is the source of many early panther reports is not all that important, but we should recognize that it is a very real possibility.

As we have seen in this review, most state and provincial wildlife agencies agree that there is every likelihood that a few panthers may very well be roaming the wilds of their respective jurisdictions. But most are equally certain that these are escaped or released captive panthers, brought here from Florida, the western United States or Central and South America. Any of these cats can be readily purchased through the pet trade, especially from the state of Florida (panthers legally purchased in Florida as pets would be of imported stock), and there are few enforceable restrictions on their transport throughout the United States. Although some states do require a specific permit for their ownership, and permits are only issued for good reason (e.g. to zoos and wildlife parks, or for research purposes), the precise number of "panthers" kept illegally in eastern United States is unknown. But this reservoir of large cats certainly is a potential source for panther sightings. A number of escaped or released captive panthers have been shot or captured in recent years. Young and cuddly panther kittens often become large and unmanageable, and occasionally, if not properly cared for, dangerous. We can only imagine how many of these "pets" have been released back into the wilds of Massachusetts, New York or other eastern states. Here are a few examples.

In the early 1980s the Law Enforcement Division of the Vermont Department of Fish and Wildlife confiscated a "mountain lion" from a biker gang at a state campground. The cat had attacked and injured a three-year-old girl. The bikers were glad to turn the cat over to the authorities.[2] Although regulations restricting ownership of non-indigenous wildlife are quite stringent in Massachusetts, an illegally possessed panther was recently seized from a person walking it on a leash, while another, purchased in Florida, was removed from a chicken (-less) coop on Cape Cod.[3] A panther, believed to have been an escaped captive, was shot in the backyard of a home in Anderson County, South Carolina in the early 1990s.[4] General possession of panthers was made illegal in Connecticut in 1983. Shortly thereafter, two illegally held immature panthers were confiscated, and a non–resident had a leashed panther which escaped (with leash) but was shortly recaptured.[5] In Rhode Island, a juvenile panther was found by authorities tied to a light pole at a highway rest area in Norton.[6] Two western mountain lions recently escaped from an animal staging facility for a small zoo in Virginia, but only one was recovered.[7] Two western cougars recently released in Florida by the Florida Game and Freshwater Fish Commission were shot by bowhunters in Georgia.[8] Three panthers have been recovered in North Carolina in the past decade. Two were shot in Tyrrell County in the eastern part of the state. Both had been lip-tattooed indicating former captivity. A third was captured alive near a home in Rutherford County, near the border with South Carolina. It was a young animal weighing only seven pounds. It was taken to the state zoo, where it was found to be quite tame, and it would purr when petted. It died despite efforts to save its life.[9]

But back to the controversy of panther sightings. The argument, it seems, is over the origin of these panthers, and over the perceived lack of interest by wildlife agencies towards these occasional "eastern panthers." But let's be open and objective about this. Where there are established viable populations of breeding panthers or cougars, such as in Florida and in the west, it is not extremely difficult to find their sign, or, if the effort is mounted, to "tree" one with the use of cat hounds. Even in Florida, where there may be fewer than fifty panthers, one or more of these animals are killed each year on the highways, shot by hunters or in some fashion fall into the hands of state wildlife officials. Although several have been shot and captured by hunters and wildlife personnel in states north of Florida, most if not all are believed to have been formerly captive, as revealed by clipped claws, lip tattoos, neck wear from collars, an unnatural lack of fear towards humans, and, more recently, DNA fingerprinting.

The great American lion has adapted to survival in the harshest of climates: the swamps of southern Florida, the slopes of the Andes and Rocky mountains, parched western badlands, temperate rain forests and the sub-boreal spruce-fir forests. There is every reason to believe that mountain lions brought into the east and released could survive and breed successfully. This may have happened in Newfoundland. Throughout much of the northeast we have large areas of suitable forested habitat and abundant supplies of white-tailed deer, the panther's preferred food. And I do not necessarily subscribe to the concern expressed by some that there are too many roads and too little wilderness left for panthers in the east. The panther, like many predators, is capable of adapting to specific environmental conditions. Yes, I initially blamed its demise on its inability to be ecologically flexible and to adapt and cope with changing conditions in the eighteenth and nineteenth centuries. But times and human attitudes have changed. We recognize and respect the growing public intolerance of widespread deforestation—deforestation in the sense of near absolute, not in today's sense of sustainable forest management. Not that I condone all current forest-management practices, but these are more environmentally considerate than the uninformed highgrading forestry operations which devastated much of the Appalachians 150 years ago. Vancouver Island may support the highest density of mountain lions in North America, but clearcut forestry operations have continued there for years.

No, the main threat to the mountain lion, wherever it is found, is the trap, the gun and the dog. An exception may be in Florida where large tracts of remaining wilderness, and panther habitat, are being lost to urban and agricultural sprawl. In California, a moratorium on hunting has seen a significant increase in mountain lions there, and an increase in the number of lion-human encounters. If not shot, trapped and pursued on sight, I really question the often-repeated assumption that mountain lions require wilderness sanctuaries. Once, when all hands were raised against them, they needed somewhere to hide. But today, when they receive the benefit of conservative hunting regulations, and total moratoriums, that need is not nearly so great.

A few panthers have been killed in the east over the past fifty years, but no more than a handful—hardly a sufficient number to threaten the survival of a viable and healthy population. Farmland, second-growth forests and recent cuttings are all prime white-tailed deer habitat. The Waasis panther of New Brunswick, if it was a panther, was crossing a back field only several hundred yards from occupied dwellings and only a few miles from the city of Fredericton, the capital of New Brunswick. It did not race off in fear when approached; it appeared to be accustomed to the presence of humans. The track followed through the snow in New Brunswick by Rod Cumberland was not in the deepest and most secluded wilderness retreat of the province. Quite to the contrary. The track, positively identified as that of a panther from hairs in a scat, was on industrial timberlands intensively managed for wood fiber. Much of the immediate area had been harvested and replanted in softwood seedlings. In the scat was a large amount of snowshoe hare. The panther does kill deer, but it also kills other prey. Early naturalists commented on the dependency of eastern panthers on porcupines. A cougar killed in eastern Manitoba a few years ago, not far from the Ontario border, had porcupine quills in its mouth. Predation by panthers on deer usually occurs in the winter, the time of year when coyotes in the northeast also prey most heavily on deer. When snows get deep and times get tough, the panther, like the coyote, turns to the most readily available food.

What about black panthers? Unless people are seeing the occasional escaped or released black (melanistic) leopard or jaguar, I think they are mistaken. They may have seen a panther, but it appeared dark due to poor lighting or because the animal was wet. As we have heard from early Appalachian hunters, in winter, eastern panthers took on the darker color of the deer. The rufous red of summer changed to a darker grey or dusky color. Most of us have seen how dark a deer can appear, especially in the fall or winter when it is raining, or when the animal is concealed in the shadows of the darkened forest.

The suggestion has been made that melanistic leopards (black panthers) were brought to North America during the early period of slave importation. Their use, we can only assume, was to strike fear in the hearts of the human cargos. Such animals, the theory goes, were subsequently released by their captors once safely on the shores of North America. Another theory put forth suggests that black panthers were imported and kept as pets and mascots by some members of the Black Panther movement, a radical black organization popular in the 1960s. But as many as one-quarter of all panther sightings throughout the east are black, including Ontario and the Maritime provinces of Canada. It hardly seems probable that black panthers were released over the length and breadth of the Appalachians. No, most black panther sightings are most likely misidentified black bears, fishers, Labrador dogs, otters or very large house cats, just as most sightings of tawny panthers are misidentified bobcat, housecats, coyotes and dogs. If all reported sightings were of real panthers, the eastern forests might indeed be a dangerous place to spend your vacation. More of us would have concern for our safety and, like the people of Dryman's Mountain in 1884, might not let our children go in the woods alone or after dark. Some reports of panthers do appear to be authentic; the exact proportion, of course, is unknown. We do know that in Florida, where the distribution of panthers is quite limited but fairly well defined, a statewide search for sightings to confirm range limits produced a flood of sightings throughout the state, so much so that the value of the program was seriously questioned, and it was eventually discontinued.

I was professionally involved in the collection of panther sightings in the Maritime provinces of Canada from 1977 through 1984, and I have maintained a personal interest in the program since then. During that time, hundreds of panther sightings were received and the maps of Nova Scotia and New Brunswick became literally cluttered with pins showing individual sightings. Recent panther sightings from throughout the Maritime provinces have been skillfully summarized by Rudy Stocek of the Maritime Forest Ranger School in Fredericton.[10] My colleagues and I investigated many of the more promising reports, but none were ever confirmed as panther. Most were coyote or dog. But many firsthand accounts could not be discounted; the descriptions and the observers were too credible. People were seeing something. Now, as to confirmation of panther tracks and hair in Vermont and New Brunswick, were they eastern panther? We just don't know. And I, for one, don't really find that a problem. The fact that we may once again share the Appalachians with Klandagi, Lord of the Forest, is sufficient reason to rejoice. Now we must hope that these few can propagate and reoccupy old haunts.

In June 1994 the first Eastern Cougar Conference was held at Gannon University, Erie, Pennsylvania. This inaugural meeting of persons interested in the eastern cougar, or panther, developed through the combined efforts of many, but especially due to the dedication and determination of Jay Tischendorf, John Lutz and Ted Reed. We met John and Ted earlier. Jay Tischendorf lives in Colorado and has studied cougars in the western United States. He also has an interest in the mystery of the eastern panther. In 1992 he joined Ted Reed in organizing a series of panther tracking workshops from New Brunswick to Massachusetts, and in 1992 again joined Ted in a winter search for panthers in New Brunswick. Although that search proved unsuccessful, he and others involved in the project feel that their efforts helped to convince many people they met on the trip of the possible continued presence of panthers in the province.

The purpose of the Erie conference was to develop an open dialogue among the participants, both believers and non-believers, and through such positive interchange, to encourage state and federal agencies to become more proactive in dealing with the issue. The conference organizers wished to see both levels of American government assume the lead role in learning more about an animal which is recognized by the United States Fish and Wildlife Service as an endangered species. Although I had originally planned to attend the conference, unforeseen work-related responsibilities forced a last-minute cancellation. But I did receive a copy of the proceedings and suggest that anyone interested in eastern panthers should do likewise.[11]

What more should wildlife agencies be doing? To be honest, aside from complete protection, and assigning any and all unrestrained members of *Felis concolor* in any eastern state or province absolute endangered status, probably little else. To set aside large tracts of wilderness for the sole purpose of preserving potential panther habitat hardly seems politically or ecologically prudent. The concept of preserving wilderness is certainly valid, but there are many reasons for doing so other than saving panther habitat. There is every likelihood that, if unrestrained panthers are as common as sightings would suggest, even conservatively speaking, they are doing quite nicely just as things are.

But Jay Tischendorf and others feel more strongly. They do not believe that federal, state and provincial governments are fulfilling their threatened and endangered species obligations. They propose that government agencies should be more active in determining whether there are viable populations of panthers breeding in eastern North America. And if not, are there ecological reasons why panthers, or their western cousins, cannot be re-established in parts of the Appalachians? Also, why are there so few laws regulating the ownership and trade of non-indigenous wildlife throughout the east, especially Florida panthers and cougars from western states? Good questions.

In the United States the eastern panther (*Felis concolor cougar)* was listed as endangered under the 1973 federal Endangered

Species Act. The Florida panther *(Felis concolor coryi)* received federal protection in 1967. As well, many states (e.g. North Carolina; Tennessee; Maine; Vermont) list the eastern panther as endangered under state legislation. Although the eastern panther is officially listed as extirpated in some states (e.g., New Jersey, New Hampshire, Connecticut, Indiana and Ohio), it retains fully protected status within the federal Endangered Species Act, and is absent from the list of animals allowed to be trapped or hunted in respective state hunting and trapping regulations. As well, the "similarity of appearance" clause in endangered species legislation provides additional protection of all free-ranging members of the species *Felis concolor* in states east of the Mississippi River (former ranges of the endangered subspecies *Felis concolor cougar* and *Felis concolor coryi*). In Canada, the eastern panther received endangered species recognition in 1978 by the Committee on the Status of Endangered Wildlife in Canada (COSEWIC). Similar federal recognition was also to be assigned the eastern panther in the forthcoming Canadian Endangered Species Act, although on non-federal lands ultimate responsibility for research and management was to remain with the respective provinces. In eastern Canada the panther is protected under provincial endangered species legislation in Ontario, Quebec and New Brunswick, and will most likely be under the newly proposed Endangered Species Act for Nova Scotia.

Both the U.S. and Canadian governments have been involved in developing preliminary "eastern cougar recovery plans." Robert Downing was instrumental in preparing the U.S. document. But both initiatives have stalled, and no cougar or panther recovery teams are presently active on either side of the border. The reason given remains the lack of verifiable evidence that there are breeding populations of eastern panthers out there around which a recovery action plan might be implemented. Of course, the obvious response to such reasoning is that the presence of panthers is difficult to establish unless a significant, well-funded and properly coordinated, government-sponsored search is initiated. It remains a circular debate.

And what are my feelings? Fully aware that my views are not shared by all, I suggest that most confirmed sightings of panthers and their signs in the east are of former captive western mountain lions, or Florida panthers, or offspring of former captives. And as much as I would like to think otherwise, I seriously doubt that there are self-propagating populations with numbers that meet minimum viable population limits. The Florida panther is a good example. Inbreeding has reduced population vitality and affected individual panther health and reproductive success, and population projection models predict eventual extinction. Concern is so great that female cougars from Texas have been introduced into Florida panther range to increase genetic diversity and, hopefully, thwart extinction. This was done even though the genetic uniqueness of Florida panthers may be threatened. But, given the widespread historic interbreeding of North American mountain lions, perhaps the Florida panther never was particularly unique. The perceived uniqueness may be an unnatural consequence of recent isolation, a situation created by the influence of humans. Could isolated pockets of eastern panthers to the north continue to survive and breed successfully, given the consequences of just such an event in Florida? It hardly seems probable. And the number of "eastern panthers" interbreeding to the north would most likely be fewer than the fifty now in Florida.

Some of my colleagues feel differently. Rudy Stocek, a respected ecologist who teaches at the Maritime Forest Ranger School in Fredericton, and who also has a long association with the mystery of panthers in the Maritime provinces, is more "cautiously optimistic": "Many apparently reliable observations suggest that there could be a small number of cougars in New Brunswick and Nova Scotia. The wide distribution of sightings throughout the region could imply that animals other than escaped captive or released cats are at large. Cougars could possibly be moving into the region from further west. Only recently there have been specimens (of unknown origin) collected in the field in Ontario and Quebec.... There are not many captive cougars registered in both provinces; less than 12 are currently known in zoos, wildlife parks or as pets. Illegally possessed animals would likely constitute a very small number. There may have been escaped cougars at large in past years but this remains unconfirmed. However, these very few animals would not account for the increase in sightings over the region. Whether the cougars reported are of the eastern subspecies ... is speculation since no recent confirmed wild specimens have been examined."[12]

Other scientists remain equally optimistic, some more so than others. Robert Downing, like Rudy Stocek, is cautious when assessing the possibility that native eastern panthers may still be found in the Appalachians.[13] But at the recent Eastern Cougar Conference, Helen McGinnis left little doubt about which side of the debate she favors: "Pennsylvania may have a small breeding population of pumas, descended from survivors of the nineteenth-century population, occasional escapes and releases of captives, and perhaps from immigration from Maryland, Virginia and West Virginia. The preconceived opinion that pumas do not occur in the state and people's inability to identify sign may be responsible for the lack of physical evidence."[14]

And after a study of the literature and personal interviews, Nicole Culbertson concluded that a small breeding population of panthers remained in the Great Smoky Mountains National Park as recent as the mid-1970s.[15] Helen Gerson, with the Ontario Ministry of Natural Resources, compiled cougar sightings from Ontario,[16] similar to the effort by Rudy Stocek in New Brunswick. Although she remains impartial, the evidence for cougars in that province is very compelling.

I remain an optimistic fence-sitter. I may not be an authentic Pantherite, in the true Reverend Ballou sense, nor perhaps as enthusiastic as Jay Tischendorf, Ted Reed or John Lutz, but with the new information being collected in the northeast, I am more hopeful than only a few short years ago. But let's work together. The Florida situation is a good example of what can happen when there are too many cooks in the kitchen.

It has been my experience that most state and provincial wildlife agencies are quite willing to receive reports of panther sightings. Most agencies now have rare and endangered species biologists on staff, and these are the people to contact with reports of panther sightings. They are usually more receptive to such information than biologists concerned with the management of so-called game species. Yes, there are many biologists, wardens and rangers who do not believe that panthers are present in the east. And yes, some of these people can, on occasion, appear unconcerned, perhaps even rude, over yet another sighting of the elusive eastern panther. Most of them have, at one time or another, pursued such leads unsuccessfully. Their outward expressions of frustration should not be taken personally, nor should their apparent lack of enthusiasm for panthers be misconstrued as a general lack of concern for wildlife in general. Identify those who offer encouragement and seem genuinely interested and concerned for your personal report of a panther.

Avoid the others. There is little sense in inciting confrontation and building barriers to productive dialogue and information exchange.

I have recently ended a thirty-year career as a wildlife research biologist, a career which took me from the frozen waters of the High Arctic to the tidal shores of the Bay of Fundy. I have camped among the caribou, wolves and muskoxen on the frozen northern tundra. I have trailed lynx through the spruce bogs on the highlands of Cape Breton Island, and coyotes in northern New Brunswick. It has been a highly rewarding and satisfying career. But I have never seen what I thought was an eastern panther. I did once see tracks in the snow in southern New Brunswick which I thought might have been those of a panther, and I have heard from hundreds of people who think they saw a panther. I remain encouraged that the panther may again be among us.

One of the most persuasive and eloquent articles on the eastern panther was written by Herbert Ravenel Sass and appeared in a 1954 issue of *The Saturday Evening Post*. Commenting on a published scientific presumption that panthers were no longer found in the Appalachian Mountains, he offered the following words of rebuttal: "That is the official verdict. But the big fellow dies hard. His strange fascination persists long after the 'last panther' has been killed, and in a hundred places you will hear rumors that the old forest king still lives and has even, in some mysterious way, renewed his youth."[17]

So let us end with this review of the eastern panther from Alex McKay, one of those fortunate to have seen what he believed in his heart to be Klandagi, Lord of the Forest: "A century ago, an old guide ruefully commented, 'I have seen the footprints of the Indian and the panther, where now the fields are white with harvest; they have passed away with the wilderness.' The panther now represents for me all the lost wilderness of the vast, virgin American continent and the mystery and challenge of its Adirondack forests. I like to think with Clinton Hart Merriam, who wrote in 1884, 'some years may yet pass before the last panther disappears from the dense evergreen swamps and high rocky ridges of this Wilderness.' I like to think that among these Adirondack fields and woods I have seen and heard the panther. I like to think our paths may cross again."[18]

Notes

Preface

1 Gerry Parker, *Eastern Coyote: The Story of Its Success* (Halifax: Nimbus, 1995), 254 pp.

Chapter One: Introduction

1 Letter describing the slaying of the Bernard Panther, deposited with Vermont Historical Society, Montpelier.
2 J. Herbert Walker, "Pioneers and Panthers," *Pennsylvania Game News* 40 (1960), 30-31.

Chapter Two: Klandagi, Lord of the Forest

1 Henry W. Shoemaker, *In the Seven Mountains* (Reading: Bright, 1913), 131-53.
2 George Laycock, *The Hunters and the Hunted* (New York: Meredith, 1990), 3.
3 Ibid., 16-17.
4 Karen McCall and Jim Dutcher, *Cougar, Ghost of the Rockies* (Vancouver/Toronto: Douglas and McIntyre, 1992), 9.
5 Stanley Young and Edward Goldman, *The Puma: Mysterious American Cat* (New York: Dover, 1964), 5-7.
6 Chris Bolgiano, *Mountain Lion: An Unnatural History of Pumas and People* (Mechanicsburg, Pa.: Stackpole, 1995) 26-27.
7 Bruce S. Wright, "The cougar in New Brunswick," *Symposium on the Native Cats of North America* (1971), 108-19.
8 Sydney Greenbie, *Frontiers and the Fur Trade* (New York: 1929), 208, in Stanley Young and Edward Goldman, *The Puma: Mysterious American Cat* (New York: Dover, 1964), 24-25.
9 John Seidensticker and Susan Lumpkin, "Mountain lions don't stalk people. True or false?" *Smithsonian* (February 1992), 117.
10 R. H. Major, *Select letters of Christopher Columbus*, with other original documents relating to his four voyages to the new world (London: Hakluyt Society, 1847) 193, in Young and Goldman, 180.

11 Kevin Hansen, *Cougar: The American Lion* (Flagstaff: Northland, 1992), 2.
12 John Smith, *Captain John Smith's works* (1608-1631), edited by Edward Arber, Birmingham, in Young and Goldman, 180.
13 Bolgiano, 39.
14 Ibid., 39.
15 The family Felidae has long been recognized as in need of revision. In 1993 the American Society of Mammalogists changed *Felis concolor* to *Puma concolor*, one of several taxonomic changes adopted by the Cat Specialist Group of the World Conservation Union. However, as these changes are still not universally endorsed, I have chosen to follow the more conventional use of the genus *Felis*, and the traditional subspecific taxonomy proposed by Young and Goldman in 1946.
16 Hansen, 1-2.
17 John Spargo, *The Catamount in Vermont* (Bennington, Vt.: Bennington Historical Museum and Art Gallery, 1950), 5.
18 Henry W. Shoemaker, *Extinct Pennsylvania Animals* (Baltimore: Gateway, 1993), 15-17 (first published in 1917).
19 Stephen L. Williams, Suzanne B. McLaren and Marion A. Burgwin, "Paleo-archaeological and historical records of selected Pennsylvania mammals," *Annals of Carnegie Museum* 54 (1985), 120-21.
20 Philip Tome, *Pioneer Life: or, Thirty Years a Hunter* (Baltimore: Gateway, 1992), 110-11 (first published in 1854).
21 Shoemaker, 1917, 14-15.
22 Ibid., 1917, 34-35.
23 C. H. Merriam, "The vertebrates of the Adirondack Region, Northeastern New York," *Transactions of the Linnaean Society of New York* (1882), 30.
24 Ibid., 33.
25 Ibid., 32, 34.
26 A. W. F. Banfield, *The Mammals of Canada* (Toronto and Buffalo: University of Toronto Press, 1974), 348.
27 Paul Beier, "Cougar attacks on humans in the United States and Canada," *Wildlife Society Bulletin* 19 (1991), 403-12.
28 Ibid., 409.
29 Young and Goldman, 100.
30 Henry W. Shoemaker, "Those Pennsylvania panthers,"

Frontiers (Academy of Natural Sciences of Philadelphia) 19 (1954), 57-58.

31 Herbert J. Walker, "Pioneers and Panthers," *Pennsylvania Game News* 40 (1960), 26-27.

32 Merriam, 33.

33 Ibid., 36.

34 Alex McKay, "The panther—still roaming?" *Adirondack Life* 5 (1974), 44.

35 Nancy Hugo, "A catamount tale," *Virginia Wildlife* (February 1987), 12.

36. Laycock, 195-96.

37 Seidensticker and Lumpkin, 114-22.

Chapter 3: A Legacy of Persecution

1 Meshach Browning, *Forty-four Years of the Life of a Hunter* (Baltimore: Gateway Press, 1994; first published in 1859).

2 George Laycock, *The Hunters and the Hunted* (New York: Outdoor Life Books, Meredith Press, 1990), 40-51.

3 Browning, 77-79.

4 Ibid., 112.

5 Ibid., 122-24.

6 Ibid., 345.

7 Ibid., 352.

8 Thomas B. Allen, *Vanishing Wildlife of North America* (Washington, D.C.: National Geographic Society, 1974), 12.

9 Laycock, 22.

10 Jack Greene, "Recent Developments in the Historiography of Colonial New England," in Margaret Conrad, ed., *They Planted Well, New England Planters in Maritime Canada* (Fredericton: Acadiensis Press, 1988), 61-96.

11 Laycock, 28.

12 Ibid., 39.

13 Ibid., 62.

14 Allen, 16.

15 Laycock, 193.

16 Henry W. Shoemaker, *Extinct Pennsylvania Animals* (Baltimore: Gateway, 1993), 9, 26 (first published in 1917).

17 Ibid., 30-32.

18 Milton B. Trautman, "The Ohio Country from 1750 to 1977—A Naturalist's View." Ohio State University, Ohio Biological Survey, *Biological Notes* No. 10, 1977.

19 Shoemaker, 51.

20 Ibid., 42.
21 Ibid., 26.
22 J. Herbert Walker, "Pioneers and Panthers," *Pennsylvania Game News* 40 (1960), 29.
23 George W. Davis and Leonard E. Foote, "A History of Wild Game in Vermont," Vermont Fish and Game Service, State Bulletin, Pittman-Robertson Series No. 11 (1944).
24 Ranier H. Brocke, "Reintroduction of the cougar *Felis concolor* in Adirondack Park: a problem analysis and recommendations," Final report to New York State Department of Environmental Conservation (1981), 17.
25 Ibid., 17, 22.
26 Alex McKay, "The panther ... still roaming?" *Adirondack Life* 5 (1974), 44-45.
27 Hansen, 57-58.
28 Monte Hummel and Sherry Pettigrew, *Wild Hunters: Predators in Peril* (Toronto: Key Porter, 1991), 244 pp.
29 George Laycock, "Cougars in Conflict," in Les Line, ed., *Audubon Nature Year Book* (Des Moines: Meredith, 1991), 13.

Chapter 4: Ghosts from the Past

1 Henry W. Shoemaker, *Extinct Pennsylvania Animals* (Baltimore: Gateway, 1993), 60–61 (first published in 1917).
2 Ned Dearborn, "An old record of the mountain lion in New Hampshire," *Journal of Mammalogy* 8 (1927), 311-12.
3 Betty Murray, "The Weathersfield Panther," *The Weathersfield Vermont Weekly*, January 31, 1966.
4 John Spargo, *The Catamount in Vermont* (Bennington: Bennington Historical Museum and Art Gallery, 1950), 19.
5 Ibid., 4.
6 Dayton Stoner, "Extant New York State Specimens of the Adirondack Cougar," *New York State Museum Circular* 25 (1950), 25.
7 Ibid., 26.
8 Don Stearns, "Susquehanna County's last mountain lion," *Montrose Independent*, February 24, 1966.
9 Stoner, 27-28.
10 James Cardoza, Wildlife Biologist, Massachusetts Division of Fisheries and Wildlife, personal communication , April 5, 1994.

11 Land Records of the Town of Wardsboro, Vermont, 1875, 48.
12 Stoner, 17.
13 Ibid., 19.
14 Ibid., 29.
15 Bruce S. Wright, "The latest specimen of the eastern panther," *Journal of Mammalogy* 42 (1961), 278-79.
16 W. Schorger, "A Wisconsin specimen of the cougar," *Journal of Mammalogy* 19 (1938), 252.
17 Ibid., 252.
18 Frank Iwen, Curator of Birds and Mammals, University of Wisconsin, Madison, personal communication, April 1, 1997.

Chapter 5: Pushed to the Edge

1 Don Stearns, "Susquehanna County's last mountain lion," *Montrose Independent*, February 24, 1966.
2 Henry W. Shoemaker, *Extinct Pennsylvania Animals* (Baltimore: Gateway, 1993), 24 (first published in 1917).
3 J. A. Allen, "The former range of some New England carnivorous mammals," *American Naturalist* 10 (1876), 709.
4 D. S. Lee, "The status of the panther in North Carolina," *Wildlife in North Carolina* 41 (1979), 6.
5 James P .McMullen, *Cry of the Panther: Quest of a Species* (Englewood: Pineapple, 1984), 372.
6 Charles B. Cory, *Hunting and Fishing in Florida* (Boston: Estes and Lauriat, 1896), 109.
7 Outram Bangs, "The land mammals of peninsula of Florida and the coast region of Georgia," *Proceedings of the Boston Society of Natural History* 28 (1898), 234-35.
8 Stanley P. Young and Edward A. Goldman, *The Puma: Mysterious American Cat* (New York: Dover, 1964; first published in 1946), 18.
9 McMullen, 375.
10 Ibid., 374.
11 Ronald M. Nowak, "The cougar in the United States and Canada," Report to the U.S. Fish and Wildlife Service and New York Zoological Society (1974), 108-9.
12 R. C. Belden, "Florida panther investigation—a progress report," 123-33, in R. R. Odom and L. Landers, eds., *Proceedings of the Rare and Endangered Wildlife*

Symposium, Technical Bulletin WL4, (Athens: Georgia Department of Natural Resources, 1978).

13 R. C. Belden, "The Florida panther," 523, in W. J. Chandler, ed., *Audubon Wildlife Report* 1988/1989 (New York: National Audubon Society, 1989).

14 Belden, 1989, 526-28.

15 Ibid., 528.

16 Peter Radetsky, "Cat fight," *Discover* (July 1992), 59.

17 Robert C. Belden and Bruce W. Hagedorn, "Feasibility of translocating panthers into northern Florida," *Journal of Wildlife Management* 57 (1993), 388-97.

18 Radetsky, 62.

19 Ibid., 63.

20 U.S. Seal, "A plan for genetic restoration and management of the Florida panther (*Felis concolor coryi*)," report to the U.S. Fish and Wildlife Service, Conservation Breeding Specialist Group, SSC/IUCN, Apple Valley, Minnesota, 1994.

21 David S. Maehr and Gerard B. Caddick, "Demographics and genetic introgression in the Florida panther," *Conservation Biology* 9 (1995), 1295-98.

22 Ibid., 1297.

23 Ronald M. Nowak, "Some thoughts on panther study: a personal view," *Endangered Species Technical Bulletin* 18 (1993), 8.

24 William Bartram, *The Travels of William Bartram*, edited by Mark Van Doren (Macy-Masius, 1928), 34, 63.

25 Francis Harper, "The mammals of the Okeefenokeee Swamp region of Georgia," *Proceedings of the Boston Society of Natural History* 37 (1927), 317-20.

26 Young and Goldman, 12.

27 Keith Guyse, Assistant Chief, Wildlife Section, Alabama Department of Conservation and Natural Resources, Montgomery, Alabama, personal communication, April 21, 1994.

28 Anonymous, "Mountain lion killed in St. Clair County," *Alabama Conservation* (April 1948), 11.

29 Young and Goldman, 25.

30 Cathy Carter and Richard Rumel, "Status of the Florida panther in Mississippi," unpublished report to Mississippi Museum of Natural Science, 1980.

31 Nowak, 1974, 128-29.

32 D. B. Warden, Statistical, political, and historical account of the United States of North America, from the period of their first colonization to the present day, 3 vols. (2, Edinburgh, 1891), 411.
33 John James Audubon and John Bachman, *The Viviparous Quadrupeds of North America* (New York, Vol. 1, 1851), 256-57.
34 F. B. Golley, *South Carolina Mammals* (Charleston Museum, Contribution XV, 1966), 156-57.
35 Ibid., 157.
36 John Lawson, *The History of North Carolina* (London: Printed for T. Warner, 1718), 117.
37 Audubon and Bachman, 311.
38 Charles R. Humphreys, *Panthers of the Coastal Plain* (Wilmington: Fig Leaf Press, 1994), 187–93.
39 Lee, 6.
40 Robert M. Hatcher, Coordinator of Nongame and Endangered Species, Tennessee Wildlife Resources Agency, Nashville, personal communication, May 18, 1994.
41 Young and Goldman, 22.
42 Roger W. Barbour and Wayne H. Davis, *Mammals of Kentucky* (Lexington: University of Kentucky Press, 1974).
43 Young and Goldman, Ibid., 37.
44 Ibid., 33.
45 Ibid., 33.
46 Stephen L. Williams, Suzanne B. McLaren and Marion A. Burgwin, "Paleo-archaeological and historical records of selected Pennsylvania mammals—*Felis concolor*—Mountain lion," *Annals of Carnegie Museum* 54 (1985), 121, 130.
47 Young and Goldman, 28–29.
48 Ibid., 28.
49 Ibid., 37.
50 Ibid., 37.
51 George W. Davis and Leonard E. Foote, "A History of Wild Game in Vermont," *Vermont Fish and Game Service, State Bulletin*, Pittman-Robertson Series No. 11 (1944), 22.
52 Thomas L. Altherr, "The catamount in Vermont folklore and culture, 1760–1900," *Proceedings of the Eastern Cougar Conference*, June 3–5, 1994, Erie, Pennsylvania, 50–91.
53 Altherr, 57–58.
54 Ibid., 68.
55 Young and Goldman, 27.

56 Ibid., 27.
57 Ibid., 23.
58 Ibid., 23.
59 Ibid., 23.
60 Ibid., 17.
61 Ibid., 24.
62 Paul Rego, Wildlife Biologist, Connecticut Department of Envrionmental Protection, Burlington, personal communication, April 4, 1994.
63 James Cardoza, Wildlife Biologist, Massachusetts Division of Fisheries and Wildlife, Westborough, personal communication, April 5, 1994.
64 Ibid., 33.
65 John M. Cronan and Albert Brooks, "The mammals of Rhode Island," Rhode Island Department of Natural Resources, *Wildlife Pamphlet* No. 6 (1968), 109–110.
66 Samuel Nicholson Rhoads, *The Mammals of Pennsylvania and New Jersey* (Philadelphia: privately published, 1903), 266 pp.
67 Rollin H. Baker, *Michigan Mammals* (East Lansing: Michigan State University Press, 1983), 540.
68 David C. Evers, ed., *Endangered and Threatened Wildlife of Michigan* (Ann Arbor: University of Michigan Press, 1994), 60–61.
69 Adrian P. Wydeven and James E. Ashbrenner, "History and status of cougars in Wisconsin," *Proceedings of the Eastern Cougar Conference*, June 3–5, 1994, Erie, Pennsylvania, 170–71.
70 Marcus Ward Lyon, Jr., "Mammals of Indiana," *The American Midland Naturalist* 17 (1936), 158–60.
71 Russell E. Mumford, "Distribution of the mammals of Indiana," Indiana Academy of Science, Monograph No. 1 (1969).
72 Donald F. Hoffmeister, *Mammals of Illinois* (Urbana and Chicago: University of Illinois Press, 1989),34.
73 Edward J. Heske, Center for Wildlife Ecology, Illinois Natural History Survey, Champaign, personal communication, April 19, 1994.
74 Milton B. Trautman, "The Ohio Country from 1750 to 1977—a Naturalist's View," Ohio State University, Ohio Biological Survey, Biological Notes, No. 10 (1977).

75 Geological Survey of Ohio, Vol. IV. *Zoology and Botany. Part I. Zoology* (Columbus: Nevins and Myers, State Printers, 1882).
76 Denis Case, Assistant Administrator, Wildlife Management and Research, Ohio Department of Natural Resources, Columbus, personal communication, March 31, 1994.
77 C. W. Nash, "Manual of vertebrates of Ontario," Department of Education, Toronto, Section 4 (1908), 96.
78 Rev. John Doel, "The panther in Canada," *Biological Review of Ontario* 1 (1894), 23.
79 James E. Orr, "Some old reminiscences of Old Ontario," *Rod and Gun and Motor in Canada* 10 (1909), 840.
80 C. H. D. Clark, "The puma in Ontario," *Ontario Fish and Wildlife Review* 8 (1969), 7–12.
81 Young and Goldman, 43.
82 Ibid., 43.
83 B. S. Wright, "Survival of the northeastern panther (*Felis concolor*) in New Brunswick," *Journal of Mammalogy* 29 (1948), 235–46.
84 Young and Goldman, 42.
85 Hon. Arthur Hamilton Gordon, *Wilderness Journeys in New Brunswick in 1862–63* (St. John: J. and A. McMillan, 1864), 49.
86 Wright, 1948, 235–46.
87 B. S. Wright, "Further notes on the panther in the north east," *Canadian Field-Naturalist* 67 (1953), 12–28.

Chapter 6: I Saw a Panther—Really!

1 Bruce S. Wright, *The Ghost of North America* (New York: Vantage, 1959), 140 pp.
2 Bruce S. Wright, *The Eastern Panther: A Question of Survival* (Toronto, Vancouver: Clarke, Irwin & Company, 1972), 180 pp.
3 Bruce S. Wright, *The Monarch of Mularchy Mountain* (Fredericton: Brunswick Press, 1963), 45–69.
4 For those of you interested in greater detail of recent panther sightings in several regions of the east, I refer you to the following summaries: Ontario—H. B. Gerson, "Cougar *Felis concolor*, sightings in Ontario," *Canadian Field-Naturalist* 102, 1988; Maritime Provinces—R. F. Stocek, "The cougar, *Felis concolor*, in the Maritime Provinces," *Canadian Field-Naturalist* 109, 1995; Pennsylvania—H. J.

McGinnis, "Reports of pumas in Pennsylvania," *Proceedings of Eastern Cougar Conference*, 1994, Erie; Eastern United States—write Eastern Puma Research Netwrok, P.O. Box 3562, Baltimore, Maryland, 21214.

5 S. Hardison, "Carolina cougar: an update," *Wildlife in North Carolina* 40 (1976), 15–16.

6 Robert Downing, "The search for cougars in the eastern United States," *Cryptozoology* 3 (1984), 46.

7 R. E. Cumberland and J. A. Dempsey, "Recent confirmation of a Cougar, *Felis concolor*, in New Brunswick, *Canadian Field-Naturalist* 108 (1994), 224–26.

8 Robert M. Hatcher, Coordinator, Nongame and Endangered Species, Tennessee Wildlife Resources Agency, Nashville, personal communication, May 18, 1994.

9 Ibid.

10 Gene Letourneau, "Man claims photo proves Maine has mountain lions," in outdoor column "Sportsmen Say," *Maine Sunday Telegram*, February 6, 1994.

11 *Bridgetown Evening News*, June 25, 1992.

12 H. Hitchcock, "A Vermont road kill report: and other selected evidence," *Panther Prints* (Spring 1993).

13 John W. Goertz and Roland Abegg, "Pumas in Louisiana." *Journal of Mammalogy* 47 (1966), 727.

14 L. S. Dear, "Cougar or Mountain Lion Reported in Northwestern Ontario," *Canadian Field-Naturalist* 69 (1955), 26.

15 Kenneth J. Doutt, "Mountain Lions in Pennsylvania?" *American Midland Naturalist* 82 (1960), 281–85.

16 Ibid, 281–85.

17 Helen J. McGinnis, "Reports of pumas in Pennsylvania, 1890–91," *Proceedings of Eastern Cougar Conference* (1994), 92–125.

18 Arnold Hayden, Pennsylvania Game Commission, Supervisor Furbearer Unit, Wellsboro, Pennsylvania, personal communication, April 17, 1994.

19 Jason Kahn, "Cougar kitten shot near Adirondack Park," *Northern Forest Forum* 2 (1994), 10.

20 Bruce S. Wright, "The cougar is alive and well in Massachusetts," *Massachusetts Wildlife* 24 (1973), 2–8, 19.

21 Ibid., 2–8, 19.

22 Ibid., 4–6.

23 Ibid., 4–6.

24 Harold B. Hitchcock, "Panther in Vermont?" *Vermont*

Natural History, Vermont Institute of Natural Science (1986).
25 John Lanzenby, "The Cat is Back," *Vermont Life*, (Winter 1994), 20–23, 25.
26 Ibid., 20–23, 25.
27 Kathleen Hentcy (staff writer), "Do cougars feel at home in Vt.?" *Sunday Rutland Herald* and *Sunday Times Argus*, September 18, 1994.
28 Sheila C. Thompson, "Sight record of a cougar in northern Ontario," *Canadian Field-Naturalist* 88 (1974), 87.
29 Helen McGinnis, "A puma puzzle," *Mississippi Outdoors* (July/August 1990), 20–21.
30 Tom Mooney, "Vermonters say panthers are back," *Providence Journal-Bulletin*, April 19, 1995, A8.
31 Ibid., A8.
32 Alex McKay, "The panther ... still roaming?" *Adirondack Life* (Winter 1974), 18–19.
33 *Adirondack Life*, editorial, (Spring 1974), 58.
34 Mike Sajna, "Storyteller," *Pennsylvania Game News* (March 1993), 15.
35 Ibid, 15.
36 Ibid, 16–18.
37 Henry W. Shoemaker, *Extinct Pennsylvania Animals* (Baltimore: Gateway Press, 1993; first published in 1917).
38 John Lutz, personal communication, May 29, 1995.
39 Ibid.
40 Charles R. Humphreys, *Panthers of the Coastal Plain* (Wilmington: Fig Leaf Press, 1994).
41 Friends of the Eastern Panther (FOTEP), P.O. Box 102, Exeter, New Hampshire 03833.
42 Jack Cawthon, "The day the panther prowled," *Virginia Conservation* 21 (1957), 12–13.
43 Dave Snow, "A report of a cougar near Port Rexton, Newfoundland," *Osprey* 25 (1994), 45.

Chapter 7: The Great Debate

1 D. C. Peattie, ed., *Audubon's America: The Narratives and Experiences of John James Audubon* (Biston: Houghton Mifflin, 1940), 73-75.
2 Steve Parren, Vermont Department of Fish and Wildlife, personal communication, April 14, 1993.

3 James Cardoza, Massachusetts Division of Fisheries and Wildlife, personal communication, May 10, 1994.
4 John Cely, South Carolina Wildlife and Marine Resources Department, personal communication, April 20, 1994.
5 Paul Rego, Connecticut Department of Environmental Protection, personal communication, May 16, 1994.
6 Christopher Raithel, Rhode Island Department of Environmental Management, personal communication, April 12, 1994.
7 Dennis Martin, Virginia Department of Game and Inland Fisheries, personal communication, April 7, 1995.
8 Bradford Winn, Georgia Department of Natural Resources, personal communication, July 6, 1994.
9 Allen Boynton, North Carolina Wildlife Resources Commission, personal communication, May 5, 1994.
10 R.F. Stocek, "The Cougar, *Felis concolor*, in the Maritime Province," *Canadian Field-Naturalist* 109 (1995), 19-22.
11 Steven J. Ropski and Jay Tischendorf, eds., *Proceedings of the Eastern Cougar Conference*, Erie, Pennsylvania, June 3-5, 1994, 245 pp. Available from Jay Tischendorf, American Ecological Research Institute, P.O. Box 380, Fort Collins, Colorado, 80522.
12 Stocek, 22.
13 Robert L. Downing, "The cougar in the east," *Proceedings of the Eastern Cougar Conference*, Erie, Pennsylvania, June 3-5, 1994, 163-166.
14 Helen J. McGinnis, "Reports of pumas in Pennsylvania, 1890-1981," *Proceedings of the Eastern Cougar Conference*, Erie, Pennsylvania, June 3-5, 1994, 92.
15 Nicole Culbertson, "Status and history of the mountain lion in the Great Smoky Mountains National Park," Great Smoky Mountains National Park Management Report No. 15, (1976)
16 Helen B. Gerson, "Cougar, *Felis concolor*, sightings in Ontario," *Canadian Field-Naturalist* 102 (1988), 419-24.
17 Herbert Ravenel Sass, "The panther prowls the east again," *Saturday Evening Post*, March 13, 1954, 134.
18 Alex McKay, 1974, "The panther —still roaming?" *Adirondack Life* 5 (1974), 47.

Bibliography

Adirondack Life, Editorial, Spring 1974.

Allen, J. A. "The former range of some New England carnivorous mammals." *American Naturalist* 10, 1876.

Allen, Thomas B. *Vanishing Wildlife of North America*. Washington, D.C.: National Geographic Society, 1974.

Altherr, Thomas L. "The catamount in Vermont folklore and culture, 1760–1900," Proceedings of the Eastern Cougar Conference, Erie, Pennsylvania, June 3–5, 1994.

Anonymous. "Mountain lion killed in St. Clair County: Huge 109–pounder slain by A. D. Hare in his pasture near Springville." *Alabama Conservation* 19, 1948.

Audubon, John James, and John Bachman. *The Viviparous Quadrupeds of North America. Vol. 2.* New York, 1851.

Baker, Rollin H. *Michigan Mammals*. East Lansing: Michigan State University Press, 1983.

Banfield, A. W. F. *The Mammals of Canada*. Toronto and Buffalo: University of Toronto Press, 1974.

Bangs, Outram. "The land mammals of peninsula of Florida and the coast region of Georgia." Proceedings of the Boston Society of Natural History 28, 1898.

Barbour, Roger W., and Wayne H. Davis. *Mammals of Kentucky*. Lexington: University of Kentucky Press, 1974.

Bartram, William. *The travels of William Bartram*. Edited by Mark Van Doren. Macy-Masius, 1928.

Beier, Paul. "Cougar attacks on humans in the United States and Canada." *Wildlife Society Bulletin* 19, 1991.

Belden, R. C. "Florida panther investigation—a progress report." In R. R. Odum and L. Landers, eds. Proceedings of the Rare and Endangered Wildlife Symposium. Georgia Department of Natural Resources Technical Bulletin WLr Athens, Georgia, 1978.

______. "The Florida panther." In W. J. Chandler, ed. Audubon Wildlife Report 1988/1989. New York: National Audubon Society, 1989.

———, and Bruce W. Hagedorn. "Feasibility of translocating panthers into northern Florida." *Journal of Wildlife Management* 57, 1993.

Bolgiano, Chris. *Mountain Lion: An Unnatural History of Pumas and People*. Mechanicsburg: Stackpole Books, 1995.

Brocke, Ranier H. "Reintroduction of the cougar *Felis concolor* in Adirondack Park: a problem analysis and recommendations." Final report to New York State Department of Environmental Conservation. 1981.

Browning, Meschach. *Forty-four Years of the Life of a Hunter*. Baltimore: Gateway, 1994 (first published in 1859).

Carter, Cathy, and Richard Rummel. "Status of the Florida panther in Mississippi." Unpublished report to Mississippi Museum of Natural Science, 1980.

Cawthon, Jack. "The day the panther prowled." *Virginia Conservation* 21, 1957.

Clark, C. H. D. "The puma in Ontario." *Ontario Fish and Wildlife Review* 8, 1969.

Cory, Charles B. *Hunting and Fishing in Florida*. Boston: Estes and Lauriat, 1896.

Cronan, John M., and Albert Brooks. "The Mammals of Rhode Island." Rhode Island Department of Natural Resources, Wildlife Pamphlet 6, 1968.

Culbertson, Nicole. "Status and history of the mountain lion in the Great Smoky Mountains National Park." Great Smoky Mountains National Park, Management Report No. 15, 1976.

Cumberland, R. E. and J. A. Dempsey. "Recent confirmation of a Cougar, *Felis concolor*, in New Brunswick." *Canadian Field-Naturalist* 108, 1994.

Davis, George W., and Leonard E. Foote. "A history of wild game in Vermont." Vermont Fish and Game Service, State Bulletin 11, 1944.

Dear, L. S. "Cougar or mountain lion reported in north–western Ontario." *Canadian Field-Naturalist* 69, 1955.

Dearborn, Ned. "An old record of the mountain lion in New Hampshire." *Journal of Mammalogy* 8, 1927.

Doel, Rev. John. "The panther in Canada." *Biological Review of Ontario* 1, 1894.

Doutt, L. S. "Mountain lions in Pennsylvania?" *American Midland Naturalist* 82, 1969.

Downing, Robert L. "The search for cougars in the eastern United States." *Cryptozoology* 3, 1984.

Evers, David C., ed. *Endangered and Threatened Wildlife of Michigan*. Ann Arbor: University of Michigan Press, 1994.

Geological Survey of Ohio. Vol. IV. Zoology and Botany. Part 1. Zoology. Columbus, Ohio: Nevin and Myers, State Printers, 1882.

Gerson, H. B. "Cougar, *Felis concolor*, sightings in Ontario." *Canadian Field-Naturalist* 102, 1988.

Goertz, John W. and Roland Abegg. "Pumas in Louisiana." *Journal of Mammalogy* 47, 1966.

Golley, F. B. "South Carolina Mammals." Charleston Museum, Contribution XV, 1966.

Gordon, Hon. Arthur Hamilton. *Wilderness Journeys in New Brunswick in 1862–63*. St. John: J. and A. Mc Millan, 1864.

Greenbie, Sydney. "Frontiers and the Fur Trade." In Young, Stanley P., and Edward A. Goldman. *The Puma: Mysterious American Cat*. New York: Dover, 1964 (first printed in 1946).

Greene, Jack. "Recent Developments in the Historiography of Colonial New England." In Margaret Conrad, ed. *They Planted Well, New England Planters in Maritime Canada*. Fredericton: Acadiensis Press, 1988.

Hansen, Kevin. *Cougar: The American Lion*. Flagstaff: Northland, 1992.

Hardison, S. "Carolina cougar: an update." *Wildlife in North Carolina* 40, 1976.

Harper, Francis. 1927. "The mammals of the Okeefenokee Swamp region of Georgia." Proceedings of the Boston Society of Natural History 37: 317–20.

Hatcher, Robert M., Coordinator, Nongame and Endangered Species, Tennessee Wildlife Resources Agency, Nashville, personal communication.

Hentcy, Kathleen. "Do cougars feel at home in Vermont?" *Sunday Rutland Herald*, September 18, 1994.

Hitchcock, Harold B. "Panther in Vermont?" Vermont Natural History. Vermont Institute of Natural Science, 1986.

______. "A Vermont road kill report: and other selected evidence."

Panther Prints. Newsletter of the Friends of the Eastern Panther, 1993.

Hoffmeister, Donald F. *Mammals of Illinois*. Urbana and Chicago: University of Illinois Press, 1989.

Holt, David. "The great cat scat mystery." *Eastern Woods & Waters* 9, 1993.

Hugo, Nancy. "A catamount tale." *Virginia Wildlife*, February 1987.

Hummel, Monte, and Sherry Pettigrew. *Wild Hunters: Predators in Peril.* Toronto: Key Porter, 1991.

Humphreys, Charles R. *Panthers of the Coastal Plain*. Wilmington: Fig Leaf Press, 1994.

Kahn, Jason. "Cougar kitten shot near Adirondack Park." *Northern Forest Forum* 2, 1994.

Kelly, J. Michael. "Cougars gone but not forgotten." ESF Quarterly, Winter 1993.

Lawson, John. *The History of North Carolina*. London: T. Warner, 1718.

Laycock, George. *The Hunters and the Hunted*. New York: Outdoor Life Books, Meredith Press, 1990.

_______. "Cougars in conflict." In Les Line, ed. 1991 Audubon Nature Year Book. Des Moines: Meredith Press, 1991.

Lazenby, John. "The cat is back." *Vermont Life*, Winter 1994.

Lee, D. S. "The status of the panther in North Carolina." *Wildlife in North Carolina* 41, 1979.

Letourneau, Gene. "Man claims photo proves Maine has mountain lions." *Maine Sunday Telegram*, February 6, 1994.

Loxton, Howard. *The Beauty of Big Cats*. London: Triune Books, 1973.

Lyon, Marcus Ward, Jr. "Mammals of Indiana." *The American Midland Naturalist* 17, 1936.

Maehr, David S., and Gerard B. Caddick. "Demographics and genetic introgression in the Florida panther." *Conservation Biology* 9, 1995.

Major, R. H. "Select letters of Christopher Columbus, with other original documents relating to his four voyages to the New World." Hakluyt Society, 1847. In Young, Stanley P., and Edward A. Goldman. *The Puma: Mysterious American Cat.* New York: Dover, 1964 (first published in 1946).

McCall, Karen, and Jim Dutcher. *Cougar, Ghost of the Rockies*. Vancouver and Toronto: Douglas and McIntyre, 1992.

McGinnis, Helen J. "A puma puzzle." *Mississippi Outdoors*, July/August, 1990.

______. "Reports of pumas in Pennsylvania, 1890–1981," Proceedings of the Eastern Cougar Conference, Erie, Pennsylvania, June 3–5, 1994.

McKay, Alex. "The panther … still roaming?" *Adirondack Life* 5, 1974.

McMullen, James P. *Cry of the Panther: Quest of a Species*. Englewood: Pineapple Press, 1984.

Merriam, C. H. "The vertebrates of the Adirondack Region, Northeastern New York." *Transactions of the Linnaean Society of New York* 1, 1882.

Mooney, Tom. "Vermonters say panthers are back." *Providence Journal–Bulletin*, April 19, 1995.

Mumford, Russell E. "Distribution of the mammals of Indiana." Indiana Academy of Science, Monograph No. 1, 1969.

Nash, C. W. "Manual of vertebrates of Ontario." Toronto: Ontario Department of Education, 1908.

Nowak, Ronald M. "The cougar in the United States and Canada." Report to the U.S. Fish and Wildlife Service and New York Zoological Society, 1974.

_______. "Some thoughts on panther study: a personal view." *Endangered Species Technical Bulletin* 18, 1993.

Orr, James E. "Some old reminiscences of Old Ontario." *Rod and Gun and Motor in Canada* 10, 1909.

Parker, Gerry. *Eastern Coyote: The Story of Its Success*. Halifax: Nimbus, 1995.

Peattie, D. C. ed. *Audubon's America: The Narratives and Experiences of John James Audubon*. Boston: Houghton Mifflin, 1940.

Radetsky, Peter. "Cat fight." *Discover*, July 1992.

Rhoads, Samuel Nicholson. *The Mammals of Pennsylvania and New Jersey*. Philadelphia: privately published, 1903.

Ropski, Steven J., and Jay Tischendorf, eds., Proceedings of the 1994 Eastern Cougar Conference. Erie, Pennsylvania: AERIE, 1996.

Sanja, Mike. "Storyteller." *Pennsylvania Game News*, March 1993.

Sass, Herbert Ravenel. "The panther prowls the east again." *Saturday Evening Post* 13, 1954.

Schorger, A. W. "A Wisconsin specimen of the cougar." *Journal of Mammalogy* 19, 1938.

Seal, U. S. "A plan for genetic restoration and management of the Florida panther (*Felis concolor coryi*)." Report to the U.S. Fish and Wildlife Service. Conservation Breeding Specialist Group, SSC/IUCN, Apple Valley, Minnesota, 1994.

Seidensticker, John, and Susan Lumpkin. "Mountain lions don't stalk people. True or false?" *Smithsonian*, February 1992.

Shoemaker, Henry W. *In the Seven Mountains*. Reading: Bright Printing, 1913.

________. *Extinct Pennsylvania Animals*. Baltimore: Gateway Press, 1993 (first published in 1917).

________. "Those Pennsylvania panthers." *Frontiers* (Academy of Natural Sciences of Philadelphia) 19, 1954.

Smith, Captain John. "Captain John Smith's works (1608–1631)." Edited by Edward Arber. In Young, Stanley P., and Edward A. Goldman. *The Puma: Mysterious American Cat.* New York: Dover, 1964 (first published in 1946).

Snow, Dave. "A report of a cougar near Port Rexton, Newfoundland." *Osprey* 25, 1994.

Spargo, John. *The Catamount in Vermont.* Bennington: Bennington Historical Museum and Art Gallery, 1950.

Stearns, Don. "Susquehanna County's last mountain lion." *Montrose Independent*, February 24, 1966.

Stocek, Rudolph F. "The Cougar, *Felis concolor*, in the Maritime Provinces." *Canadian Field-Naturalist* 109, 1995.

Stoner, Dayton. "Extant New York State specimens of the Adirondack Cougar." New York State Museum Circular 25, 1950.

Thompson, Sheila. "Sight record of a cougar in northern Ontario." *Canadian Field-Naturalist* 88, 1974.

Tome, Philip. *Pioneer Life: or, Thirty Years a Hunter*. Baltimore: Gateway Press, 1992 (first published in 1854)

Trautman, Milton B. "The Ohio country from 1750 to 1977—a naturalist's view." Ohio State University, Ohio Biological Survey, Biological Notes No. 10, 1977.

Walker, J. H. "Pioneers and panthers." *Pennsylvania Game News* 40, 1960.

Warden, D. B. Statistical, political, and historical account of the United States of North America, from the period of their first colonization to the present day. 3 vols. Edinburgh, 1819.

Williams, Stephen L., Suzanne B. Mclaren and Marion A. Burgwin. "Paleo–archaeological and historical records of selected Pennsylvania mammals." *Annals of Carnegie Museum* 54, 1985.

Wright, Bruce S. "Survival of the northeastern panther (*Felis concolor*) in New Brunswick." *Journal of Mammalogy* 29, 1948.

________. "Further notes on the panther in the northeast." *Canadian Field-Naturalist* 67, 1953.

________. *The Ghost of North America*. New York: Vantage Press, 1959.

________. "The latest specimen of the eastern panther. "*Journal of Mammalogy* 42, 1961.

________. *The Monarch of Mularchy Mountain*. Fredericton: Brunswick Press, 1963.

________. "The cougar in New Brunswick." Symposium on the Native Cats of North America, 1971.

________. *The Eastern Panther: A Question of Survival*. Toronto and Vancouver: Clarke, Irwin & Company, 1972.

________. "The cougar is alive and well in Massachusetts." *Massachusetts Wildlife* 24, 1973.

Wydevan, A. P. and J. E. Ashbrenner. "History and status of cougars in Wisconsin." Proceedings of Eastern Cougar Conference, Erie, Pennsylvania, June 3–4, 1994.

Young, Stanley P., and Edward A. Goldman. *The Puma: Mysterious American Cat*. New York: Dover, 1964 (first published in 1946).